Thika

Nairobi

Kajiado

Magadi

KENYA

D0404385

SOMALIA

Lake Natron

Dolnyo Lengai 2980

Ngorongoro Conservation Area

Arusha

Loolmalassin

**NORTHERN
SAFARI CIRCUIT**

Mt Meru 4566

**ARUSHA AND
KILIMANJARO**

Arusha

Moshi

Mbulu

B1

Lake Manyara

Tarangire National Park

Babati

Kilimanjaro

Mkomazi National Park

Voi

Malindi

Manyara

Same

Pare Mts

Mombasa

Massai
Steppe

Lushoto

Usambara Mts

Korogwe

Dodoma

Kondoa

**THE NORTH COAST
AND USAMBARA**

Tanga

Pemba

Chake Chake

Dodoma

T A N Z A N I A

Saadani National Park

ZANZIBAR AND PEMBA

Zanzibar
(Unguja)

Mtera Reservoir

Kilosa

Uluguru Mts

A7

Morogoro

Pande Game Reserve

Bagamoyo

Zanzibar

Great Ruaha

Mikumi National Park

Pwani

Dar es Salaam

DAR ES SALAAM

Iringa

A7

Udzungwa Mountains National Park

A104

**SOUTHERN PARKS AND
TANZAM HIGHWAY**

Mikumi

Morogoro

Kilimahera

Kisiju

Mafia Island

Iringa

Kibiti

Rufiji

Ikwiriri

Kilindoni

I N D I A N

O C E A N

Kilombero Floodplain

Mahenge

Mbarika Mountains

Selous Game Reserve

Utete

Mafia Island Marine Park

Njinjo

Kilwa Kivinje

Lindi

Liwale

Lindi

THE SOUTH COAST

Mnazi Bay-
Ruvuma Estuary
Marine Reserve

B4

Nachingwea

B5

B2

Mtwara

Ruvuma

Msanjesi Game Reserve

Masasi

Palma

A19

Lukwita-Lumesule Game Reserve

Mtwara

Ruvuma

Songea

Tunduru

Rovuma

Mocimboa da Praia

MOZAMBIQUE

TANZANIA & ZANZIBAR

◉ Walking Eye App

YOUR FREE DESTINATION CONTENT AND EBOOK AVAILABLE THROUGH THE WALKING EYE APP

Your guide now includes a free eBook and destination content for your chosen destination, all for the same great price as before. Simply download the Walking Eye App from the App Store or Google Play to access your free eBook and destination content.

HOW THE WALKING EYE APP WORKS

Through the Walking Eye App, you can purchase a range of eBooks and destination content. However, when you buy this book, you can download the corresponding eBook and destination content for free. Just see below in the grey panels where to find your free content and then scan the QR code at the bottom of this page.

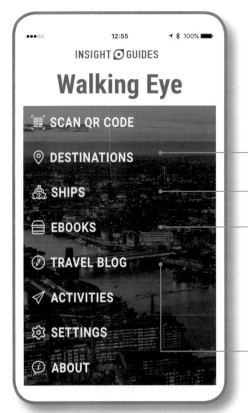

Destinations: Download your corresponding essential destination content from here, featuring recommended sights and attractions, restaurants, hotels and an A–Z of practical information, all for free. Other destinations are available for purchase.

Ships: Interested in ship reviews? Find independent reviews of river and ocean ships in this section, all available for purchase.

eBooks: You can download your free accompanying digital version of this guide here. You will also find a whole range of other eBooks, all available for purchase.

Free access to travel-related blog articles about different destinations, updated on a daily basis.

HOW THE DESTINATION CONTENT WORKS

Each destination includes a short introduction, an A–Z of practical information and recommended points of interest, split into 4 different categories:

- Highlights
- Accommodation
- Eating out
- What to do

You can view the location of every point of interest and save it by adding it to your Favourites. In the 'Around Me' section you can view all the points of interest within 5km.

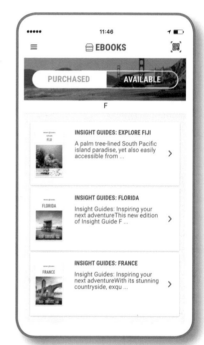

HOW THE EBOOKS WORK

The eBooks are provided in EPUB file format. Please note that you will need an eBook reader installed on your device to open the file. Many devices come with this as standard, but you may still need to install one manually from Google Play.

The eBook content is identical to the content in the printed guide.

HOW TO DOWNLOAD THE WALKING EYE APP

1. Download the Walking Eye App from the App Store or Google Play.
2. Open the app and select the scanning function from the main menu.
3. Scan the QR code on this page – you will then be asked a security question to verify ownership of the book.
4. Once this has been verified, you will see your eBook and destination content in the purchased ebook and destination sections, where you will be able to download them.

Other destination apps and eBooks are available for purchase separately or are free with the purchase of the Insight Guide book.

CONTENTS

LEGEND
⚲ Insight on
📷 Photo Story

THE BEST OF TANZANIA & ZANZIBAR: TOP ATTRACTIONS

△ **Serengeti National Park.** Arguably East Africa's finest game reserve, this is the main setting for the Great Migration, where some 8 million hooves – mostly belonging to wildebeest and zebra – pound the plains in search of fresh grass. See page 170.

▽ **Ngorongoro Crater.** This vast and immensely scenic caldera supports around 25,000 large animals, including the world's densest population of lions and spotted hyenas, several massive old tuskers, and some of East Africa's last black rhinos. See page 166.

△ **Mount Kilimanjaro.** The world's tallest free-standing mountain, and the highest peak anywhere in Africa, snowcapped 'Kili' is spectacular; it is one of the highest walkable summits on the planet. See page 153.

▽ **Stone Town, Zanzibar.** With its wealth of 19th-century Omani architecture and laid-back Swahili atmosphere, the historic Stone Town on the legendary Spice Island of Zanzibar is Tanzania's most satisfying urban destination. See page 217.

△ **Chimp tracking (Mahale/Gombe).** There is no better place in Africa to track man's closest relative than these two parks on the eastern shore of Lake Tanganyika; researchers have studied the chimp communities here since the 1960s. See page 184.

△ **Kilwa Kisiwani.** Once home to the most important medieval trading centre along the East African coast, the island of Kilwa is studded with impressive ruins of abandoned mosques, palaces and other Swahili buildings. See page 210.

△ **East coast beaches, Zanzibar.** There is no shortage of superb beaches along the coast of mainland Tanzania and the islands, but none surpass the east coast of Zanzibar for dazzling white sand and impossibly blue sea. See page 232.

△ **Selous Game Reserve.** Dominated by the sluggish brown Rufiji, a riverine wilderness inhabited by immense numbers of hippos, crocodiles and water birds, Africa's largest game reserve offers excellent opportunities for game viewing from a boat or on foot. See page 189.

△ **Lake Natron and Ol Doinyo Lengai.** Bordering Kenya, Natron is the largest and most remote of the lakes that line the floor of Tanzania's eastern Rift Valley, overlooked by Ol Doinyo Lengai, the Maasai 'Mountain of God' and the region's most active volcano. See page 162.

▽ **Ruaha National Park.** Game viewing in this remote reserve begins as soon as you arrive, with the banks of the Ruaha River supporting elephants, lions, leopards and antelopes – including the localised sable and greater kudu. See page 192.

THE BEST OF TANZANIA & ZANZIBAR: EDITOR'S CHOICE

On an elephant safari.

BEST OUTDOOR ACTIVITIES

Balloon safari. Flights take off as dawn breaks over the Serengeti, illuminating the amazing natural habitat of the world's most famous game reserve. See page 173.

Equestrian safaris. Galloping alongside a herd of zebra or wildebeest is a lifelong dream for many horse riders. www.makoa-farm.com

Climbing Kilimanjaro. Requiring a minimum of five days, the ascent to the snowcapped peak of Kilimanjaro is among the world's most iconic climbs. See page 153.

Diving and snorkelling off the Swahili Coast. The best dive sites are Mnemba Atoll, Mafia Marine Park and Misali Island. These and several other sites also offer great snorkelling, with hundreds of species of colourful reef fish on display. See page 236.

Hiking the Usambara. Wonderful scenery, interesting local culture and plenty of rare forest wildlife make this a great budget alternative to a Kili hike. See page 137.

Camping on Mount Kilimanjaro.

BEST EXCLUSIVE CAMPS & LODGES

&Beyond Klein's Camp. Superlative guided game drives on a large private concession bordering the Serengeti are matched by the beautifully decorated and well-appointed hillside cottages. www.andbeyond.com/kleins-camp

Manyara Ranch. In a wildlife corridor linking Lake Manyara and Tarangire National Parks, this exclusive camp offers excellent guided game walks and night drives. www.manyararanch.com

Sayari Camp. This stylish and wonderfully sited small camp in the Northern Serengeti is ideally placed to catch the amazing wildebeest crossings of the Mara in migration season. www.mirusjourneys.com/africa/tanzania

Lamai Serengeti. This ultra-luxurious lodge straddles a group of well-wooded rocky outcrops in a part of the northern Serengeti famed for its large lion prides. www.nomad-tanzania.com

&Beyond Ngorongoro Crater Lodge. The last word in over-the-top decor, this extraordinary lodge on the edge of the magnificent Ngorongoro Crater brings Baroque to the African bush. www.andbeyond.com/ngorongoro-crater-lodge

Chumbe Island. Combines a bush-lodge feel with a beach setting on a small private island whose offshore reefs offer some of the finest snorkelling in East Africa. www.chumbeisland.com/accommodation

BEST FOR BIRDWATCHING

Amani Nature Reserve.
At the top birding spot in the Usambara, it's possible to see the likes of green-headed oriole and half-a-dozen Eastern Arc endemics in the headquarters' gardens. See page 137.
Udzungwa and Kilombero. The biodiverse Udzungwa Mountains, partially protected within a national park, and nearby Kilombero Valley are home to numerous local endemics. See page 195.

Lake Manyara National Park. Best known for its famous tree-climbing lions, this gem of a park on the northern safari circuit also hosts a dazzling array of raptors and water birds. See page 161.
Arusha National Park. Highland forest specialities such as the gaudy Hartlaub's turaco can be seen here alongside flamingos and other water birds. See page 143.

Balloon safari over the wildebeest migration in Serengeti National Park.

BEST OFF-THE-BEATEN-TRACK SAFARIS

Tarangire National Park. Huge herds of elephants rival this underrated park's ancient baobab trees as its most prominent feature. See page 156.
Katavi National Park. The most remote and least visited of East Africa's major safari reserves is home to profligate numbers of hippos, buffalo, elephants and lions. See page 186.
Saadani National Park. Billed as the reserve

where the bush meets the beach, oft-neglected Saadani is the last place in East Africa where elephants and lions might be seen on Indian Ocean shore. See page 134.
Singita Grumeti. This game reserve abutting the Serengeti's western corridor comes into its own in June and July, when hundreds of thousands of northbound wildebeest cross the Grumeti River. See page 175.

Elephants and baobab tree at sunset, Tarangire National Park.

BEST CULTURE & HISTORY

Hadza at Lake Eyasi. Walk with Tanzania's last Hadza hunter-gatherers, armed with bows and arrows, honey-gathering and looking for healing plants and food. See page 164.
Oldupai Gorge. Groundbreaking palaeontological discoveries here include fossil remains of hominids dating back 1.75 million years, and numerous extinct animals. See page 169.
Bagamoyo and Kaole ruins. Once the mainland centre of the slave and ivory trade to Zanzibar, the historic 19th-century port of Bagamoyo lies close to the ruined medieval city of Kaole. See page 131.
Kondoa Rock-Art Site. Tanzania's least-publicised Unesco World

Heritage Site is a treasury of prehistoric rock art decorating the granite faces of north-central Tanzania. See page 159.
Maasai *Manyatta*. Several *manyattas* – the family homesteads of the charismatic Maasai pastoralists – in the vicinity of Manyara and Ngorongoro are open to visits. See page 166.
Mwaka Kogwa. This four-day celebration of the Shirazi New Year takes place at the end of July in the southern Zanzibari village of Makunduchi. See page 231.
Tingatinga. The best Tingatinga painting is vibrant and appealing in its depictions of Tanzania's animals and people, sometimes with political undertones. See page 63.

Fishing dhows at low tide, Nungwi, Zanzibar.

African elephant browsing,
Ngorongoro Crater.

Maasai herding camels in front of the active volcano Ol Doinyo Lengai, Lake Natron.

Hadza girl, Lake Eyasi.

THE STUFF OF LEGENDS

Tanzania – with vast swathes of stunning wilderness – is one of the most complex, romantic and friendly countries in Africa.

Maasai giraffe in front of Longido Mountain, West Kilimanjaro.

Tanzania has some of the world's finest game parks, two of Africa's highest mountains, superb white-sand beaches and coral reefs, and delightfully friendly and hospitable people. The names are the stuff of legend: the great Serengeti plains; Lake Victoria, birthplace of the Nile; the towering bulk of Mount Kilimanjaro; the red-clad Maasai cattle herders; the spice islands of Zanzibar and Pemba. Traders sailing the East African coast named the Swahili people and provided the inspiration for the tales of Sinbad the Sailor, while Sultan Said built glamorous baths for his Persian wife. Inland, the great Victorian explorers, Burton, Speke, Livingstone and Stanley, led convoys of porters across the vast terrain. Imagination can run riot here; the reality more than matches the fantasy.

The United Republic of Tanzania came into being in 1964 when the newly independent mainland nation of Tanganyika merged with offshore Zanzibar (the 'tan' and 'zan' in 'Tanzania' respectively). Little more than a century before that, much of the region fell under the influence of Zanzibar – which in turn was part of the vast Omani Empire. However, only the coast and islands were developed; the Swahili traders never tried to conquer or develop the hinterland, seeing it simply as a vast natural storehouse of their main cash crops – ivory and slaves.

Traditional Swahili dhows, Zanzibar.

Since then, the balance of power has shifted, purely on weight of numbers: about 45 million people on the mainland to just over 1 million on the islands. There is still a great divide between the two main cultures, and the link remains fragile. Economic power remains in the east. Dusty little Dodoma is the official capital, chosen for its central location, but it is largely ignored – people prefer to hang out with the money in Dar es Salaam.

President Nyerere's post-independence government gave Tanzania a true sense of nationhood: the country has more than 120 different tribal groups, each with its own language and traditions, but no one tribe is large enough to dominate the others. Tanzania has also strived to develop its tourism industry without destroying the natural beauty on which it is based. And while most tourists come to enjoy these fantastic natural assets, combining an exciting safari with downtime on the beaches, those who take the time to look further will discover a nation whose cultural wealth is matched by a rich history stretching back millions of years to man's first upright steps.

Maasai dance in a traditional manyatta.

PEOPLE

In an African success story, Tanzania's many different tribes and cultures have developed a harmonious and hospitable way of life.

A pair of Maasai warriors draped in red-checked togas, metal-tipped wooden spears clutched protectively to their sides, stroll loose and languid down Arusha's Sokoine Avenue, animatedly conversing in their guttural Maa mother tongue. A bleeping sequence forms a half-recognisable tune as one of the warriors fumbles deep in his toga to pull out a mobile phone. He lifts it to his ear, presses a button and barks a colloquial KiSwahili greeting – 'Mambo!' – then, on recognising his caller, switches over to Tanzania's second national language, English: 'Me? Ah, I'm well, very well, thank you!'

It is such mildly surreal encounters that subvert Western preconceptions about African modernity and traditionalism to reveal Tanzania's true human essence. Superficially, the country can often come across as a mass of seemingly irreconcilable contradictions. This proudly unified nation is comprised of more tribes than any other African country, a land where Islam and Christianity co-exist alongside ancient animist cultures, while its people are steeped in conservatism yet eager to embrace the latest technology.

Tanzania's 'safari capital' of Arusha must surely have the highest pro rata concentration of four-wheel drives, internet cafés and satellite televisions in equatorial Africa. And yet, only 20km (12 miles) out of town, the road to the country's renowned northern game reserves speeds through open plains where traditionally attired herdsmen cling defiantly to a lifestyle little changed from that of their forefathers.

THE PEOPLING OF TANZANIA

Where between these two opposite worlds does one locate the real Tanzania? Tanzania's modern population – over 55 million – consists of at least

A tailor in Pangani.

120 tribes (a word used widely within Tanzania) of diverse origin. The country's oldest inhabitants, though numerically insignificant today, are the Hadza of Lake Eyasi (see page 164), the sole cultural heirs to the nomadic hunter-gatherers who once roamed much of the Tanzanian interior, leaving behind a rich artistic legacy in the form of numerous rock paintings scattered through the hills of Kondoa district. In about 1000 BC, the first agriculturists arrived in the region, Cushitic speakers represented today by the Iraqw, who live in the highlands around Karatu and Mbulu, and claim distant Arabian ancestry.

The pivotal event in the populating of modern Tanzania was the arrival, some 2,000 years ago, of Iron Age Bantu-speaking agriculturists from West

Africa. In most parts of the region, the Stone Age hunter-gatherers were displaced by, or absorbed into, these more technologically advanced migrant societies. Today, the country's most populous tribes, such as the Sukuma of Lake Victoria, the Nyamwezi of Tabora, the Chagga of Kilimanjaro and the Hehe of Iringa, all speak languages of the Bantu family. While most such tribes have ancient roots within Tanzania, others are more recent arrivals – the Ngoni, for instance, are refugees from South Africa who settled around Songea in the 1850s.

For visitors, the most romanticised of Tanzania's people are its traditional pastoralists, in particular the Maasai of the northern Rift Valley and Ngorongoro Highlands, who many see as epitomising the soul of ancient Africa. Ironically, the Maasai are among the most recent arrivals to Tanzania, having crossed the modern-day border with Kenya in the late 18th century, at the end of an all-conquering southward migration through the Rift Valley. The Datoga of the central Rift Valley, like their Maasai neighbours, are dedicated cattle herd-

Boat in Bagamoyo.

⊘ THE IRAQW

The Iraqw, who inhabit fertile areas of Arusha province, are Tanzania's last true Cushitic-speaking tribe, with an estimated population of 600,000. Their houses are built cave-style on hillsides, with thick wooden frameworks covered in mud planted with grass. Men sleep on one side and women and children on the other. Society is run by a series of councils for youths, women, men and elders, with the men's council having the final say. Although regarded as equal, all tribe members are divided into black, red and white, according to their skin tone, with paler skin being viewed as equating to greater physical beauty.

ers who speak a Nilotic tongue and migrated south from western Ethiopia, but they were resident in Tanzania hundreds of years before the Maasai.

THE COASTAL PEOPLE

The coast, like the interior, has been subject to numerous intra-African and local population movements over the centuries. But nearly 1,500 years of trade links with Arabia and Asia have also left their mark on the coastal Swahili. Over the centuries, merchants from all over the world settled in East Africa's trade ports and intermarried with the indigenous African inhabitants. KiSwahili, the main coastal tongue, is a virtual linguistic mirror of this maritime history and trade: a Bantu language whose vocabulary is liberally spiced with words derived from Arabic and Hindi, and more recently Portuguese, German and English.

Having spread along the coast as the lingua franca of medieval commerce, KiSwahili played a similar role along the 19th-century slave caravan routes into the interior. Today, it is the first official language of Tanzania, spoken as a first or second language by around 95 percent of the populace and a similar proportion of Kenyans, and it still performs its

established throughout the interior from the late 19th century onwards. Tanzanians of Islamic and Christian persuasion generally live side by side without noticeable rancour, though both are likely to express surprise, if not outright shock, at any visitor who professes to the unfamiliar concept of atheism.

In keeping with this atmosphere of religious tolerance, many practising Muslims and Christians in Tanzania adhere concurrently to apparently conflicting animist beliefs. Traditional healers and spiritualists are frequently

Schoolgirls in Stone Town, Zanzibar.

traditional role as a trade language in bordering parts of Mozambique, Malawi, Zambia, Burundi, Rwanda and Uganda.

RELIGION

The most significant Arab implant in Tanzanian culture has been religious. Numerous ruined medieval mosques, some dating back to the 12th century, line the country's coastline, while its modern ports have a deep and pervasive Islamic mood. In the 19th century, Islam followed KiSwahili along the caravan routes, taking root in important trade depots such as Ujiji and Tabora.

In general, however, the interior is essentially Christian in feel, the result of various missions consulted in times of ill health or misfortune; in the Islamic port of Tanga, the football team routinely prepares for a crunch match by leaving a sacrifice to the powerful spirits thought to inhabit the nearby Amboni Caves.

Localised religions hold little sway among the pastoralists of the Rift Valley. However, the Maasai traditionally worship a dualistic deity, Engai, who resides in the tempestuous volcanic crater of Ol Doinyo Lengai near the Kenyan border (see page 163). Mount Hanang, in the central Rift Valley, is the home of Aseeta, the

Collecting coconuts from a palm tree, Pangani.

god of the Datoga, who has little influence over earthly affairs, but monitors them through his all-seeing eye, the sun.

Of all Tanzania's people, the Barabaig, a sub-group of the Datoga, have proved least mutable to evangelical persuasion – 99 percent of them adhere exclusively to their traditional beliefs.

FOOD

For most Africans, the wide selection and easy availability of foodstuffs in Western societies is difficult to comprehend. In rural Tanzania, choice of food more or less amounts to whatever one can cultivate or lay one's hands on – indeed, one of the first questions rural Tanzanians like to ask foreigners is what crops they grow in London, Paris, New York, or from wherever the visitor hails. Thus, in coastal areas and around lakes, the main source of protein is fish, while people living away from water generally herd cattle and goats, and keep poultry.

In most parts of Tanzania, the main staple is *ugali*, a stiff porridge made from maize meal. Served in a large solid heap, the *ugali* is customarily hand-rolled into mouth-sized balls by the diner, then dunked into a bland, watery stew of meat, fish or beans, often accompanied by a local vegetable very similar to spinach. Until the European introduction of maize, the staple would have been millet, still regarded by the Iraqw as an 'oath' plant, used when making solemn vows, from marriage to curses.

In moister and more fertile areas – parts of the Lake Victoria hinterland, for instance, and the slopes of Kilimanjaro – *ugali* is replaced by *batoke*, a dish made with cooked plantains. A popular snack throughout Tanzania, the local equivalent of a quick burger, is *chipsi mayai* (literally 'chips eggs'), basically an omelette made with thick potato chips.

More interesting to most foreign palates is traditional Swahili food. Fish and shellfish feature strongly, and rice becomes the main carbohydrate. Thanks to centuries of Arabic, Asian and Portuguese trade and influence, it is distinguished by the liberal use of spice (in particular peri-peri) and coconut milk.

Even insects are not safe from the cooking pot. Termites and flying ants are popular, eaten raw or fried in butter. Other edible insects include locusts, grasshoppers, mopane worms and lake flies.

Swahili cooking is also permeated with the culinary influence of the many Indians who are settled along the coast, and in many instances the line between traditional Swahili and Indian dishes is blurred. Indians have also settled all over the Tanzanian interior, and tourists in need of a decent meal should always consider seeking out Indian eateries in smaller towns where there is not a huge choice of restaurants.

The British colonial influence is discernible less perhaps in the 'steak, chips and one vegetable' style of menu favoured by many mid-range hotels than in the breakfast fry-ups offered by the majority of lodges.

TRADITIONAL MEDICINE

Many Tanzanians depend on their surroundings as a source not only of food, but also of *dawa* (medicine). To outsiders, the relationship between Western and traditional medicine can be difficult to comprehend, especially

A MODERATE NATION

Within East Africa, Tanzanians are regarded as egalitarian and peaceful people, not publicly demonstrative but imbued with a deeply ingrained sense of tolerance, justice and respect for other cultures. Without wishing to reinforce national stereotypes, few outsiders who have spent significant time here would strongly disagree with these sentiments. Tanzania's transition to independence occurred with a unique absence of bloodshed, as did its subsequent evolution from benign dictatorship to full

Prawns for sale at Kivukoni fish market, Dar es Salaam.

as it varies regionally and from one individual to the next.

But while Westernised clinics are increasingly visited to treat serious diseases such as malaria and HIV/Aids, traditional healers still play an important role, particularly in rural society, where many ailments are alleviated using medicine made from herbs, bark and other organic materials. In some areas, for instance, the bark of the striking sausage tree is boiled in water to cure cramps, while the stem is used to treat pneumonia. The bark of the whistling thorn – a common tree in the Serengeti – is said to alleviate diarrhoea, and throughout East Africa frayed ebony stems serve as handy organic toothbrushes for many people.

⊘ MAASAI COWS

The Maasai believe every cow in the world is theirs by godly ordain, and recognise cattle as the sole measure of material wealth. Since cows have no value once dead, they are slaughtered for eating only on special occasions. The traditional Maasai diet, a blend of fermented cow's blood and milk, is no longer consumed regularly. The Maasai view tribes who hunt, fish or eat vegetables with contempt, and their proprietary claim on every last breathing cow has often made life difficult for neighbouring pastoralists. Such attitudes have mellowed, but intertribal cattle raids still occur occasionally on territorial boundaries.

democracy. It is one of the few African countries to enter its sixth decade of independence without ever having experienced a coup, sustained civil unrest, or the rule of an unpopular leader who refused to stand down.

A principled stance on international politics was reflected in staunch support of the ANC at the height of apartheid, and the strong denouncement and eventual overthrow of the bloodthirsty Ugandan dictator Idi Amin. Tanzania, poor though it is, has long opened its arms to refugees fleeing regional conflicts,

Maasai woman.

mainly in neighbouring Democratic Republic of Congo, Rwanda and Burundi. Their presence has caused little internal tension, although a recent influx of Burundian refugees (beginning in 2015) has seen Tanzania's refugee population explode, resulting in the creation of two new refugee camps and putting immense strain on the system.

Tanzania's pervasive sense of nationhood is generally attributed to two main factors. The first, ironically, is the country's very cultural diversity. Elsewhere in Africa, national politics is often dominated by the jostle for supremacy between two numerically dominant tribes. In Tanzania, the most populous tribe accounts for just 16 percent of the populace, so that tribal

self-interest plays no significant role in determining national affairs. The other factor is the guiding influence of first president Julius Nyerere – affectionately remembered by the name *Mwalimu* (Teacher) – whose actions, words and policies repeatedly stressed the importance of nationhood over more parochial concerns. Tanzanians generally hold their tribal roots in deep regard, but as a source of cultural pride rather than political divisiveness.

ECONOMIC UPS AND DOWNS

Nyerere, for all his virtues, was the instigator of the misguided *Ujamaa* (familyhood) scheme of centralised collective villages (see page 56), implemented in 1967. By the mid-1970s, some 85 percent of the rural population lived in *Ujamaa* villages. The result was a disaster, since many of the villages lay in areas without sufficient water or arable land to support a large community. Tanzania, already one of the least developed African colonies, retreated further into economic torpor, to be ranked among the world's 10 poorest countries.

Since Nyerere's voluntary retirement from the presidency in 1985, Tanzania has undergone a dramatic economic transformation (see page 57). Its sustained growth rate since 2000 (6.5% per annum on average between 2006 and 2016) has been among the highest on the continent, and the healthy aura of commercial bustle that envelops Dar es Salaam today would render the city virtually unrecognisable to anybody who last visited it during the economic nadir of the mid-1980s. Yet it is difficult to determine the extent to which the bustling city centre, with its smartly dressed businessmen, burgeoning shopping malls and fancy restaurants, reflects an improvement in the lot of the average Tanzanian. The outskirts of Dar es Salaam are lined with slums. The city's population far exceeds that of the next 10 largest urban centres in the country combined. The vast majority of Tanzanians live rurally as subsistence farmers, fisherfolk or livestock herders, and poverty is manifest, with 12 million Tanzanians living below the poverty line. Unemployment is high in rural areas. Meanwhile, the population has virtually trebled in number since independence – and continues to grow rapidly. Inadequate health-care facilities have been stretched thinner in recent years by the Aids pandemic. The average life expectancy now stands close to 65 years, which is higher than most parts of Africa, but still lower than the global average (71.4 years in 2015).

Education received a major boost when president John Magufuli introduced free secondary education in 2015 and set aside more than $7 million to implement the new law. However, many schools are struggling to cope with burgeoning numbers of new students. Further problems, such as low completion rates among girls,

but rural Tanzanian women typically bear the full burden of rearing children, housekeeping, raising crops and fetching water. Some case studies show women doing up to 85 percent of the work required to support the family.

Polygamy, customary in most traditional societies, is on the decline, partly due to the infiltration of Christianity, partly for economic reasons, though the pastoralists of the Rift Valley remain actively polygamous, while also (almost uniquely among Tanzanians) practising initiation rites centred on the (illegal) genital mutilation of pubescent girls.

School children in uniform, Lushoto, Usambara Mountains.

still need to be addressed. This mainly affects rural areas, where large families with limited resources – still necessary to pay for indirect costs, such as transport and exam fees – accord priority to the education of their male progeny.

THE ROLE OF WOMEN

Even after years of socialist, supposedly egalitarian rule, the inferior education and literacy rate of modern Tanzanian women is reflected by their relatively low profile in national politics and the formal business sector. It is a disparity rooted in traditional tribal structures, which are almost exclusively patrilineal and governed by males.

The traditional division of day-to-day labour varies significantly from one tribe to the next,

A modern phenomenon, and a major factor in the spread of the HIV virus, is prostitution, which is rife in most towns, linked to the economic necessity for many men to seek employment away from their family home.

While it would not do to gloss over the economic and social concerns raised above, it should be stressed that similar problems are endemic throughout the world's poorest continent. What distinguishes Tanzania – a colonial creation in which disparate tribes were forced to co-exist within arbitrarily imposed national borders – is the way it has transcended its hotchpotch tribal beginnings to become a genuinely united and forward-looking nation.

People gather outside a mosque in 1860s Zanzibar.

DECISIVE DATES

Ancient tools, Isimila Stone Age Site.

c.3.6 million years ago
Australopithecus Afarensis leaves footprints in the Laetoli mud.

c.2 million years ago
Australopithecus Boisei living at Oldupai Gorge; Homo habilis first appears.

c.1 million years ago
Homo erectus appears.

c.130,000 years ago
The first signs of modern man, *Homo sapiens*.

c.10,000 years ago
Identifiable Bushman people in central Tanzania create early rock art at Kondoa.

c.1000 BC
Cushitic tribes begin to move in from the Ethiopian highlands.

THE HISTORIC ERA
c.AD 60
Author of the *Periplus of the Erythraean Sea* gives the first recorded account of the East African coast in a guide to Indian Ocean shipping.

c.AD 150
In his *Geography*, Ptolemy mentions the island of Menouthesias (Zanzibar).

2nd–4th centuries AD
Indian and Persian ships trade along Tanzanian coast. The first Bantu-speaking peoples arrive from West Africa.

7th century AD
Islam is brought south by traders and early Arab settlers.

11th century
First Nilotic people move south into Tanzania from Egypt and the Sudan.

1107
Earliest known mosque is built at Kizimkazi on Unguja Island, Zanzibar, by Shirazi settlers.

Medieval picture of an Arab dhow.

1332
An Arab traveller, Ibn Battuta, visits the prosperous trading port of Kilwa.

15th century
There are 30 Swahili city-states along the East African coast, each ruled by a Sultan. Zanzibar is visited by Chinese admiral Cheng Ho.

EUROPEANS ARRIVE
1489
Pedro de Covilhan sails south from Alexandria along the East African coast.

1497–8
Portuguese explorer Vasco da Gama finds the sea route around the Cape of Good Hope to India, visiting Zanzibar on his way home.

1503
The Portuguese capture Unguja Island, the *Mwinyi Mkuu* becomes a subject king and allows Portuguese ships free passage, food and water.

1506
The Portuguese capture Pemba.

1510
When the locals refuse to pay their tribute, the Portuguese, led by Duarte de Lemos, loot and plunder Unguja and Pemba.

1560
The Portuguese build a small chapel and fort on the west coast of Unguja. The fledgling settlement eventually becomes Zanzibar Town.

1591
Sir James Lancaster visits Zanzibar in the British ship the *Edward Bonaventure*.

OMANI RULE

1650
The Omani Arabs sail south to help the *Mwinyi Mkuu* overthrow the Portuguese in Zanzibar.

1668
The Omanis gain control of the whole coast, apart from Mombasa and Stone Town.

1695
The last Portuguese settlers on Pemba leave.

1698
The Omanis drive the Portuguese from Mombasa and Zanzibar. Queen Fatuma, a Portuguese supporter, is taken to Muscat where she spends 12 years in exile while her son, Hassan, takes the title, paying tribute to the Omanis. The Omanis rule through a series of local governors.

18th century
The Omanis raid inland Africa for non-Muslim slaves for their plantations and for sale overseas. Numbers of slaves rise from about 500 a year to 8,000 a year at the beginning of the 19th century. The Maasai arrive in Tanzania, taking over the northern highlands.

Early 19th century
First clove plantations created in Zanzibar.

1840
Sultan moves the capital of Oman from Muscat to Zanzibar. By now, at least 40,000 slaves a year are being traded along the coast.

1840s
Ngoni (Zulu) people arrive from the south, terrorising much of southern Tanzania and disrupting the balanced system of chiefdoms. The first European missionaries, Johann Krapf and Johannes Rebmann, arrive at Mt Kilimanjaro.

1858
Burton and Speke 'discover' Lake Tanganyika; Speke finds Lake Victoria; Livingstone reaches Lake Nyasa.

1871
Livingstone and journalist Henry Stanley famously meet.

1873
Slave trade abolished; David Livingstone dies.

Illustration showing Stanley meeting Livingstone at a village in Ujiji, near Lake Tanganyika.

THE COLONIAL YEARS

1885
Karl Peters' German East Africa Charter Company (DOAG) forms bogus treaties with several inland tribes and is mandated by the German government to administer the territory.

1890
Britain and Germany carve up Africa. Britain gets Uganda and Malawi; Zanzibar and the coast becomes a British Protectorate; the rest of Tanzania becomes a German colony, German East Africa.

1905–7
The Maji Maji Rebellion in southern Tanzania is crushed.

It is the last of several unsuccessful uprisings against the Germans.

November 1914
British and Indian expeditionary force arrives; World War I reaches East Africa.

November 1918
German commander Paul von Lettow-Vorbeck surrenders undefeated to the British.

1919
Treaty of Versailles gives Rwanda and Burundi to the Belgians and mandates rule of the rest of German East Africa to the British.

1929
The formation of the Tanganyika African Association (TAA) marks the start of the nationalist independence campaign.

1939–45
Nearly 100,000 Tanganyikans fight as Allied troops in Europe during World War II.

1947
The UN affirms Tanganyika's status as a Trustee Territory, to be administered by Britain.

1954
The TAA is rebranded as the overtly political Tanganyika African National Union, led by Nyerere.

INDEPENDENCE

9 December 1961
Tanganyika gains full independence, with Julius Nyerere as prime minister.

1962
Tanganyika becomes a republic, with Julius Nyerere the first executive president.

1963
Zanzibar is given independence.

1964
Sultan of Zanzibar is deposed in a bloody revolution; Nyerere and the Zanzibari leader, Karume, sign the Act of Union, creating modern Tanzania from Tanganyika and Zanzibar.

1967
The Arusha Declaration sets out Nyerere's vision of African Socialism, leading to the disastrous policy of *Ujamaa* collective villages.

Nyerere becomes the first prime minister of newly independent Tanganyika in 1961.

Jakaya Kikwete, former president of Tanzania.

1977
With Tanzania now among the world's poorest countries, *Ujamaa* is abandoned.

1979
Tanzania invades Uganda and topples the brutal dictator Idi Amin.

1985
Nyerere resigns. Ali Hassan Mwinyi becomes president.

1995
Mwinyi retires. Benjamin Mkapa becomes president. The World Bank and IMF agree to help rebuild the economy on a Western, capitalist model.

1998
An Al-Qaeda bomb explodes outside the US Embassy in Dar es Salaam, killing 11 people.

1999
Tanzania is one of the first countries to be awarded Highly Indebted Poor Country (HIPC) status, qualifying for billions of dollars of debt relief.

2005
Violence mars the Zanzibar elections as Karume returns to power as president amid allegations of vote-rigging. Jakaya Kikwete becomes president of Tanzania.

2005–6
A large part of Tanzania's massive external debt is cancelled.

2008
President Kikwete is elected Chairman of the African Union. Prime Minister Lowassa stands down after the Richmond Development energy scandal and is replaced by Mizengo Pinda.

2010
President Kikwete is re-elected.

2012
The country's largest known gas reserves are discovered off the south coast.

2015
John Pombe Magufuli becomes president of Tanzania and scraps tuition fees in secondary schools.

2016
Tanzania and Uganda announce the construction of East Africa's first major oil pipeline.

2017
President Magufuli begins relocation process of government from Dar es Salaam to Dodoma, due for completion by 2020.

President John Magufuli meets a Chinese official in 2016.

Isimila Stone Age Site.

THE EARLIEST INHABITA ITS

Tanzania's human history goes back several million years to mankind's first steps, and is being pushed back further with every new find.

The earliest history of human beings is pieced together from a handful of bones and a few broken tools scattered across thousands of miles, from South Africa to the Gobi Desert, and a biological and social study of chimpanzees and gorillas, our closest genetic relatives. One new find – a skull or set of fossilised footprints – can rewrite the books. At best, it is an inexact science.

Yet one thing cannot be disputed – as things stand at present, practically all of the key discoveries on which we base our knowledge of our earliest ancestors have been made in or around East Africa's Rift Valley – in the Afar Region of northeast Ethiopia, at Koobi Fora on Kenya's Lake Turkana, and in the Oldupai Gorge in northern Tanzania (see page 169), where erosion has exposed ancient fossil beds to modern excavations.

FIRST STEPS

It is now commonly accepted that man's earliest roots do lie in Africa, a theory first postulated by Charles Darwin in the 1870s, and that we are not descended from apes, but share a common ancestor with them. The apes evolved into forest dwellers, while humans, who lived more vulnerably in the open, learned first to stand upright, for better vision, thus freeing their hands to use tools. With no natural defences against predators or weapons for hunting, the use of strategy and tools became essential for survival. And as social creatures, the use of language for communication was an inevitable mark of progress.

It is not known exactly when the evolutionary paths of humans and apes diverged, but molecular studies suggest it was perhaps 6 to 8 million years ago. Two relatively recent discoveries have been put forward as candidates for the title

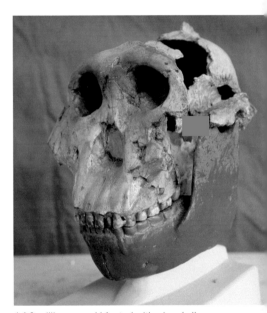

A 1.8-million-year-old Australopithecine skull, unearthed by Mary Leakey.

of the world's oldest known hominine fossil, though neither is universally accepted as such by palaeontologists. These are *Sahelanthropus tchadensis*, discovered in Chad in 2001 and dated to about 7 million years ago, and the arboreal *Orrorin tugenensis*, which lived about 6 million years ago and was first unearthed in Kenya's Tugen Hills in 2000. Some scientists believe that the Orrorin fossils from Tugen represent a common ancestor of all subsequent hominine species, as well as chimpanzees.

The Afar region of northern Ethiopia has yielded the world's oldest undisputed hominine remains, thought to be around 5.5 million years old and ascribed to the species *Ardipithecus kadabba*.

Ethiopia is also the only place where *A. ramidus*, a probable descendent of *A. kadabba* that lived at least 4.4 million years ago, has been located.

First identified in South Africa in 1924, the most widespread of early hominine primates, and possibly the first to be full bipedal, are placed in the genus *Australopithecus* (literally 'southern ape'). They stood 1.2 to 1.4 metres (3ft 8ins to 4ft 7ins) high and had a chimp-like face. They left no stone tools, but probably used sticks.

Australopithecine fossils have been found all over eastern and southern Africa, and several species have been identified, many of which lived at the same time. These include *A. Africanus*, the species first unearthed in South Africa in 1924, as well as *A. Anamensis*, found in northern Kenya, and *A. Afarensis*, identified in Ethiopia. Two sets of footprints discovered by Mary Leakey in 1976 at Laetoli, near Tanzania's Oldupai Gorge, are thought to have been made by *A. Afarensis* around 3.6 million years ago. More recently, new sets of footprints, also believed to belong to *A. Afarensis*, were discovered at Laetoli in 2016. Large strides suggest one individual to be among the tallest *A. Afarensis* ever identified.

The oldest Australopithecine fossils, unearthed in northern Kenya, date to more than 4 million years ago, and the genus evidently thrived for several millions of years. Indeed, current paleontological thinking, subject to regular revision as new evidence emerges, is that the Australopith-

> *For a long time, the oldest known member of our genus was Homo habilis. That changed in 2010 when scientists at South Africa's Sterkfontein Caves discovered H. gautengensis, thought to be significantly more than two million years old.*

Louis and Mary Leakey excavating Oldupai Gorge in 1961.

ecines were not necessarily ancestral to modern humans and that they co-existed with our direct Homo ancestors until around 500,000 years ago, when they became extinct.

THE FIRST TRUE HUMANS

In 1964, Louis Leakey, Phillip Tobias and John Napier announced another milestone in evolutionary understanding when they found and named *Homo habilis* ('handy' man). Originally thought to be a true ancestor to modern man, this has now been disproved, with several similar species found at other dig sites.

A more certain candidate for one of our direct ancestors is *Homo erectus* ('upright' man), which first emerged on the fossil record about

1.8 million years ago, and survived until some 25,000 years ago. *Homo erectus* was tall and relatively upright with a 950-cubic cm (58-cubic ins) brain. It had a flatter face than earlier hominines, with an external nose, and a smaller jaw, making it look far more recognisably human. It was also probably the first human to live in a hunter-gatherer society, to make a sophisticated range of purpose-built tools, and to control fire.

Homo erectus is probably the first hominine species that crossed the Sahara to range outside Africa. Fossils, some more than one million years

Although we now come in all shapes, sizes and colours, these genetic variations are relatively young, and a compelling combination of fossil and DNA evidence asserts that modern man evolved in Africa and spread across the planet from there.

By the Acheulean era, *Homo erectus* was crafting elegantly designed, highly efficient hand axes, cleavers, scrapers and knives. Fine collections have been found at several sites in Tanzania, including Oldupai and Isimilia, near Iringa in central Tanzania (see page 197), an erosion gully that was once the shore of a large freshwater

Later Stone Age rock painting interpreted by recent scholars as recording a shamanistic trance dance.

old, have been found as far afield as Europe and the Far East, though it seems that our ancestors didn't venture beyond warm, open, grassy environments until about 50,000 years ago.

THINKING MAN

Evolution rarely seems to follow a straight line and, for a time, *H. erectus* lived side by side with our own species *Homo sapiens* ('thinking' man), who first appeared on the scene about 130,000 years ago. *H. sapiens* is significantly taller but less bulky than his predecessors, with a much larger brain (about 1,300 cubic cm/79 cubic ins). His success has led not only to total domination of the plant and animal kingdoms, but the eventual extinction, en route, of all other hominid species.

lake. The oldest tools of this type, dated to 1.75 million years ago, come from the vicinity of Lake Turkana in Kenya. By 10,000 years ago, these tools had been refined into microliths – small, ultra-efficient flakes of stone, used for spears, arrows or as knife blades inserted into a wooden handle. Families lived in rock shelters, their walls frequently decorated with pictures of animals, hunting and dancing.

THE BUSHMEN

Throughout sub-Saharan Africa, the oldest surviving aboriginal people are the so-called Batwa (Bushman) races, small, relatively sharp-featured, slightly yellowy-skinned people whose hunter-gatherer culture and click-based

Khoisan language are thought to date back 40,000 years. Even today, the last few groups live as nomadic hunter-gatherers, providing us with a direct link to the late Stone Age. However, as other groups have dominated, they have been integrated, enslaved, exterminated or simply pushed back to the inhospitable fringes of the continent, such as the southern Namib and Kalahari deserts.

In Tanzania, they are represented by the Hadza people, who live in the remote Lake Eyasi region (see page 164), and the Sandawe, who

Paleolithic rock painting, Kondoa.

live in the area around Kondoa (see page 159), famed for its ancient rock art.

THE FIRST AGRICULTURISTS

Over the past 3,000 years, the pace of change has quickened as wave after wave of invaders have arrived and taken root, leading to the complex web of people that now inhabit Tanzania.

First to arrive were the Cushitic-speaking tribes, who began to drift south from Ethiopia about 3,000 years ago. With them, they brought agriculture. These were more settled people than their hunter-gather predecessors, living in villages and clearing the bush to plant millet and vegetables, while their herds of domestic cattle, sheep and goats competed for grazing with the local wildlife. The

balance between man and nature began to shift. The Cushitic-speaking tribes settled the fertile northern highlands, pushing the nomadic hunter-gatherers south to the lowland plains. Of the true Cushitic-speaking people, only the Iraqw (in the area between Ngorongoro and Lake Manyara) remain (see page 20).

THE BANTU-SPEAKERS

The most important event in the course of populating modern Tanzania was the arrival of the Bantu-speakers from their original home in West Africa about 2,000 years ago. Various Bantu-speaking tribes have meandered across much of the continent ever since, with the Ngoni fleeing north from Zulu aggression in the 19th century. The massive shifts of 20th- and 21st-century refugees continue the theme. Today, 95 percent of Tanzanians speak a home language in the Bantu subgroup, which includes KiSwahili, the coastal lingua franca that is also the national language.

Most Bantu-speakers are farmers and cattle herders, living in villages, with a strong family and clan structure. Where they gained superiority over all existing inhabitants was in their ability to work metal. Their iron tools were not only infinitely more effective weapons, but enabled them to cultivate more difficult ground, clearing woodland and invading the less hospitable reaches that had, until then, been the preserve of the hunter-gatherers. Iron was so important that the ironworkers became the local aristocracy, appointing administrators to rule their web of chiefdoms. They were also traders, with the early long-haul trade in salt and iron gradually being joined by gold, ivory and slaves.

THE NILOTIC TRIBES

The last ethno-linguistic group to reach Tanzania was the Nilotic-speaking people who came south from Egypt and the Sudan in a sequence of migrations from the 11th century AD onwards. Tanzania's Nilotic-speakers fall into three main branches. The 'highland' branch, represented by the Datoga people, settled the area around Ngorongoro, before being pushed back to Lake Eyasi. The 'river-lake' people (the Luo in Kenya) infiltrated the area around Lake Victoria. Both have been partially assimilated by the local Bantu population, learning to farm and fish as well as herding cattle. The last to arrive, in the early 19th century, were the 'plains' people – the Maasai.

THE LEAKEYS

Louis Leakey, father of East African palaeontology, founded a scientific dynasty that includes his wife Mary, son Richard and granddaughter Louise.

Louis Leakey was born in 1903, in Kenya, the son of English missionaries. Always fascinated by early history, he studied anthropology and archaeology at Cambridge in the 1920s, returning to East Africa to conduct digs in several areas. He carried out his first serious excavation of Oldupai Gorge in 1931.

In 1933, he met Mary Nicol, an English scientific illustrator who had spent much of her childhood in Dordogne (France) and was fascinated by the area's rich prehistory. She never took a degree, but followed a number of university courses and was, in later life, inundated with honorary degrees. The two married in 1936, after Louis' divorce from his first wife.

Louis and Mary's joint excavations at Oldupai Gorge completely rewrote our evolutionary history. Mary's first major discovery there, in 1948, was the first fossil skull of the Miocene primate, *Proconsul*. In 1959, she discovered *Australopithecus Boisei*. In 1964, Louis led the team that found and identified *Homo habilis*.

During World War II, Louis became involved in intelligence work, and in 1945 he became the curator of what is now the National Museum of Kenya. In 1947, he organised the first Pan-African Congress of Prehistory. A flamboyant speaker and excellent fundraiser, he used his international fame to generate finance not only for the family's archaeological expeditions, but also for ventures such as Jane Goodall and Diane Fossey's acclaimed primate studies. Poor health dogged the last years of his life, and he died in 1972, aged 69.

Meanwhile, Mary, who is generally recognised to have been the better scientist, remained in her husband's shadow, quietly getting on with excavating Oldupai and surrounding archaeological sites. With their three children grown up and her marriage disintegrating due to Louis' womanising and global wandering, she moved almost full-time to Oldupai in the 1960s, living there for the next 20 years. In 1976, she discovered the 3.6-million-year-old Laetoli footprints.

In 1983, Mary retired to Nairobi, where she remained until her death, aged 83, in 1996. However, this was not the end of the story. Their middle son, Richard, led his first fossil-hunting expedition in 1964. Two years later, he started work with the National Museum of Kenya and began a series of excavations at Koobi Fora on Lake Turkana in northern Kenya, where he added significant new species to the early catalogue of hominids.

In 1966, he married an archaeologist, Margaret Cropper, who also began to work in the family 'firm'. In

Louis Leakey, father of a respected archaeological dynasty.

1970, after their divorce, he married a primate researcher, Meave Epps. He headed the National Museum of Kenya, the Kenya Wildlife Services, and eventually the entire Kenyan Civil Service, before taking a seat in parliament from 1997 until 2001. He is still active in conservation and works as a professor of anthropology at Stony Brook University, New York. In 2013 the American Humanist Association honoured him with the prestigious Isaac Asimov Science Award.

Meave started and has continued to work as a palaeontologist, discovering *Australopithecus Anamensis* in 1995 and the 3.5-million-year-old *Kenyanthropus platyops* in 2001, the same year their daughter, Louise, completed her PhD in palaeontology. The dynasty continues.

Khalifa bin Haroub (seated),
Sultan of Zanzibar from 1911
to 1960.

SWAHILI TRADERS

The arrival of the Arabs created a new world with the introduction of Islam, bringing a vibrant culture and international trade.

There has been trade along the East African coast since at least the 4th century BC. In about AD 60, an anonymous Greek wrote the *Periplus of the Erythraean Sea*, a guidebook to the Indian Ocean shipping routes. In about AD 150, Ptolemy discussed the region in his *Geography*. Both mention the island of Menouthesias, thought to be Zanzibar.

By the 2nd century AD, Indian and Persian ships were trading regularly along the Tanzanian coast. It was also about this time that the Bantu-speaking precursors of the Swahili arrived at the coast from the interior. When the first Arab traders arrived a century later, they named the region *Zinj el Barr* (Land of the Blacks, later to be corrupted to Zanzibar). However, it was far from being a single country. Instead, the coast and islands were split into numerous small kingdoms, each of which had its own dynasty of leaders.

From the 7th century AD onwards, Arab traders brought Islam to the coast. A century later, they began to settle and intermarry with the local people. Legend has it that the first to arrive were the Sultan of Shiraz and his six sons, who fanned out to colonise Mombasa, Pemba and Kilwa. Over the years, the language, customs and blood of the local Bantu-speakers were infused with Shirazi and other Arabian influences to form a distinct coastal people called the Swahili – a term derived from the Arabic word *sahel* (coast or edge).

TRADE WINDS

Life was governed by the trade winds. The Arab dhows, their design little altered today, would head south on the northeast monsoon between October and February, carrying trade goods such as cloth, beads and porcelain, returning north on the southwest monsoon between March and

Dhow at sunset, Bagamoyo.

September, laden with gold, ivory and slaves. It was a pattern that was to continue right up to the birth of the steamship and nominal abolition of the slave trade in the late 19th century.

The area and trade flourished, with enough wealth for all and little squabbling by rival power bases. By the 11th century, there were significant cities on Zanzibar and Pemba. Zanzibar's earliest surviving building is the Kizimkazi Mosque, dated to 1107.

By the end of the 12th century, Kilwa had become a major port, its initial wealth founded on trading gold with the southern city-state of Sofala (in present-day Mozambique). Kilwa and, in later years, Mombasa, dominated the coast, but 13th-century chronicles also talk of Zanzibar as a

SLAVES AND SPICE

The mercantile culture of the Swahili Coast, founded on the export of gold and ivory, eventually came to be dominated by the slave trade.

Spices on sale in modern Zanzibar.

The history of slaving in Africa is at least 2,000 years old. Many local tribes traditionally practised some sort of slavery, and the international slave trade with Arabia probably dated back to the 4th century AD, though it was less significant than the trade in ivory, gold and spice in the early days.

The slave trade out of East Africa peaked in the 19th century. Tribes around lakes Tanganyika and Nyasa, the inland termini of the Tanzanian caravans, set up profitable careers as ivory and people hunters, leading to the virtual extinction of elephants, bitter tribal clashes and the depopulation of some areas. In exchange, the local chiefs received iron, copper, salt, guns, cloth and beads.

The slaves, who were captured in raids or simply sold by their families, were used as porters to carry ivory to the coast. Up to 90 percent are thought to have died on this tortuous journey. Those who survived were sold on, primarily to Arabia and Persia. In total, about 1.5 million people are thought to have been sold through the slave markets in Zanzibar, Bagamoyo and Kilwa.

The other highly prized cargoes, including rhino horn, animal pelts, tortoiseshell, ambergris and, of course, ivory, were traded on to China and India, in exchange for spices, silk and porcelain. These in turn were traded in Europe for guns, cloth and beads.

Zanzibar's spice plantations were a by-product of this lucrative triangular trade. Not only did the Arabs realise that they could cut out the long, expensive sea voyages to the Far East, but that those surplus slaves, used as porters on the caravans, could be readily employed on the islands. Clove trees from Indonesia were smuggled out to Mauritius in the mid-18th century, and were first brought to Zanzibar from Réunion in 1812 by an Arab plantation owner, Saleh bin Haramil al Abray.

In 1822, the British Captain Fairfax Moresby persuaded the Sultan of Zanzibar to limit the international passage of slaves to Oman, cutting off the lucrative French and Dutch islands. In 1827, Sultan Said annexed al Abray's plantations along with other land and set up 45 commercial clove plantations, decreeing that all Zanzibaris should plant three clove trees for every coconut palm. Failure resulted in confiscation of their land.

In 1873, amid growing international pressure fuelled by missionaries' heart-rending tales of the slave caravans, the British finally persuaded the Sultan to ban the sale of slaves altogether. This curbed the volume of trade greatly, but it continued to operate underground, in remote corners of Zanzibar such as Mangapwani, until 1919, when Britain took complete control of the island. A hurricane wiped out Unguja's plantations in 1872. They never fully recovered, and today around 80 percent of Zanzibar's cloves are grown on Pemba. The trade is in crisis: the government of Zanzibar has long operated a state monopoly with an artificially low price, meaning growers could make more money smuggling cloves to Kenya. But in 2011, the government decided to revive the official industry and discourage smuggling by raising the price paid to farmers from US$2.50 per kilogram to US$6.50. As a result, the official 2012 harvest of almost 5,000 tonnes was the largest in a decade. Over the next few years further protective measures and incentives were adopted as Zanzibar's authorities embarked on an ambitious plan to double clove production by 2020.

wealthy city with fine stone houses. By the early 15th century, direct trade with China was sufficiently important for Admiral Cheng Ho to make an official visit, returning home with a giraffe as a present to the Emperor from the Sultan of Malindi. The Chinese trade stopped abruptly in 1443 when the Ming Emperor cut off foreign trade, but trade with India and the Middle East remained buoyant.

The equilibrium was rudely shattered in 1498 by the arrival of the Portuguese, with their superior ships and firepower.

SEARCH FOR THE SEA ROUTE

With the Renaissance in full swing, Europe was rich and self-indulgent. Luxuries, from silk to spices, came from the East and reached Europe the hard way, by sea to Arabia, then by camel caravan to the Mediterranean. Much of the journey was through the hostile Ottoman Empire, and supplies were precarious. There was a fortune waiting for those who could find a shipping route to India.

The Portuguese and Spanish were the first to try. Christopher Columbus sailed west and inadvertently discovered America in 1492. Vasco da Gama was more successful. In 1497, he rounded the Cape of Good Hope and, with the aid of the amenable but short-sighted Sultan of Malindi, who lent him his finest pilot, discovered the secret of the trade winds. On 20 May 1498, da Gama arrived in Calicut, in southern India, causing mayhem, and returning via Zanzibar.

Other ships soon followed, and the Portuguese were permitted to build repair bases on both Zanzibar and Pemba. In 1503, however, their ambition got the better of good relations. Portuguese captain Rui Lourenço Ravasco attacked Zanzibar, capturing 20 dhows and killing some 35 people. To stop the carnage, the Sultan of Zanzibar had to pay tribute, provide fresh food and water, and offer free access to all Portuguese shipping. In 1505, the Portuguese captured Sofala, with its lucrative gold trade, established a military garrison and trading post at Kilwa, and sacked Mombasa. They took over Pemba in 1506, and by 1511 had spread north to grab Muscat and Hormuz on the Gulf of Arabia. By 1525, they controlled the whole of the African coast from the Red Sea to Sofala, while mirror colonies in India ensured their total domination of Indian Ocean shipping routes.

It was not always plain sailing, however, with a constant rumble of protest. In 1510, the

Portuguese brutally suppressed uprisings on both Pemba and Unguja. In 1512, they realised that Kilwa was of no use to them, as they already controlled the gold trade, and withdrew, leaving the city virtually bankrupt. The traders of Kilwa, in search of a way to rebuild their fortunes, looked to the interior for luxury trade goods including ivory, rhino horn and beeswax. Eventually they linked up with the Yao people who were moving north from Mozambique, hungry for iron and cloth. The first of Tanzania's infamous caravan routes was born.

Rare photo of chained slaves awaiting sale in 19th-century Zanzibar.

OMANI REVOLUTION

By the end of the 16th century, the British were also taking a keen interest in the area. In November 1591, the *Edward Bonaventure*, under the command of Sir James Lancaster, sailed into Zanzibar. It was the first of an increasing number of British ships stopping off for supplies and repairs. Relations remained outwardly friendly, but Portugal now faced a potential rival with serious military muscle. In 1593, they built a fort at Chake Chake on Pemba and began work on the imposing Fort Jesus in Mombasa. In the end, however, the British remained on friendly terms. It was the subject Arabs who proved to be the real threat. In 1622, the Omanis succeeded in throwing the Portuguese out of Hormuz. In 1631, Pemba helped Mombasa regain its independence. In 1650, the Omanis retook Muscat. Two years later, they sailed south to 'liberate' Unguja while Pemba attacked pro-Portuguese Kilwa. The Portuguese won that encounter and struggled on, propped up by a series of increasingly feeble alliances, for another 50 years. However, it signalled the beginning of the end.

In 1682, the Christian, pro-Portuguese Queen of Pemba was thrown out by her own people, and the Portuguese were pushed off the island altogether in 1695. The following year, the Omanis besieged Mombasa, and in March 1696 attacked Zanzibar, killing hundreds. By 1698, Mombasa had fallen, closely followed by Zanzibar. Portugal's only remaining property on the East Coast was Mozambique.

The revolution was over, but far from helping the coastal states regain their independence, the Queen of Zanzibar was taken to Muscat, where she lived in exile for the next 12 years, while her son was installed as a puppet king. Real power was in the hands of the Omani governor. East Africa had new imperial masters.

A TRADING NATION

The Arabs paid relatively little attention to their new possessions in the early years, while the enfeebled Yarubi dynasty struggled to hang onto power at home. On Zanzibar, the first obvious sign of the new occupation was the immediate building of a formidable fort on the site of the Portuguese church, right next to – and totally dominating – the existing Sultan's palace. The next, as it was forbidden to enslave Muslims, was the huge growth of the slave trade to provide workers for the Omani date plantations. Old trading centres such as Kilwa were revived, and new towns, including Tanga, Bagamoyo and Dar es Salaam, sprang up along the coast.

In 1744, the Yarubis were finally overthrown by the dynamic trading Bu Said dynasty. Minor members of the family were installed as governors of many regions, including Zanzibar, but elsewhere, local governors had enough autonomy to give them ideas above their station. In 1753, the rival

An 1882 engraving of a slave market in Zanzibar.

⊘ THE RIDDLE OF RHAPTA

The *Periplus of the Erythraean* Sea and Ptolemy's *Geography* both describe a port called Rhapta as 'the metropolis of Barbaria, set back from the sea' on the river Rhapton, whose source lay a 25-day trek distant, close to a pair of snowcapped peaks and two large lakes.

Nobody knows exactly where Rhapta was situated, but the circumstantial evidence points to somewhere on the Tanzanian mainland. Two specific candidates stand out. One is present-day Pangani, on the mouth of the Pangani River, which rises close to Moshi, at the base of snowcapped Kilimanjaro. But no trace of such a settlement has ever been found in the vicinity of Pangani, leading some historians to suggest that Rhapta lay further south, in the Rufiji Delta, whose shifting channels would almost certainly have submerged all trace of the old town by now.

Both the ancient documents give directions to Rhapta, but these do little to help resolve the mystery. The author of the *Periplus* states that Rhapta lay 'two days' sail' south of a 'flat and wooded' island he calls Menouthesias (almost certainly Zanzibar), which would tally closely with a location on the Rufiji Delta. Contradictorily, Ptolemy indicated that Rhapta lay to the north of the island of Menouthesias, at a sailing distance that supports advocates of the theory that Pangani was Rhapta.

Mazrui family, governors of Mombasa, broke away, declared independence and attacked Zanzibar, which repelled the invasion to stay loyal to Oman.

With Mombasa back under Mazrui rule, and Sofala, the traditional gold port, in the hands of the Portuguese, Zanzibar stepped in to fill the gap, rapidly becoming the commercial and political hub of the coast. Meanwhile, the Arabs and Swahilis began to venture further inland, taking control of the previously African-operated slave and ivory caravans to maximise profits. New markets opened up when the Dutch and French arrived to

Tippu Tip was the most notorious of all the slavers to traffic out of Zanzibar.

buy slaves for their plantations in Indonesia, Mauritius and Réunion.

Although they had banned slavery at home in 1772, the British proved happy to deal with slavers, signing a Treaty of Commerce and Navigation with Oman in 1798 in order to block Napoleon's proposed takeover of the Middle East. The British East India Company set up shop in Muscat, and from then on the British played an increasingly important role in the administration of the coast.

SULTAN SAID

One of the longest-living and most influential of the Omani rulers, Sultan Said came to the throne in 1804, aged 13, initially reigning with his cousin,

Bedr, as regent. In 1806, suspicious that his life was in danger, he acted first, had Bedr killed and assumed full power. From the first, he showed himself to be an astute player of international power politics. In 1822, he took the first official step towards breaking the power of the slave trade, by signing a British accord abolishing the transport of slaves beyond the so-called Moresby Line. This still allowed traffic between Zanzibar and Oman, but supposedly stopped sales to the rest of the Indian Ocean.

Five years later, Said made his first visit to Zanzibar, where he founded huge clove plantations, not only providing a lucrative new market for slaves, but annexing a considerable portion of Indonesia's spice trade. Meanwhile, French and Dutch slave ships continued to trade freely. The number of slaves passing through Zanzibar each year went up from 3,000 in the 1780s to 13,000 in the 1840s.

Sultan Said signed trade agreements with the United States (1833), Great Britain (1839), France (1844) and the Hanseatic League (1859), and set up diplomatic relations with the United States, France and Great Britain.

In 1837, with British help, Said overthrew the Mazruis and brought Mombasa back into the empire. In December 1840, he moved his capital to Zanzibar, leaving his son, Thuwaini, as Governor of Oman. Within a couple more years, Arab traders had set up posts at Tabora and in the Kingdom of Buganda (Uganda). They also opened up routes to Mount Kenya, southern Ethiopia and the Congo.

Said encouraged the immigration of Asian businessmen, and from 1840 to 1860, the number of Asians in Zanzibar grew from 300 to 5,000. Heavily involved in financing the slave trade, these immigrants followed the caravan routes inland to establish shops and trading posts, founding many of Tanzania's small towns. Everywhere the caravans went fell under the nominal control of Zanzibar, creating an empire that covered most of the interior, although it was used as a supply depot and never developed.

In 1845, the British forced another supposed reduction in the slave trade on the Sultan. This time the trading limits were set between Lamu and Kilwa, cutting off trade with Oman. The ban was policed by a British naval blockade which proved so ineffective that over the next 20 years the number of slaves passing through Zanzibar rose to 20,000 a year.

Henry Morton Stanley.

STANLEY IN AFRICA.

IMPERIAL AMBITIONS

Faced with European military might, the Sultan of Zanzibar could only stand aside and watch as the British and Germans carved up his empire.

Although Vasco da Gama had opened the flood-gates to European involvement on the coast nearly 350 years before, it was not until the 1840s that any Westerners ventured more than a few miles into the East African interior. By then, Europe's second wave of empire building was getting under way.

In 1788, the Africa Association (later merged with the Royal Geographical Society) was founded in Britain, with the aim of exploring and exploiting the continent. In South Africa, the British were dogging the heels of the Boers, as they colonised the interior, finding rich farm-land and mineral resources. The businessmen, bedazzled by Portuguese tall tales of gold nuggets as big as fists lying on the ground waiting to be picked up, were beginning to take an interest in the seemingly endless wealth pouring into Arab coffers. The Church, having abolished slavery at home, was beginning to take a serious interest in cutting it off at the roots.

Vasco da Gama.

It was the Victorian age of optimism, adventure and, above all, arrogant certainty about the superiority of Western ideas. The mood of the age, and the contradictory motives behind European expansion into Africa, are encapsulated by David Livingstone's conviction that the slave trade – which he had ample opportunity to witness first hand, and described as an 'open sore upon the world' – could be conquered by the spread of 'civilisation, commerce and Christianity'. The three Cs went neatly hand in hand into the unknown.

THE GREAT EXPLORERS

The first European to venture into the Tanzanian hinterland was a German missionary, Johann Krapf, sent out to East Africa by the English Church Missionary Society in 1844. Two years later, he was joined by Johannes Rebmann, who 'discovered' Mount Kilimanjaro in 1848. In 1856, the Royal Geographical Society dispatched an official expedition in search of the White Nile, led by the mismatched and quarrelsome lieutenants Richard Burton and John Hanning Speke. They reached the Lake Tanganyika terminus of the slave caravan route in January 1858. Burton then had to turn back, due to ill health, but Speke continued north to find and name Lake Victoria. He returned in 1860 with James Grant, and the two found the source of the Nile in present-day Uganda. Proving their discovery was actually the feted source was more difficult, however, and Speke died amid professional ridicule, led by Burton (see The riddle of the Nile, page 181).

Meanwhile, the celebrated Scottish explorer Dr David Livingstone was turning his attention to East Africa. He arrived in Zanzibar in January 1866, funded by the British government to solve the question of the source of the Nile once and for all. Convinced it was to be found at Lake Tanganyika, he headed south, eventually finding the source of the Lualaba, which he remained convinced until his dying day would prove to be the Nile. His journeys took him far off the beaten path and kept him totally out of touch for several years. With alarm bells ringing back home, three separate expeditions set out to find him. The first, led by the Welsh journalist Henry Morton Stanley, actually did so in 1871 (see box). The second, led by Lieutenant Llewellyn Dawson, met Stanley in Bagamoyo in 1872, heard the news and went home. The following year, when Livingstone had failed to appear, a third expedition, led by Lieutenant Verney Lovett Cameron, set out from Zanzibar. By this time, it was too late.

Livingstone had grown weak from dysentery and died on 2 May 1873, in the village of Chitambo (in modern Zambia). Two of his servants, Susi and Chumah, buried his heart under a tree, dried his body and carried it to Bagamoyo, a journey of several months. En route, they met Cameron, who decided to keep going, and became the first European to cross Africa from east to west. Livingstone was finally buried in Westminster Abbey on 18 April 1874.

A DIVIDED KINGDOM

At court, life was getting fraught. Sultan Said died at sea in 1856, leaving behind three of his sons to slug it out for control: Thuwaini, governor of Oman, Majid, governor of Zanzibar, and Barghash, who had no real claim to the throne but was with his father when he died.

Barghash's first hasty bid for the throne was abortive, and after much posturing, the kingdom was split, with Thuwaini ruling Oman and Majid becoming the Sultan of Zanzibar. Barghash staged a second unsuccessful coup in 1859 with

John Hanning Speke (right).

⊘ STANLEY AND LIVINGSTONE

In 1866, Livingstone was charged by the Royal Geographical Society with resolving the hotly debated issue of the source of the Nile. By 1869, however, the mystery of Livingstone's whereabouts had become more topical than the riddle he had been sent to resolve. The *New York Herald*, hoping for the scoop of the decade, contacted a young reporter named Henry Morton Stanley with a telegram bearing the plain instruction, 'Find Livingstone'.

Two years later, Stanley arrived at Ujiji where, he later recalled, 'The great Arabs, chiefs and respectabilities... disclosed to me the prominent figure of an elderly white man clad in a red flannel blouse, grey trousers, and a blue cloth, gold-banded cap. All around me was the immense crowd, hushed and expectant, and wondering how the scene would develop itself... I could do no more than exercise some restraint and reserve, so I walked up to him, and, doffing my helmet, bowed and said in an inquiring tone: "Dr Livingstone, I presume?" Smiling cordially, he lifted his cap, and answered briefly: "Yes."'

Stanley recorded his mission to find Livingstone in his book *How I Found Livingstone*. After Livingstone's death, Stanley decided to continue his research on the Congo and the Nile. His journey to the sources of the Nile, *Through a Dark Continent*, was published in 1878.

the help of his sisters Salme (see page 220) and Khole, then spent the next two years in exile in India. In 1861, the British Governor General of India, Lord Canning, was asked to mediate in the dispute. He decreed that the two states should be split, with Zanzibar paying an annual tribute to Oman, but existing as a sovereign state with the Sultan at its head. The island's traditional ruling dynasty was completely sidelined, and the last of the line, Ahmed, died almost unnoticed in 1873.

In 1866, Sultan Thuwaini was murdered, Majid promptly stopped paying tribute and,

David Livingstone is seen 'unlocking' Central Africa.

from then on, Oman withdrew from international affairs, only re-emerging in the 1970s. Zanzibar was left on its own. In 1870, Majid died, and Barghash finally gained the throne he had coveted for so long.

THE BUILDER KING

Barghash was undoubtedly one of Zanzibar's most influential rulers. Zanzibar Town had been growing by leaps and bounds, but there was no town planning or even basic sanitation. The place was awash with disease, and the stench could be smelt miles out to sea. Influenced by the British Vice-Consul, Sir John Kirk, who was also a doctor, Barghash built the town a freshwater supply, as well as building his family a series of opulent

palaces, based on the luxurious royal residences he had seen in India.

Only two years into his reign, Zanzibar was hit by a freak hurricane that decimated the clove plantations on Unguja, although those on Pemba remained largely intact. Barghash decided to replant, and the slave trade sprang into overdrive to provide the workers. It was the last straw. In 1873, faced by a total British blockade, he was eventually persuaded by Sir John Kirk to sign a treaty closing the slave market and protecting liberated slaves. It wasn't perfect – the treaty didn't free all slaves; Zanzibaris were still permitted to import slaves from the mainland as domestic workers; and above all, there was no real will to crack down on the thriving underground traffic. However, it was the beginning of the end.

In 1875, Barghash was invited on a state visit to Britain to ratify the treaty. Between various engagements, he became fascinated by the wonders of modern technology and, on his return home, set to work to provide his city with paved roads, electric street lighting, telephones, a telegraphic link to Europe, an ice factory and a police force. He also bought a fleet of steamships, which could be used free by pilgrims travelling to Mecca for the Haj, as well as for commerce.

He also appointed a British officer, William Lloyd Matthews, as Commander-in-Chief of a revamped army, aiming to take greater control of his vast mainland empire. However, he had left it too late. The European empire builders were on their way.

GERMAN EAST AFRICA

In 1885, a German doctor, Carl Peters, arrived in Zanzibar disguised as a mechanic. From here, he headed into the interior, armed with a series of official-looking treaties. As far as the many local chiefs who signed them were concerned, they were merely treaties of 'Eternal Friendship'. What they actually did was hand their lands over, lock, stock and barrel, to Dr Peters' Society for German Colonisation. They weren't worth the paper they were written on, and the land technically still belonged to the Sultan, but they were sufficiently impressive for Peters to get a German imperial charter from Bismarck for his

Deutsche Ostafrikanische Gesellschaft (the German East Africa Charter Company), with official sanction to colonise and run German East Africa. The speed with which he moved was phenomenal, and the Sultan could only watch as his empire was stripped from him.

In dismay, Barghash turned to his supposed British allies. The ensuing series of high-level European summits neatly sliced his empire up between the British, Germans and Portuguese, leaving Zanzibar only the islands and a 16km (10-mile) wide strip along the coast,

The battle between German troops and Hehe warriors in 1891.

although Germany took Dar es Salaam. In 1887, the British leased the northern part of the strip (now the Kenya coast), which included Mombasa; the Tanzanian portion was ceded to the Germans.

Barghash died in 1888. The following year, his successor, Khalifa, agreed to abolish slavery within his territories, before dying the following year. In 1890, Sultan Ali bin Said signed a treaty forbidding the sale or purchase of slaves. The same year, with Carl Peters attempting to claim Uganda, the British and Germans held a final summit, recognising German control over mainland Tanganyika, giving Britain Kenya and Uganda

and formalising Zanzibar's position as a British Protectorate. In 1891, Zanzibar got its first constitutional government, with General Sir Lloyd Matthews as First Minister. European control of East Africa was complete, and with the loss of slaving revenues and the mainland ports of Mombasa and Dar es Salaam now coming to the fore, Zanzibar began to slide slowly but inexorably into the atmospheric backwater it remains today.

GERMAN OCCUPATION

On the mainland, the Germans moved swiftly, efficiently and often harshly to consolidate their new possession. Local resistance began in the Pangani area in 1888 and spread to Tanga and Bagamoyo before it was eventually suppressed.

In May 1889, an Imperial Commissioner, Major Von Wissmann, was appointed with the aim of suppressing the uprisings. In 1891, the German government took over administration of the colony from the charter company.

Administrative towns were set up across the country, connected by a network of roads and railways. German missionaries were encouraged to settle, with their stations becoming a focus for new rural settlements. Local people were moved into less productive areas, allowing the Germans to develop the fertile agricultural land. Those who managed to stay on their lands were forced to grow cash crops, often at the expense of their own foodstuffs.

In 1891, the Germans killed peaceful envoys from a southern Hehe chief, Mkwawa, due to a misunderstanding, sparking off a war that lasted until 1898. In 1892, the Kilimanjaro area erupted into violence, and in 1894 it was the turn of the German garrison at Kilwa to come under fire. Other uprisings were more localised and caused little harm to the Germans, until the devastating Maji Maji Wars of 1905–7.

The Germans had been forcing the Matumbi Highlanders to grow cotton on unsuitable soil. Sparked by a rumour that a potion had been discovered that would turn the white man's bullets to water before they could strike, they rebelled. It was the first uprising to cross tribal boundaries and spread throughout the south. By the end, 100,000 people had died in bitter fighting, and the Germans' scorched-earth policies led to a three-year famine.

MISSIONARIES

Perhaps the most crucial – and least acknowledged – role in the colonisation of Africa was that of the missionaries, who were among the earliest and most dedicated European explorers.

Even the Portuguese and Spanish navigators sailed with priests, the call of the Catholic Monarchs and the Inquisition ringing in their ears. In Tanzania, Krapf and Rebmann, the first Westerners to venture into the interior, were sent there by the English Church Missionary Society. Livingstone was actually an employee of the London Missionary Society, although he proved to be far more efficient as an explorer, leaving others to follow behind to do the conversions. The first German governor used Lutheran and Moravian missionaries to open up the Mbeya region to colonisation.

The relationship between the missionaries, the traders and the administration was always a pragmatic one. The missionaries believed sincerely that the way to God was through Western civilisation and that commerce would help produce the desired result. They also were prepared to use any means to justify the end result.

From the first, they found the slave trade abhorrent and campaigned rigorously against it. Livingstone's graphic first-hand accounts of conditions on the caravans led to a huge anti-slaving campaign back in Britain and the near saint-like status he still enjoys in Tanzania today. However, he and most of his colleagues used Zanzibar as a base and supply depot; they were happy to accept the generous hospitality of the Sultan and travelled long distances under the protection of Arab slavers. Livingstone even stayed in the home of the infamous slave trader Tippu Tip.

From the point of view of local tribes, the missionaries were generally welcomed, first as a curiosity, but then for the benefits they brought with them. The chiefs frequently used these educated Westerners as translators, scribes and advisers during negotiations. Some actively became involved in trading such items as much sought-after cloth, and were welcomed for the wealth their activities provided. Others

were seen as political allies and buffers against intertribal violence.

Life was not all plain sailing. Some missions faced a rougher reception, particularly in areas where the traditional priests had great power. One of the forces behind the Maji Maji Rebellion (see page 48) was a last-ditch attempt to reassert traditional religious views. Its disastrous outcome led

Missionaries teaching tribespeople in 1907.

directly to a mass conversion of the south, as the disillusioned people resigned themselves to colonial rule, and gratefully took the missionaries' food during the ensuing famine.

The missionaries were most persuasive when the message came from other African converts, such as freed slaves from the model village in Mbweni set up by Universities' Mission in Central Africa (see page 226) or graduates of St Andrew's College, the country's first really good school, also founded by the UMCA, in 1869. Then, people could see the tangible benefits of adopting this foreign God in exchange for food, clothes, education and health care. It was, to a great extent, mission-educated men who created the Tanganyikan civil service, the first nationalist movements and the first independent government. Today, although the coast and islands remain essentially Islamic, the vast majority of mainlanders are Christian, although many hedge their bets, worshipping their traditional gods alongside Christ.

A 1915 cartoon shows the British in their surprising struggle to defeat Germany in East Africa.

Zeichnung 7

D. O. Afrika

THE COLONIAL ERA

World War I had repercussions far beyond Europe: in East Africa, dogged German resistance was followed by 40 years of British colonial rule.

When the Austrian Archduke Franz Ferdinand was assassinated by Serbian nationalists in Sarajevo in 1914, a major European conflict was clearly imminent. Kaiser Wilhelm II immediately affirmed German support for Austria-Hungary, while France and Russia stood behind the Serbians. For six weeks, Britain was indecisive. However, it had long held concerns about the growing international influence and military power of Germany. As a result, in early August, when German troops marched through Belgium to attack France, thus violating the Treaty of London (which declared that Belgian neutrality was to be respected by all European nations), Britain had little hesitation in entering the war on the side of Serbia, Russia and France.

The European war was to have a significant consequence on Germany's scattering of far-flung African colonies. In 1914, German East Africa was wholly surrounded by rival colonial territories. The British ruled over Kenya and Uganda to the north, as well as Northern Rhodesia (now Zambia) to the south, and the islands of Zanzibar and Pemba to the east, while the colony's western border was shared with the Belgian Congo. Furthermore, Germany's forces in East Africa were not only surrounded by Allied troops, but also heavily outnumbered.

AN INSPIRED PRUSSIAN

The German commander, Oberst (Colonel) Paul von Lettow-Vorbeck, had fewer than 4,000 men under his command. They included several hundred German officers and non-commissioned officers, and a handful of European volunteers, but the bulk of his force were *Askari*, native African recruits. If the British expected German East Africa to capitulate without a fight, however, they

Colonel Paul von Lettow-Vorbeck, commander of the German forces in East Africa.

had reckoned without the skill and daring of Paul von Lettow-Vorbeck, the descendant of distinguished Prussian army officers and an inspired commander. Far from capitulating, or even taking a defensive stance, Lettow-Vorbeck launched a series of effective attacks on the railway in Kenya, and even attempted to capture Mombasa, although he was beaten back.

In November 1914, a large British and Indian invasion force landed at Tanga with orders to 'secure German East Africa'. Although they heavily outnumbered Lettow-Vorbeck's troops, they were poorly organised and indecisively led. They walked into a German trap, suffered heavy casualties and retreated to their landing craft, leaving behind large quantities of weapons and ammunition which Lettow-Vorbeck gratefully seized. Unsurprisingly, the British government hushed up this humiliating defeat until long after the end of the war.

Encouraged and rearmed, Lettow-Vorbeck proceeded to make raids into Kenya and Zambia (then Northern Rhodesia), attacking and laying waste to a number of forts, 20 trains, several bridges and many miles of British railway line.

In 1916, Britain launched another major attack on German East Africa, led by the South African General, Jan Christiaan Smuts. But even with

Farming in the 1950s; a worker carries millet home for processing.

40,000 troops under his command, including reinforcements from the Belgian Congo, Smuts was unable to rout Lettow-Vorbeck's 4,000.

By 1917, with the British attacking from Kenya and Rhodesia, the Belgians from the Congo, and the Portuguese from Mozambique, the overwhelming odds began to tell on the German commander. Running low on ammunition, food and supplies, Lettow-Vorbeck resorted to guerrilla warfare. His *Askari* showed him how to live off the land, and how to make their own clothing and medicines. Munitions were acquired by surprise attacks on Portuguese forts on the Mozambique border. The unique combination of Prussian tactics and discipline and *Askari* knowledge of the African

bush made Lettow-Vorbeck's force perhaps the finest guerrilla army in military history.

THE AFTERMATH OF WAR

In November 1918, Lettow-Vorbeck was planning a large-scale attack on a British command centre in Zambia when news arrived of the Armistice in Europe. He reluctantly surrendered to the British, undefeated after a brilliant four-year campaign. The East African campaign had weakened the country disastrously. Apart from the many thousands of Europeans and Africans killed in the fighting, food production had been disrupted, and famine (especially severe in the Dodoma region) claimed many more lives. The 1919 Treaty of Versailles assigned Germany's former African territories to the new League of Nations. Ruanda-Urundi (now Rwanda and Burundi) was handed to Belgium; the rest of German East Africa was renamed Tanganyika and mandated to Britain. In theory, under the League of Nations mandate, it was to be managed by the British in the interests of the 'native inhabitants'. In practice, Tanganyika became another country coloured pink on world maps, administered by the Colonial Office in London.

In 1925, Sir Donald Campbell was appointed governor. Adapting the former German policy of 'indirect rule', he included tribal leaders in local decision-making, while denying them access to central government. Chiefs were nominated to preside over 'native' courts, collect taxes, recruit labour and enforce other colonial edicts. In some areas this worked fairly well. In others, tribal leaders commanded little respect, and were unable or unwilling to perform their duties.

FOOD BOOM

The British devoted much energy to organising agriculture, concentrating on export crops, produced both on plantations, owned and managed by Europeans, and on peasant farms. To encourage locals to commit themselves to growing cash crops, the British persuaded village families to move to the plantations by building schools and health facilities nearby, and offered technical support and price inducements for cultivation on family land.

These incentives greatly increased the production of export crops – but also led to a dangerous neglect of food production for local use. With most of its fertile land devoted exclusively to cash crops,

Tanganyika suffered several serious food short-ages during the interwar years. Although the new plantation communities may have disrupted tradi-tional social systems, they did foster the formation of African associations and community collectives, which later provided the foundation for political organisation. Some groups, such as the Bahaya Union in Bukoba, sprang up in agricultural com-munities. Others began in towns: the Tanganyika African Association was formed in Dar es Salaam in 1929 and later spread to rural areas. In time, these groups became more political, and joined the campaign for self-government.

GROWING PROSPERITY

World War II strengthened Tanganyika's economy as dramatically as World War I had weakened it. The country saw no fighting, so food production continued unabated – while international food prices soared. An increased world demand for sisal, cotton and pyrethrum also boosted exports. Tanganyika's revenue from overseas trade grew by 600 percent between 1939 and 1949.

After the war, the League of Nations evolved into the United Nations, and in 1947, Tanganyika's status was affirmed as a UN Trustee Territory. Implicit in the trusteeship was the goal of self-government: observed by visiting UN missions, the British colonial administration was expected to work to that end. The governor, Sir Edward Twin-ing, took steps towards self-rule by making 'native' authorities responsible for devising and imple-menting development plans, with funds available from government agencies. He went further and set up local councils on which Europeans, Asians and Africans would take equal numbers of seats – even in areas with small or non-existent European or Asian populations.

These plans were at best ineffective. More often they provoked serious and even violent opposition, which soon found a collective voice in one organi-sation: the Tanganyika African National Union (TANU). The Tanganyika African Association (TAA) had begun life as a social organisation, but in the post-war years it became a focus for nationalist feeling. In 1953, a former schoolteacher, Julius Nyerere (see page 59), was elected its presi-dent, and immediately redrafted its constitution. In 1954, the TAA became the TANU, an overtly politi-cal organisation with the slogan *Uhuru na Umoja* (Freedom and Unity). Nyerere embarked on a

vigorous recruitment campaign, and within a year, TANU had become the largest political organisa-tion in Tanganyika. It entered candidates for the 1958 elections for the Legislative Council, an advi-sory body that had always been dominated by non-Africans. Governor Twining continued to reserve two-thirds of the council seats for Europeans and Asians, and voter registration was restricted, yet TANU picked up a large share of the popular vote and won five seats. As tensions mounted, the Brit-ish government replaced Twining with a new gov-ernor, Sir Richard Turnbull, with instructions to

Sir Richard Turnbull, the last British colonial governor of Tanganyika, and his wife wave farewell to the newly independent Tanzania.

guide Tanganyika towards independence. His first act was to scrap the tripartite (European-Asian-African) council. In the 1960 elections, with no restrictions along ethnic lines, TANU candidates were returned in all but one seat. The message to Britain was clear. Hasty constitutional reform instituted a Government of Internal Affairs, domi-nated by TANU. By May 1961, the governor had lost all effective power. Tanganyika was effectively self-governing, with Julius Nyerere as its chief minister.

On 9 December, the Union flag was replaced by a new green, black and gold flag. Tanganyika had achieved full independence, without a shot being fired or a single life being lost.

COMPLETE

INDEPENDENCE

1961

INDEPENDENCE

The first three decades of independence were dominated by Julius Nyerere's radical socialist policies, but these have since given way to a free-market economy.

Prime Minister Nyerere had big plans for the newly independent Tanganyika. His first aim was to forge a sense of national unity. To this end, he made Swahili the national language and ordered that it should be taught in all schools. Swahili, already widely spoken among the country's many different ethnic groups, soon became the lingua franca, even in areas where it had not been much used before.

But that was just the beginning. Nyerere planned to make Tanganyika economically self-sufficient. Internally, he was determined that rural Africans should not be oppressed by a rich elite. Internationally, his stance was theoretically non-aligned, yet he expressed support for the disenfranchised Africans in South Africa, Angola and Mozambique. It was not long before his leftist egalitarian ideals caused watchful concern among some Western states.

In December 1962, Tanganyika became a republic within the Commonwealth, and Julius Nyerere smoothly progressed from being prime minister to president.

REVOLUTION IN ZANZIBAR

Although Tanganyika was independent, Zanzibar was still a British Protectorate. In 1962, a constitutional conference in London thrashed out a plan for independence for the island, with the Sultan as head of state. Elections the following year left legislative power in the balance: the predominantly Arab Zanzibar National Party (NZP) held most of the seats in the Legislative Council, although the left-wing Afro-Shirazi Party (ASP), led by Sheikh Abeid Amani Karume, won 54 percent of the popular vote.

When independence arrived in December 1963, tension between the two factions was mounting.

Putting Tanganyika's flag at the summit of Mt. Kilimanjaro to celebrate independence.

Within a month, it erupted into bloody revolution. The Sultan was deposed and driven into exile. Most of the island's Arab population fled or were killed. The NZP was ousted by the revolutionary council of the ASP, with Abeid Karume as prime minister. As old scores were settled, it is estimated that up to 20,000 people lost their lives.

Most of the world, including Britain and the US, refused to recognise Karume's left-wing regime. Feeling vulnerable, he looked to his nearest neighbour. In April 1964, Karume and Julius Nyerere signed an Act of Union between Zanzibar and Tanganyika, creating the United Republic of Tanzania, with Nyerere as president and Karume vice-president.

THE ARUSHA DECLARATION

Re-elected for a second term in 1965, Nyerere soon fell out with Britain. He loudly condemned what he saw as the tacit British acceptance of the Unilateral Declaration of Independence (UDI) in Rhodesia. In return, Britain suspended economic aid to Tanzania. Increasingly frustrated at Tanzania's slow economic growth, Nyerere made radical plans to make his country self-supporting. The 1967 Arusha Declaration outlined his vision of African Socialism, nationalising banks, plantations and major industries,

Women cultivating the soil in an Ujamaa village, 1974.

and redistributing individual wealth through selective taxation.

The cornerstone of the new policy was a system of co-operative farming that combined Maoist collectivist principles with the traditional African village. The watchword was *Ujamaa* (familyhood).

Families were to move voluntarily into large villages in which food and basic commodities would be produced collectively for the community. The state would provide incentives including piped water, electricity, schools and clinics, but the villages would be effectively self-governing.

COLLAPSE OF UJAMAA

After three years, the number of people working in collectivised villages had grown to only 500,000 – less than 4 percent of the total population. To hurry things along, Nyerere added more incentives in the form of financial and technical assistance. However, a widespread reluctance to move to the collectives meant that the ambitious production targets were still not being met. From 1973, compulsory resettlement drove literally millions of people into the villages, with dramatic results. By 1977, more than 13 million (about 85 percent of the population) had been resettled into more than 8,000 *Ujamaa* villages. The effects were socially invigorating but economically disastrous.

Rural collectivisation gave millions access for the first time to clean water, health care and education, giving Tanzania one of the highest literacy rates in Africa, but agricultural productivity actually dropped. The villages tended to be overcrowded, and the surrounding lands were usually incapable of supporting large populations. Water supplies were often inadequate to support the large herds of cattle and goats, and Tanzania's frequent droughts only exacerbated the situation.

By 1977, it was clear that rural collectivisation had failed to produce a viable economy. Reluctantly, the *Ujamaa* policy was abandoned, and Tanzania was obliged to accept loans from donor countries and the International Monetary Fund (IMF), with all the political and economic strings they entailed.

INTERNATIONAL RELATIONS

Despite its economic problems, Tanzania was not entirely inward-looking during the 1970s. It gave safe haven to African National Congress (ANC) members wanted by South Africa's apartheid government. Nyerere urged neighbouring countries to boycott South African goods and refrain from investing in South African companies. He also gave active support to the independence movements in Angola, Mozambique and Rhodesia, even offering a home and training camps for the freedom fighters. When Zambia closed its border with Rhodesia, the Tanzanians and Chinese built the TAZARA railway from Lusaka to Dar es Salaam to give the copper mines access to a port.

Since 1967, Tanzania, Kenya and Uganda had been members of the East African Community (EAC), a free-trade zone which shared some services, including immigration, telecommunications and an airline. But ideological differences between the three members soon emerged, as

Tanzania embraced socialism, Kenya adopted a capitalist stance and Uganda was oppressed by the erratic dictator Idi Amin. Things came to a head in 1977, in a dispute over the funding of the jointly run East African Airways (EAA). Kenya unilaterally seized all the planes, and Tanzania retaliated by closing the border with Kenya. The EAA was effectively dead, and the Tanzania–Kenya border remained closed until 1983, when the assets of the EAA were finally settled.

Relations with Amin's Uganda were even worse. When Tanzania gave refuge to Ugandan dissidents,

A soldier waving his gun in victory on a border post after its capture from Idi Amin's troops.

including Milton Obote (the former president) and Yoweri Museveni (the current president), Amin retaliated by invading Tanzania, bombing the lake ports of Bukoba and Musoma and occupying the region east of the Kagera River. Tanzania had virtually no regular army, but a people's militia was assembled, and in January 1979 a hastily trained Tanzanian force of over 20,000 invaded Uganda, routing the disaffected Ugandan army and marching into Kampala. Amin fled into exile, initially to Libya, while an occupying force of 12,000 Tanzanian troops kept the peace in Uganda. Thus Tanzania became the only African country to win an international war in the 20th century – although the victory has never been widely celebrated.

Elections in 1980 returned Milton Obote as Uganda's president for a second time. The Tanzanian troops withdrew the next year. Although the West – and most of Africa – were glad to see the end of Amin's regime, no other country contributed to the war effort or towards the estimated US$500-million war cost.

POLITICAL UPHEAVAL

In 1975, a law was passed making TANU the national political party. Tanzania was now officially a one-party state – although Zanzibar still had its own semi-autonomous government, controlled by the Afro-Shirazi Party. A pragmatic merger took place in 1977, TANU and the ASP combining to form Chama Cha Mapinduzi (CCM), the Party of the Revolution.

Nyerere was duly re-elected president in 1980. But by now the failure of *Ujamaa*, the collapse of the EAC and the war against Uganda had brought the economy to its knees. Poverty and corruption were rife; the infrastructure was crumbling, and improvements in education and health care were being eroded.

Western governments, the World Bank and the IMF were all prepared to help – but only if Tanzania undertook major social and economic reforms, including liberalisation and privatisation. Julius Nyerere refused to compromise his socialist principles, but in 1985 he relinquished the presidency – the first post-independence African president to do so voluntarily.

ECONOMIC ABOUT-TURN

The new president, Zanzibari Ali Hassan Mwinyi, spent the next 10 years trying to revive Tanzania's economy with IMF-sanctioned austerity measures: spending cuts, privatisation, encouraging foreign investment and anti-corruption policies.

The results were not instantaneous, but since that time Tanzania has maintained an annual growth rate of 5–8 percent. Mwinyi could not entirely eradicate corruption, although a purge of the civil service was remarkably effective. One of his notable achievements was the abolition of the one-party state.

PARLIAMENTARY OPPOSITION

In 1995, Mwinyi retired after two terms in office, and the first multi-party election in decades took place. The CCM won 186 of the 232 National Assembly seats, and Benjamin Mkapa became president. The major opposition party, the Civic United Front (CUF), accused the CCM of vote-rigging in Zanzibar – and international observers agreed that the electoral process was badly flawed. Having failed to get a rerun of the election, the CUF boycotted the National Assembly. Tension between the government and the opposition continued until 1998, when the CUF ended its three-year boycott of parliament and reached an uneasy truce with the CCM.

> *In 1999, the introduction of an East African passport let Tanzanians, Kenyans and Ugandans to cross borders freely. In 2000, the nations revived the East African Community, to be joined by Burundi and Rwanda in 2009 and South Sudan in 2016.*

In August 1998, international terrorism reached Tanzania when an Al-Qaeda-backed bomb exploded outside the US Embassy in Dar es Salaam, killing 11 people. Many more died in a similar explosion in Nairobi.

Meanwhile, President Mkapa was forced to address a number of difficult domestic problems, particularly the debt-saddled economy (most of the debt was cancelled by the US in 2002). In an effort to balance the budget and increase state revenue, he downsized the civil service and brought in stringent laws against tax evasion. He also cracked down on gold and gemstone smuggling, which had for years diverted a significant amount of government revenue. Mkapa successfully strived to attract international investment, and to revive regional trade relations by restoring the East African Community in 2000.

In 2005, the CCM's Jakaya Kikwete was elected as president of Tanzania. Kikwete's government initially received praise, both at home and abroad, for addressing issues of social justice and education, and for encouraging new investment. Kikwete also launched a national campaign on voluntary HIV/Aids testing. Kikwete was re-elected in 2010, but with a vastly reduced majority amid growing concerns about governmental corruption.

Kikwete was replaced in 2015 by his party colleague and former teacher Dr John Pombe Magufuli in a hotly contested presidential election. Muguguli's campaign was underpinned by promises to tackle corruption and the frequent power shortages paralysing the country, to boost the economy, and to introduce free secondary education. Nicknamed 'the Bulldozer' for relentlessly driving an extensive road-building programme as minister of works, Magufuli began his rule by curbing public spending, streamlining the administration and reducing the number of ministers in his

John Magufuli, president of Tanzania.

cabinet. He even cancelled Independence Day celebrations, urging citizens to take part in a nationwide clean-up campaign instead, while diverting celebration funds to public hospitals. Widely praised for his anti-corruption stance, Magufuli was nonetheless criticised by the opposition for banning political rallies until 2020 and suspending live broadcast of parliamentary sessions.

Tanzania remains one of the poorest countries in the world, and while the mainland is very peaceful, there is ongoing political tension in Zanzibar linked to religious extremism and separatist movements, as well as recent concerns over fair elections. Despite these challenges, the mood in Tanzania is optimistic, with encouraging economic growth and an ever-expanding tourist industry.

PRESIDENT NYERERE

A controversial leader whose idealistic socialist policies shaped Tanzania, the late Julius Nyerere is affectionately remembered as the Father of the Nation.

Regarded with reverence for his success in freeing his people from ethnic and civil conflict, Nyerere also attracts resentment for relocating 85 percent of the population in an attempt to develop a new brand of socialism, and for his part in creating many of Tanzania's economic difficulties.

He was born in Butiama in 1922, the eminently intelligent son of a Zanaki chief. He shone at primary school, went on to Tanganyika's only secondary school and then to Uganda's Makerere University, where he obtained a teaching degree. He then spent three years studying economics and history at the University of Edinburgh.

Although Nyerere began his working life as a teacher, he soon turned into a full-time politician. In 1953, he became president of the Tanganyika African Association, which, under his leadership, evolved into the Tanganyika African National Union (TANU), with the slogan 'Freedom and Unity'. By 1957, TANU was the largest political organisation in the country, and Nyerere was the voice of Tanganyika's bid for independence from colonial government.

He became Tanganyika's chief minister in 1960 and led his country to independence on 9 December 1961.

Passionate about eradicating the structure of colonial rule, Nyerere wanted to introduce a sense of national identity and pride in the emerging nation and a fairer system of sharing for his people. He made Swahili the national language, and also persuaded Zanzibar to form the union that became Tanzania.

In 1965, Nyerere was officially acknowledged as head of a one-party state, and began to introduce a brand of Chinese communism that embraced the African ethos of hard work, equality and *Ujamaa* (familyhood).

Two years later, his Arusha Declaration aimed to create a nation that would feed and educate itself and offer equality to all. His idea was to establish large *Ujamaa* villages combining productivity and the distribution of the nation's resources, replacing the many small, rural villages which were too scattered to allow a proper supply of water, education and health services.

In the end, 85 percent of the people were moved compulsorily, causing huge resentment. Education, health care and access to water did improve, but the villages were ultimately unable to produce enough food to feed themselves, and rural poverty became rife.

On the international scene, Nyerere was regarded as a political mover and shaker. He was one of the founders of African nationalism and one of the continent's greatest statesmen. A leading supporter of the

Julius Nyerere, first president of Tanzania.

freedom struggle in Zimbabwe and anti-apartheid movements in South Africa, he was instrumental in overthrowing Idi Amin's stranglehold on Uganda, and campaigned for developing-world debt relief. He strongly supported unity and cooperation between the regions, consistently maintaining that he would like to see Tanzania and its neighbours work together to form an East Africa Federation.

By 1985, however, Tanzania's economy was in dire straits. Nyerere took responsibility for his actions, telling his people, 'I failed. Let's admit it.' He resigned in favour of Ali Hassan Mwinyi, but continued to exercise political influence in Tanzania and across Africa until 1990, when he retired back to the place of his birth with his wife and seven children. He died in October 1999.

Maasai giraffe next to a baobab tree, Ruaha National Park.

MUSIC, DANCE AND ART

Blending traditional and contemporary influences,
Tanzania's arts scene, from the music to the
paintings, is bright with colour and full of life.

Music leads to dancing and dancing to art, and in Tanzania they are all vibrant and colourful. Music, dance and art are inextricably linked in Tanzania. Indigenous painting and carving is relatively undeveloped in comparison to music and dance. Although there are renowned examples, specifically Tingatinga painting and Makonde carving, the growth of fine art has been heavily influenced by the dictates of the tourist market. This has had a negative impact on artistic quality, but nevertheless has secured a livelihood for the many craftsmen who satisfy a voracious demand for souvenirs.

TINGATINGA

Tanzania's most notable artist is Edward Saidi Tingatinga, whose story began in the first half of the last century. He was born in 1932 in Namonchelia (now Nakapanya in the Ruvuma region) to a poor peasant family, and worked on the sisal plantations, in gardens, as a street vendor and an embroiderer. He started painting in 1968, using a brush and oil paints to depict animals and African scenes on hardboard.

His paintings began to sell in Dar es Salaam, and in time, the National Arts Company agreed that Tingatinga should supply some of his paintings. The prices doubled, and he quit his day job to become a full-time artist and train young relatives as apprentices. Tingatinga died aged 40 from gunshot wounds after being mistaken for a thief by police, abruptly ending the brief period during which he produced African naïve art but arguably increasing the popularity of his work.

His students continued to paint in his style, and currently around 50 artists work at the Dar es Salaam factory alone. This art co-operative was formed with government backing. Each year

A Dar es Salaam Tingatinga artist.

on Christmas Day, the artists clean his burial ground and cook food as a sacrifice.

Tingatinga's work is characterised by a highly decorative, patterned finish, usually in square format worked in enamel and high-gloss oil paints. Each picture tells its own story, often of rural life and sometimes with political undertones. It has a simplicity which borders on animation, a cross between Grandma Moses and Walt Disney. Stylised birds, fish or animals may be depicted against Mount Kilimanjaro in the background, or perhaps a decorative pattern of dots.

The early paintings were quite simple and usually tended to feature just one African creature on a flat, monotone background. However, since his death, imitators have appeared in several parts of the country, and the style has developed towards the extremely colourful and complex ones that we see everywhere, aimed specifically at the tourism market.

Much of the work has little artistic merit but provides a cheerful reminder of Tanzania, and can now be found in many parts of the country, including Zanzibar.

THE ART OF WOMEN

Painting is almost exclusively a male preserve, while crafts are the domain of women. Tourists

Tingatinga painting.

can find a natural development of this cultural tradition at the Bagamoyo Art Market, on the north coast, where women produce excellent weaving, tie dye, batik, pottery and printed fabrics.

The women use indigenous materials, with an emphasis on traditional design, and their work is a classic illustration of practical culture becoming an art form.

Further up in the Usambara Mountains, walking tours offer visitors the chance to visit mountain villages like Kileti, where around 30 potters work. They are all women, as decreed by ancient sacred tenets. Their knowledge is passed from generation to generation, and men are forbidden to participate. A typical pot takes a week to prepare, starting with a 2km (1-mile) walk

to dig the clay, which the potter carries back to her village on her head. The clay is broken up, mixed with water and pounded to a smooth consistency, and the pots are made from a clay ball which has been pushed and pulled into shape. Bigger pots have coil after coil of clay added to the rim. The surface is decorated with gourd scrapers and fired inside a mound of firewood.

WOOD

As in many African countries, woodcarving is a staple of traditional craft. However, it can be

Makonde carver at work, Mwenge Craft Market, Dar es Salaam.

difficult to distinguish between imported lookalikes and genuine local products. Many of the 'curios' on sale in Tanzania come from elsewhere in Africa, such as Kenya, South Africa and Zimbabwe, all of which have older tourist trades. Once you have established the provenance of a piece, you need to look carefully at the quality of the workmanship and also at the wood itself. Real ebony is exceptionally heavy and black inside as well. However, the wood is now endangered due to extensive cutting, so consider opting for 'fake' ebony instead.

Probably the best and most imaginative woodcarving in East Africa is produced by the Makonde people from southern Tanzania and northern Mozambique, who have been practising their craft for about 300 years. Some carvers still work on the Makonde Plateau, but many have gravitated to Dar es Salaam and Arusha.

One style of carving consists of distorted and highly stylised people, usually a mother and her children. These would have been carried by the male carver for good luck. More common are those with *ujamaa* motifs and those known as *shetani*, which include grotesque figures based on Makonde spirits.

owner, the larger and more elaborate the door. There are still around 560 carved doors in Stone Town, and others to be found in areas such as Bagamoyo, Kilwa and Pemba. The ornate geometric and floral decoration that typifies Swahili design can also be found on chests, jewellery boxes and tables. If you have the money, you can even commission a four-poster bed.

WHERE TO SHOP

Excellent-quality modern wood products can be obtained at most of the major souvenir

Intricately carved door in Stone Town.

Ujamaa carvings look like totem poles made up of interlocking people and animals. Made from a single piece of wood, they contain up to 50 figures and can stand several metres high.

THE SWAHILI TRADITION

The doorway was always the most elaborate feature in a Swahili home, but during the 1800s, craftsmen in Zanzibar developed a style and tradition of carving wooden doors that has no parallel in any other part of the world. They combined Indian methods with Islamic decorative styles and the home-grown Swahili tradition. When a house was built in Zanzibar, the door was the first part to be erected, and the greater the wealth and social position of the

shops, such as the Cultural Heritage Centre outside Arusha or the Zanzibar Gallery in Stone Town. In Dar es Salaam, try the markets outside The Slipway, or shops along Samora Avenue, south of the Askari Monument. There are also many craft stalls along Ali Hassan Mwinyi Boulevard. However, the best place in the country to see the diversity of these high-quality artefacts is at the Mwenge Craft Market (see page 128) on the outskirts of Dar es Salaam. Craftspeople from all over the country sell their wares in a little enclave of stalls stacked high with carvings.

There are spears, life-size warriors, masks, giraffes, lions. You name it, they've carved it – anything from a tiny hippo for a few US dollars

> 'Music is learning, music is prayer and mourning. You won't see me sing when I am happy. I sing when I have sorrow in my heart.' (Traditional song).

to life-size African women and warriors selling for upwards of US$200,000. This is as much a workshop as a showcase. The air is thick with sawdust; craftsmen sculpt under the trees; and

Dancer performing at a game lodge.

as you visit each hut you can hear the tapping of their work and watch the women polish the finished products. Other souvenirs, from slippers to drums or jewellery, are also on display. Prices are very reasonable, and the quality is generally excellent. Larger objects can be shipped.

THE RHYTHM OF DANCE

Of all the arts, music and dance have progressed most naturally and creatively. Traditional dance rhythms have been maintained, while new forms emerge as musicians and dancers are influenced by more Western sounds. The Swahili word for dance is *ngoma*, which also means drums. Of all the country's traditional instruments, the drum is supreme, used to announce arrivals and

departures and to keep morale up in farming societies through a dance called *Gobogobo*.

Among the many other musical instruments new to Western ears – and on display in the National Museum in Dar es Salaam – are the *kalimba* (a type of thumb piano), *kayamba* (shakers), rattles, bells and *silva* (horns). Dance in Tanzania serves as a way of communicating with ancestors as well as a means of entertainment and a way of expressing emotion. Although performances for tourist groups tend to dilute the message, most traditional movements and rhythms remain the same. *Taarab* is popular in Zanzibar. This evening show involves a singer backed by a 40-piece orchestra of drums, horns and strings. Women in evening wear slowly approach the singer, dancing as they ascend and offering money to sponsor lines they feel speak to their own lives. The music itself is a mix of Indian, Arabian and African.

Sauti za Busara, a music festival that attracts musicians and spectators from across the globe to Zanzibar, is a huge event in the Tanzanian calendar. Held in the Old Fort along Stone Town's waterfront during February, Sauti za Busara is foremost a celebration of Tanzanian music in all its diversity. Don't expect much sleep – performances begin early in the morning and run throughout the day and night.

Mwaka Kogwa (see page 231), in southern Zanzibar, is a colourful dance and music festival celebrating the Shirazi New Year (in July). It features mock fights with banana stems which enable the fighters to vent their grievances and enter the new year with a pure heart.

Dancing with masks is not common except in the southeast, where the Makonde and the Makua use masked dancing to celebrate coming-out ceremonies for children. Just south of Bagamoyo, on the road to Dar es Salaam, Chuo cha Sanaa is a theatre and arts college which sometimes gives performances of traditional drumming and dancing. Enquiries should be made at the school.

BAND SCENE

Many displays of traditional music and dance in Tanzania have developed in a way that art and crafts have not. During the colonial era, British and German military bands had an influence, and brass instruments were combined with traditional instruments, creating rhumba bands. There is also a Tanzanian dance called *mchirku*, which is big in the cities. Comprising seven or eight teenagers, three or four drums, a tambourine and keyboard, it is rhythmic and raucous, and was banned in the 1970s for its lewd lyrics and erotic dance style. It's now heralded as a distinctly Tanzanian sound.

The local dance-band scene is also thriving. Since the late 1960s, the radio has exclusively featured Tanzanian bands on its Swahili programme, and this in turn has helped develop a

was taught by a *ngoma* (drummer). In its original form, the dancers were bare-chested, carried a spear and had bells on their ankles. Jazz is also popular. The first local jazz band appeared in the 1940s, and you'll find many jazz musicians in Dar es Salaam, where, once again, the dance tradition is strong.

This interlinking of dance, music and art makes Tanzania's deep traditional culture very accessible. To enjoy it is to learn about Tanzanian history and lifestyle, and to discover a people with a big heart and capacity to live to the full.

Musicians playing at Zanzibar's Sauti za Busara festival.

specific national style of music. Lyrics are more important than the music, and a topical message is often incorporated. It is folk music in the making; this song from Remmy Ongala is typical of modern music with a message:

A bicycle has no say in front of a motorbike.
A motorbike has no say in front of a car.
A motorcar has no say in front of a train.
The poor person has no rights.
I am poor. I have no right to speak.
Poor and weak before the powerful.
Weak as long as the powerful likes.

The Tanzanians are natural and enthusiastic dancers. *Sedema* is a type of music during which the musicians dance as they play and the audience copies them. It has traditional origins and

⊘ BONGO FLAVA

Tanzania's home-grown hip-hop is known as *bongo flava* (*bongo*, meaning 'brain', is a nickname for Dar es Salaam, and *flava* a derivative of flavour). Derived from its American counterpart, it also draws on diverse African musical influences, and lyrics are usually sung in Swahili. The most trendy musical style among young Tanzanians, *bongo flava* is also very popular in neighbouring Kenya and Uganda, but very little has been released further afield. The most popular artists of this genre include Professor Jay, Ali Kiba and Lady Jaydee, among others.

Sanje Falls, Udzungwa
Mountains National Park.

THE LIE OF THE LAND

From the blinding white of coral sand to the snows of Kilimanjaro, Tanzania has some of Africa's most varied and dramatic natural environments.

Tanzania is remarkable for the extraordinary variety of its topography, giving it one of the greatest ranges of biodiversity in Africa. The Serengeti, Ngorongoro, Kilimanjaro and Selous are among its seven World Heritage Sites. Ancient pre-Cambrian basement rocks of gneisses, schists and granite, which form the large central plateau of the Maasai Steppe, rise from 1,000 to 1,500 metres (3,300 to 4,900ft) in the Serengeti.

Next door, violent volcanic activity has formed the Great Rift Valley and its associated mountains – including Africa's highest mountain, Kilimanjaro – over the past 20 million years. Along the narrow coastal belt are the younger sediments of the Jurassic, Cretaceous and Tertiary periods, while offshore there are even coral atolls.

VALLEYS AND MOUNTAINS

The Great Rift Valley, which stretches from Turkey through East Africa south to the Zambezi Valley, is represented by two branches in Tanzania. The western arm, which runs along the border with the Democratic Republic of Congo, is dominated by the vast expanse of Lake Tanganyika. The eastern arm is clearly visible in parts, with dramatic escarpments, as can be seen from the road to Serengeti, flanking the alkaline lakes Manyara and Eyasi, and rising sharply to the Ngorongoro Highlands. The two arms meet in the Southern Highlands around Mbeya; further south, the Rift Valley is dominated by Lake Nyasa (the name by which Tanzanians still refer to Lake Malawi).

The Ngorongoro Crater has been dubbed the eighth wonder of the world, not only as the world's largest complete caldera, the relict of a volcanic mountain that may once have been higher than Kilimanjaro, but as a natural arena, 16km (10

Beach at Pangani.

miles) in diameter, that hosts a staggering concentration of 30,000 or more large mammals.

The north of the country is dominated by the domed peaks of Kibo (5,895 metres/19,340ft) and Mawenzi (5,149 metres/16,893ft) on Kilimanjaro, which rises like a giant sugarloaf from the flat plains, making it the world's highest free-standing mountain. Kibo's crater is 200 metres (656ft) deep and contains active fumaroles. Ol Doinyo Lengai, the Maasai 'Mountain of God', near Lake Natron on the Kenyan border, is still active. Other rift mountains, such as Meru (4,560 metres/14,960ft) are deemed to be dormant, not having erupted within the past 200 years.

Elsewhere, mountain ranges include the Monduli, west of Arusha; the Pare and

Usambara of the Eastern Arcs, to the southeast of Kilimanjaro; the Uluguru, east of Morogoro; the Ugzungwa, southwest of Mikumi; and the Mahale on the shores of Lake Tanganyika.

RIVERS

Southern Tanzania is characterised by a fairly flat ancient landscape with poor soils and deciduous woodland, interspersed with sand rivers that flood during the rainy season, clearly seen in the Selous Game Reserve, which has a network of sand rivers the size of Wales linking to the Rufiji River.

Burchell's zebra, Serengeti National Park.

Surprisingly, wetland areas cover about 10 percent of the country. Apart from the Great Lakes, several major rivers flow into the Indian Ocean. The Pangani drains the Kilimanjaro region; the Great Ruaha and Kilombero join to become the Rufiji, with a catchment area in the southern highlands; while the Ruvuma forms the boundary with Mozambique.

The Malagarasi, which feeds Lake Tanganyika, also forms the Malagarasi swamps, whose international significance was recognised in 2000 when they became Tanzania's first Ramsar site – conforming to international agreements set out in Ramsar, Iran, on the conservation of wetlands.

The soda lake, Natron, in the far north, was added to the Ramsar wetland list in 2001, due to its importance as a breeding ground for the deep rose-pink lesser flamingos.

It was followed a year later by the Kilombero Valley, south of the Udzungwa Mountains, which is the only home to the Kilombero weaver. The coastal wetlands of southern Tanzania became the Rufiji-Mafia-Kilwa Marine Ramsar site in 2004.

THE HUMAN POPULATION

Tanzania's complex underlying geology and water resources have both played a significant role in the geographical distribution of the country's humans and wildlife. The third important factor is the climate. East Africa has two rains a year and does not have a long dry season. In Tanzania, the significance of this is apparent in the shorter, sweeter grasses found in the Serengeti and the Maasai Steppe, which can support higher densities of wildlife – hence there are more animals and a greater variety of species in East Africa than southern Africa. The southern part of Tanzania falls into the miombo woodland belt that continues south into Zambia, Zimbabwe and Botswana. This area has one rainy season, and consequently game densities are less high, and there are fewer species.

Tanzania's human population is mainly rural. Around 50 percent of the population is employed in the agricultural industry, which focuses on the upland areas where rich, volcanic soils and two growing seasons support high population densities.

The semi-arid lowlands are far more sparsely inhabited, by pastoralists such as the Maasai and Datoga, and are also where the major wildlife areas are concentrated. However, in recent years an increase in population has led to more permanent settlement in the marginal areas, giving rise to increasing soil erosion and potentially serious conflicts over water usage.

Another major factor influencing population distribution is the presence of the tsetse fly, which causes sleeping sickness. The 'fly-belt' is a vast area that cannot be inhabited or farmed by humans. The wildlife in these areas is in effect preserved by the presence of the pest.

There are a few large urban centres, of which Dar es Salaam is the only one with a population of more than a million. Other significant towns (listed in size order, with the largest first) include Mwanza, Arusha, Dodoma (the capital),

Mbeya, Morogoro, Tanga, Kahama, Tabora and Zanzibar Town.

COMMERCIAL FARMING

Expansive, bright-green tea plantations dominate much of the Usambara and Tukuyu regions, at an altitude of around 2,130 metres (7,000ft). At a lower altitude are the Robusta coffee farms around Bukoba, and the Arabica coffee farms found in the Moshi and Usa River area near Arusha, on the foothills of Kilimanjaro. Other crops are grown alongside coffee, such as beans, bananas – 10 types, from the tiny, sweet, yellow, finger bananas to the large, green *matoke*, which is used as a savoury staple – and increasingly a variety of horticultural products. Fruit and vegetables for the local market range from strawberries to Arusha tomatoes. A new commercial crop is flowers, grown both for seed production and for export as cut flowers to Europe.

There are wheat farms to the north of Arusha region and on the slopes of the Ngorongoro Highlands, while extensive maize production is found in the drier areas. Other cash crops include tobacco, grown by local smallholders, and pyrethrum. Cotton is produced inland from Tanga and Dar es Salaam, along the Rufiji River and south down the coast as far as Kilwa. Rice and cotton are also grown in the Shinyanga area near Lake Victoria. The Morogoro region was once the world's largest producer of sisal, until the market collapsed due to competition from synthetic materials. There are still several large plantations, but the area has also diversified into horticultural production to meet the demand of the domestic market around Dar es Salaam. Although less than 3 percent of the land is given to permanent crop production, there is enormous potential to increase yields and expand the areas under cultivation through irrigation; but this in turn needs to be balanced against traditional agricultural practices and the impact on the wetland areas.

On Lake Victoria, sardine fishing is an important industry at Kibirizi and Kigoma. While tilapia is the preferred fish for eating, Nile perch, which was introduced into the lake in 1956, accounts for 75 percent of the catch.

SPICES

Along the coast, commercial coconut plantations are harvested for copra, which produces coconut oil, coconut meal for livestock and a host of other by-products.

Clove, coconut and spice plantations dominate the Zanzibar archipelago. The island of Pemba is the world's largest producer of cloves, and some trees are as high as 24 metres (79ft). During the clove-picking season, from July to December, the air is thick with the pungent scent of cloves. Other spices include nutmeg, lemon grass, vanilla and ginger, and local factories produce clove and lemon-grass oil. In the northeast of Unguja Island, around Matemwe, the local women culti-

Coffee plantation, Karatu.

Estimated at more than 55 million in 2016, Tanzania's population comprises 120 different tribal groups. No one group has supremacy – indeed, the largest tribe, the Sukuma, accounts for just 16 percent of the population.

vate seaweed in the shallows for export to the Far East. At the coast, there's also a healthy domestic market for deep-sea fish, such as marlin and tuna, as well as more easily caught sea creatures, from octopus to crabs and snapper.

Indigenous forest and woodland account for between 30 and 40 percent of Tanzania's

> Covering 945,100 sq km (364,900 sq miles), including the Zanzibar and Mafia archipelagos, Tanzania is the world's 31st-largest country, more than four times the size of Britain, half as big as Alaska, and 35 percent larger than Texas.

land area, but deforestation is increasingly a problem, as land is cleared for agriculture, firewood and charcoal. In the mountainous regions, commercial timber is an important commodity; camphorwood, teak, mahogany and ebony are produced. At the coast, mangrove swamps are extensive in the Kilwa and Rufiji areas, where they are harvested for mangrove poles, which are much in demand by the building industry, while the bark is used for tanning leather.

MINING

In recent years, there has been a significant increase in mineral exploration and production,

Maasai woman herding goats at the hot springs of Lake Natron below Ol Doinyo Legai.

⊙ TANZANITE

Discovered in 1967 by a Maasai herder, tanzanite was given to a ruby prospector, Manuel d'Souza. He took it to Tiffany's in New York, who named and popularised the stone. Gemologically, tanzanite is called blue Zoisite, but it was renamed to avoid the similarity with the word 'suicide'. A hydrated calcium aluminium silicate mineral, it is technically only semi-precious, but as it is rarer than diamonds, and the pale-brown stone, when heated, becomes a glorious purple-blue, it is highly sought after. The world's only tanzanite mine is at Mererani, 40km (25 miles) from Arusha. The stones can be bought at jewellers in Arusha.

with the ancient rocks yielding gold, diamonds, graphite, tin and copper. Mining areas are found around Shinyanga, and gold has also been discovered in Mwanza. Mwadui has the largest pipe diamond mine in Africa. Alexandrite is mined in Tunduru, rubies in Morogoro and emeralds, rubies and rhodolite in Tanga.

Tanzanite, the mauve semi-precious stone the colour of jacaranda flowers, is mined in the hills near Kilimanjaro Airport (see box). Low-grade coal is mined in the south, and sources of power include hydroelectric schemes on the Rufiji River, together with natural gas deposits found in the Rufiji delta.

Large gas deposits are still being uncovered in Tanzania; the past decade has witnessed several major discoveries, and in 2016 another gas field was confirmed at the Ruvu basin near Dar es Salaam. The industry's rapid expansion has prompted the construction of a Uganda–Tanzania gas pipeline, as well as a liquefied natural gas processing plant in Lindi.

Manyara National Park contains only about 100 sq km (39 sq miles) of land around the lake, but the habitats range from the rift wall to the groundwater forest, acacia woodland, open grassland, the lake shore, swamp areas and the lake itself.

NATIONAL PARKS

Remarkably, 25 percent of Tanzania's land has been set aside as national parks, game reserves, game-controlled areas and wildlife-management areas – a reflection of the diverse

LOWLAND ECO-ZONES

There are varying definitions of habitat type – some sources suggest six major ecological zones, while others expand the list to around 13 or more. However, they may be broadly defined as acacia

Acacia tree at sunset, Serengeti National Park.

range of habitats and the value placed on wildlife for tourism and hunting.

The northern circuit, operating out of Arusha, is the most developed; it includes the Serengeti, Ngorongoro Crater, Lake Manyara and Tarangire, together with Mount Kilimanjaro and Arusha. The southern circuit, visited from Dar es Salaam, focuses primarily on the Selous, Ruaha and Mikumi.

Due to the tremendous topographical variation, virtually all the major habitats found elsewhere in Africa are represented in Tanzania, the only major exception being arid desert. The major division of ecological zones primarily relates to altitude. Within a small area there can be a variety of habitats – for example, Lake

Ø THE FEVER TREE

Acacia xanthophloea, better known as the fever tree, was given its ominous name by early travellers. It is most common along watercourses and lake shores, which provide good shade for pitching camp, but are also breeding grounds for mosquitoes. Travellers linked their bouts of malaria to camping in these habitats, and initially it was thought the fever was caused by the trees, whose yellow powdery bark seemed to signal danger. One of the most attractive of the acacias, it is easily recognised by its (harmless) yellow bark and flat-topped crown. It has a shallow root system to avoid being waterlogged in clay soils.

savannah grassland; miombo woodland; lowland rainforest; riverine and evergreen forest; montane forest; heath and moorland; and highland desert.

The **acacia savannah grassland** is rich in flora, with some 2,500 plant species. It forms the backbone of the central plateau and northern ranges of grassland. The Serengeti plains are dominated by the red oat grass, *Themeda triandra*, and the sedges of *Sporobolus ioclada* and *Kyllinga* species. Wooded grassland is extensive, with many regional variations, and is dominated by trees from the acacia or *Combretum* family. (Tanzania

Lowland rainforest is found in the Eastern Arc Mountains, and typified by the lower eastern slopes of the Usambaras, characterised by *Anthocleista grandiflora*, *Cephalosphaera usambarensis* and *Anisophyllea obtusifolia*. The Usambaras have the greatest altitudinal range of unbroken forest cover in East Africa, from the lowland forest communities at below 250 metres (820ft) through to montane species. They support one of the richest biological communities in Africa. Of the 276 forest trees recorded, 50 are endemic. Remarkably, over 100 species of

African elephants and baobab tree at sunset, Tarangire National Park.

has more than 40 indigenous acacia.) A typical combination, as found in parts of the Serengeti, is a woodland dominated by *Acacia tortilis* and *Commiphora schimperi*, with other common species being *A. drepanolobium*, *A. seyal*, *A. melacocephala* and *A. pseudofistula*. Interestingly, the grassland areas are dependent upon being grazed – by both wild and domestic animals. If grazing was removed from the equation, the grassland would naturally revert to acacia woodland.

The south of the country is extensively covered by **miombo woodland**, dominated by some 15 species of *Brachystegia*, tall deciduous trees with an open canopy. They shed their leaves during the six months of the dry season, while the tall grasses are prone to bush fires.

trees and shrubs in the area have been selected for their importance in terms of biodiversity.

Riverine and evergreen forest follows the major rivers and is also found at the foot of the escarpment at Manyara, fed by springs from the foot of the scarp. Here, there are magnificent stands of tall, mature trees, among them *Trichilea emetica*, *Antiaris toxicaria*, *Bridelia micrantha* and *Ficus sycamorus*, with an under-storey of *Croton macrostachys* and *Rauvolfia caffra*. Other species include the *borassus* and *phoenix* palms.

Gombe Stream and the Mahale Mountains still possess fragments of the original West and Central African forests, which became isolated during climate changes over the past 8,000 years. Among trees common to the West African forest which can be seen are species of *Anthocleista, Elaesis, Myrianthus, Pseudosponias* and *Pycnanthus*.

MOUNTAIN VEGETATION

Montane forest is found between the 1,200-metre (3,937ft) contour and the tree line at 3,000 metres (9,843ft) and shows variations, with a greater number of species in areas of higher rainfall. On the slopes of Kilimanjaro, the most common tree around Marangu is *Macaranga kilimandscharica*, which has a smooth grey bark and heart-shaped leaves. The forest on the western and northern slopes receives less rain. Here the dominant trees are juniper, *Juniperus procera*, the olives, *Olea africana* and *O. kilimandscharica*, and *Nuxia congesta*, which is often draped with moss and lichen and has attractive clusters of white flowers which bloom at the start of the rains. One of the tallest trees is the *Podocarpus milanjianus*, a conifer that can grow to 30 metres (100ft), together with the ivy, *Ilex mitis*, and the camphorwood, *Ocotea usambarensis*.

A dense understorey of shrubs and wild flowers contains familiar species such as Busy Lizzies and begonias, popular as house plants. Giant tree ferns grow up to 6 metres (20ft) high in wetter parts of the forest, while orchids, African violets and balsams are also commonly seen. In the upper reaches, stands of the feathery giant heather tree, *Erica excelsa*, grow 3 metres (10ft) high, with pink or white flowers, and giant groundsel, *Senecio johnstonii*, has cabbage-like leaves and small clusters of yellow flowers.

Typical **heath and moorland** vegetation (from 2,800 metres/9,200ft to 4,000 metres/13,100ft) is characterised by giant heathers, *Erica arborea* and *E. excelsa*, the yellow flowers of *Hypericum revolutum* and the papery, everlasting daisy-like flowers of *Helichrysum*. A yellow protea, *Protea kilimandscharica*, and the red-hot poker, *Kniphofia thomsonii*, are also easily recognised.

On the moorland, lobelias reach 3 metres (10ft) high, among tussocks of grass, *Pentaschistis minor*, and mauve-flowered herbs like *Satureia biflora* and *S. kilimandscharica*. Some species, like *Lobelia deckenii* and *Senecio kilimanjari*, are endemic to Kilimanjaro. The lobelia has adapted to the sub-zero conditions by closing its open leaves over its rosette buds at night.

The **highland desert** (4,000 metres/13,200ft to 5,000 metres/16,400ft) freezes at night, while daytime temperatures can soar to 40°C (104°F). Evaporation is high and water retention in the soil is poor, particularly when the soil is frozen. Yet some 55 plant species have adapted to these bleak conditions. Among them, coloured lichens cling to the lava rocks, free-rolling moss balls wrap themselves around a nodule of soil, and rosette plants like *Haplocarpa rueppelii* and *Haplosciadium abyssinicum* also flourish. Other plants have adapted by coating their leaves in silvery hairs, which reflect the sun and trap a layer of air around the leaves, which reduces temperature loss.

Kilimanjaro vegetation.

⊘ BAOBABS

In tribal folklore, the baobab, *Adansonia digitata* (also called the upside-down tree due to its root-like branches), is said to contain tree spirits. It is easily distinguished by its bulbous silver-grey trunk, which can be 5 metres (16ft) in diameter and hold up to 300 litres (66 gallons) of water. Some baobabs are believed to be 3,000 years old. Preferring altitudes below 1,300 metres (4,265ft), they are found throughout Tanzania, usually in isolation. The seeds in their fruit pods are made into sherbet sweets by the Swahili people. The bark fibre is used to make ropes and baskets; the trunk can be hollowed out as a canoe.

African elephants, Ngorongoro Crater.

SAFARI

In Swahili, safari simply means 'journey'; today the word is synonymous with the thrill of seeing Africa's great wildlife.

Images of the grand hunting safari, complete with an entourage of porters, still abound in Tanzania, immortalised by the adventures of glamorous big-game hunters such as Ernest Hemingway. Today, it is photographic rather than hunting safaris that form the mainstay of Tanzanian tourism, but the origins of both may be found in far more ancient interaction between humans and wildlife.

FOOD OR COMMERCE?

It was probably man's urge to hunt that led to the very first development of tools, from scrapers used to skin an animal to arrowheads for shooting them. Some of the early rock-art sites scattered around Tanzania depict men hunting. A few scattered groups of nomadic hunter-gatherers still exist around the margins of Tanzania's Lake Eyasi, southwest of Ngorongoro. Retaining an intimate knowledge of their environment and hunting terrain, the nomadic Hadza (see page 164) use different plant poisons to lethal effect on their poison arrows, and employ agility and cunning in the hunt. They are skilled trackers, reading game trails like a map, but will also use certain trees as a lookout point. At times they will even imitate an animal as part of the chase, for example, donning a headdress of impala horns when stalking impala.

Other tribal groups, such as the pastoralist Maasai, have co-existed in harmony with the wildlife over the years, referring to them as their second cattle, and only resorting to hunting for food in times of severe hardship. Yet traditionally, a young Maasai *moran* (warrior) had to kill a lion as part of the ritual to attaining manhood and status, although this is no longer a prerequisite.

The ivory trade stretches back to the days of ancient Rome. Arab caravans were certainly operating from the 7th century. By the time the

Tourists watching a herd of buffalo, Mikumi National Park.

British arrived, the slaughter of elephants for their ivory had become part of a sophisticated trading network, with the ivory transported to the coast by slaves the traders had captured en route.

The Arabs supplied guns to the African hunters, and it is estimated that 30,000 elephants were being killed a year in Kenya, Uganda and Tanzania in the 1850s. By the 1880s, this had risen to between 60,000 and 70,000.

TROPHY HUNTING

The advent of trophy hunting started with the Victorian big-game hunters, who moved up from southern Africa where much of the game had been decimated, lured by the big tuskers and large herds of East Africa.

In 1902, Frederick Courteney Selous made his first expedition to East Africa. In 1909, he returned to set up a hunting expedition for the American President, Theodore Roosevelt.

Today, wildlife areas – National Parks, National Reserves, Game Controlled Areas and Wildlife Management Areas – account for a massive 25 percent of Tanzania.

Trophies were a large part of the testosterone-fuelled pleasures of big-game hunting.

The scale of this safari, to collect specimens for the Smithsonian and American Museum of Natural History in New York, took on epic proportions, and covered a nine-month period and four countries. The attendant press entourage gave international publicity to African safaris, initiating the beginning of the commercial hunting safari in Africa. Meanwhile, Selous himself made the transition from hunter to safari guide, and began, through his writings, to influence world opinion on the need to conserve wildlife.

GREAT WHITE HUNTER

The commercial hunting safari was thus established. For the most part, however, the professional hunters were men who appreciated the wildlife, revelled in the excitement of the bush, and simply took hunting clients to earn a living. Unfortunately, they were often too efficient. The pioneering pilot, Beryl Markham, tells of watching the elephants gather round the big tuskers to hide them from her spotter plane.

Meanwhile, these romantically rugged figures became further glamorised and embellished by movies like *King Solomon's Mines*, filmed in the 1950s, the writings of hunting fanatic Ernest Hemingway, and the filming of *The Snows of Kilimanjaro*, also in the 1950s. White hunters became enveloped in the mantle of Hollywood.

Selous was by no means the only hunter to become an ardent conservationist. Another was Constantine Ionides, more renowned for his passion for snakes, who gives an interesting account of the early hunting days in his autobiography, *A Hunter's Story*.

Drawn to Tanzania by a passion for hunting, he joined the 6th King's African Rifles, arriving in 1925. After a short spell in the army, he turned to hunting and poaching elephants, where he was not averse to bribing chiefs and officials when in pursuit of big ivory. Ionides then worked as a white hunter, taking hunting safaris, where the emphasis was on tracking the game and finding suitable specimen trophies for the client, without the frills of drinks on ice and gourmet cuisine. He aptly described the development of the role of the white hunter today as combining the social skills of a travelling hotel manager with those of a hunter.

From the 1920s onwards, land had been set aside for Game Parks and Reserves. Ionides joined the Game Department in 1933; at that time, six European game rangers and around 120 African scouts were responsible for the entire country. Their remit was to conserve the game, protect human life and property from attacks by wildlife, and control hunting.

THE MODERN HUNT

Apart from a seven-year period from 1973 when a complete moratorium was imposed, the hunting safari has been a highly profitable industry for Tanzania. Licensed hunting began in 1984, when the government issued 10 hunting concessions through the Tanzania Wildlife Corporation (TAWICO), which was subsequently privatised. The Game Department is the government arm responsible for controlling hunting, issuing hunting concessions and regulating game quotas. The industry strives to maintain high ethical standards, although its very existence remains controversial. In the words of one operator: 'We are committed to maintaining a long tradition of ethical hunting, and not merely providing opportunity for indiscriminate killing of animals.'

The annual hunting season runs from 1 July to 31 December. Restrictions on certain species are laid down by the international monitoring agency, the Convention on International Trade in Endan-

is supplemented by other charismatic creatures such as cheetahs, giraffe, African hunting dogs and zebra.

While some companies retain the classic style of the traditional mobile camp complete with gourmet catering, others operate a less lavish set-up, with basic camping facilities. Increasingly, new types of permanent and sophisticated accommodation have appeared, from the permanent tented camp to lodges and opulent hotels decked out in a 1930s theme. Books have been written on safari style, catering for a new fashion of Western

Safari vehicle with Burchell's zebra, Serengeti National Park.

gered Species (CITES). Hunting is big business – overseas clients hunting buffalo, elephants, lions and leopards pay thousands of dollars for the privilege. The government gains more than US$20 million a year in trophy fees and other associated fees. Additional money is paid to local communities, and there are significant tips for the trackers.

PHOTOGRAPHIC SAFARIS

The development of the photographic safari derived from the hunting safaris, replacing the gun with the camera and attracting an increasing number of tourists on different budgets. The big five of the photographic safari are still those that were the prime hunting trophies in the past – elephant, lion, leopard, buffalo and rhino – though this list

⊙ CAMPING IN COMFORT

The classic tented safari has its origins in the camps of the early hunters, where camping in the bush did not mean stinting on luxury. A typical safari involved dozens of porters, gun-bearers and servants. People would dress for dinner, dine off fine china and drink from crystal. Karen Blixen's lover, Denys Finch Hatton, was remembered for taking his wind-up gramophone on safari. When Sir Winston Churchill's father went to Africa at the end of the 19th century, a piano was considered an essential item to his well-being in the bush. Nor were they all-male affairs. Women would go, and sometimes shoot, in full Victorian dress.

tourist, reinventing the romantic notions conjured up by Hollywood, where accommodation has become as important as the wildlife.

While the National Parks are all dedicated to photographic safaris, in the Game Reserves and Wildlife Management Areas, certain lands are allocated as hunting zones. With the advent of walking safaris in the community lands adjacent to the parks in northern Tanzania, there has been a conflict of interests between the operators of hunting and photographic safaris, giving rise to a need for more stringent zoning of activities and,

many hunting companies are affiliated to non-governmental organisations that assist the Tanzanian government with anti-poaching measures and use sustainable hunting to provide tangible economic benefits to the local communities.

COMMUNITY INVOLVEMENT

An interesting phenomenon is that both hunting and photographic safaris have increasingly become involved with the local communities. Quite rightly, some of the revenue received from hunting and photographic tourism is ploughed back

A government bonfire of animal products captured from poachers and illegal traders.

Enjoying sundowner drinks at a game reserve.

quite possibly, for buffer zones between them. Not only do many photographic tourists dislike the whole concept of hunting, but the proximity of guns makes the animals infinitely less approachable. Those looking for good pictures are likely to be very disappointed.

The role hunting plays in wildlife conservation is a contentious issue, especially among those who are against hunting in any shape or form. But whatever your personal views, there is no doubt that in Tanzania it brings in vital revenue which can be ploughed back into conservation projects. This is particularly the case in the vast Selous Game Reserve, which derives as much as 80 percent of its official revenue from trophy hunters. In addition,

into community development, building schools, providing bursaries for education, health care and water points.

On walking safaris in Maasai areas, tourists are guided by the Maasai, learning about the environment and the traditional uses of plants, as well as glimpsing Maasai culture at first hand. With the hunting safaris, local people are employed as trackers, and meat is distributed to neighbouring villages. This has resulted in a shift in the attitude of local people from seeing wildlife as a pest to valuing it as a resource.

POACHING

During the 1970s and '80s, as elsewhere in Africa, Tanzania's elephant population was decimated in the ivory wars. Some herds were poached to within 20 percent of their former size. At its worst, in the Selous Game Reserve, 20,000 elephants were slaughtered over a two-year period. Poaching was out of control, and the government did not have the resources to combat it. The timing coincided with the anti-hunting ban in Tanzania, giving the poachers carte blanche in the hunting areas.

Fortunately, the international outcry resulted in the CITES imposing a moratorium on the ivory trade in 1989, when the African elephant was

population (the remainder being split between the Ngorongoro Crater and a few specific parts of the Serengeti). The population is so fragmented and dispersed that there have been suggestions that the only way to create a viable breeding pool is to create a sanctuary within the Selous.

In 1994, the Sand Rivers Rhino Project was established by Richard Bonham and the late Elizabeth Theobold to protect rhinos from poaching. The project, now named the Selous Rhino Trust, has grown in scale and received major funding from the European Union.

Maasai giraffe on a walking safari near Lake Manyara.

placed on the critical endangered species list, which gave a total ban on trading in elephant products. In late 2002, a limited trade in ivory resumed. There was no immediate increase in poaching as a result of this, but numerous reports indicate that elephant poaching throughout Tanzania has been on the increase since 2009. In 2016, the WWF warned that elephants could disappear from the Selous Game Reserve completely by 2022 unless poaching is stopped.

ON THE ENDANGERED LIST

The current situation with black rhino is more fragile. It is estimated that there are only a few dozen animals in the Selous, and they constitute about two-thirds of Tanzania's total rhino

The rhino are difficult to see, a reflection of poaching avoidance and the dense, riverine gullies in which they live. Trackers with GPS have only a 50 percent chance of finding rhino evidence along a 1,000km (620-mile) transect.

Since the carnage of the 1970s and '80s, poaching remains a problem, but it is not on the same gross scale as before. The battle continues nevertheless, and in 2017 the government launched plans to create a paramilitary force to target poachers. At the same time, there has been an increase in the local bush-meat trade, particularly of smaller species such as antelope, where the indiscriminate killing gives great cause for concern. Undoubtedly, the future of Tanzania's wildlife remains balanced in the hands of man.

MAMMALS

Tanzania offers some of the world's finest game viewing, with an extraordinarily rich array of wildlife.

There are more large mammals in East Africa than virtually anywhere else on earth – more than 80 species in Tanzania alone. (By 'large', zoologists mean anything from the size of a domestic cat.) There are plenty of smaller ones, too, although most of these are nocturnal and can be difficult to spot. Everyone wants to see Africa's big five – elephant, rhino, lion, leopard and buffalo – and Tanzania is home to them all. But in your eagerness to tick them off, don't ignore the less dramatic creatures: the dogs and the smaller cats, the monkeys and the mongooses, and, above all, the antelopes – dozens of different species, from the imposing eland to the tiny dik-dik.

The list that follows contains more than 50 mammals – the species you are most likely to encounter on safari – with descriptions to help you identify each one, and suggestions as to where you might see them. Many mammals are restricted to one type of vegetation or habitat; others are more versatile and are found throughout the country. Some occur in a variety of subspecies, which we do not have space to describe.

LION (PANTHERA LEO)

Tawny or fawn in colour, with manes ranging from gold to black on the male, the lion is the largest of Africa's three big cats, and also the most sociable. Prides consist of six to a dozen females and their cubs, with one or more dominant males. Most of the hunting is done by females, working as a team usually at night, but males will normally be first to eat at a kill. Some prides specialise in hunting buffalo or giraffe, but most feed on impala, zebra or wildebeest, seizing the prey by the throat and suffocating it.

LEOPARD (PANTHERA PARDUS)

The elegant leopard is larger than the other spotted cats, and distinguished by dark rosettes on the back and flanks and solid spots on the face. The background colour ranges from off-white to russet. It is a solitary animal, except when a pair come together for mating, or a mother is accompanied by cubs. Hunting mainly at night, the leopard steals up on its prey, then pounces from close range. It is powerful enough to carry an antelope (impala are its favourite food) up a tree to keep it safe from other carnivores.

CHEETAH (ACINONYX JUBATUS)

Much smaller than a leopard, the cheetah is a lithe, long-legged cat with solid dark spots all over its fawn body, a small head and characteristic black 'tear-marks' from the corner of each eye. It prefers open savannah, where it uses its impressive speed – up to 100kmh/60mph over short distances – to run down its prey (typically Thomson's gazelle). Cheetahs are usually seen alone, in pairs or in small family groups consisting of a female and her cubs. They hunt by day, usually during the cooler hours soon after dawn.

CARACAL (FELIS CARACAL)

Similar in appearance to a lynx, the caracal is a medium-sized cat, anything from pale fawn to chestnut in colour, with long, pointed, tufted ears. It is a solitary hunter, preying on mammals from mice to small antelopes, birds and reptiles. It stalks its prey as close as possible, then relies on a pounce or a short run. Its powerful hind legs enable it to leap vertically 3 metres (10ft) to swat a bird. Caracals are widespread throughout Tanzania's drier regions, but are mainly nocturnal and rarely seen.

SERVAL (FELIS SERVAL)

Another spotted cat, smaller than a cheetah but with a similar build, long legs and a short tail. Its black-on-gold spots give way to black streaks near the head. The serval is usually a solitary animal, but is sometimes seen in pairs or small family groups. It hunts mainly at night, and sometimes in the early morning or late afternoon, preying on small mammals, birds and reptiles. Although it is not uncommon, its favoured habitat of long grass and reed beds, and its elusive habits, mean it is rarely seen.

AFRICAN WILDCAT (FELIS LYBICA)

This small carnivore resembles a tabby cat – in fact, it is the ancestor of most domestic cats – but is distinguished by striped legs and ginger fur on the backs of its ears. It is a solitary nocturnal hunter (except when a female is accompanied by kittens), feeding on small mammals up to the size of hares, and birds, including ostrich chicks. The wildcat is found throughout Africa, especially in areas where rodents are plentiful. This often means the outskirts of human settlements, where it may interbreed with domestic cats.

AFRICAN WILD DOG *(LYCAON PICTUS)*

Unlikely to be mistaken for any other canid, the wild dog (or hunting dog) has long legs, huge ears, a bushy white-tipped tail and a body covered in black, white and tan blotches. No two animals have exactly the same markings. It is a superb hunter, customarily working in packs of 10 to 15 animals, which can maintain a chase over several kilometres, overwhelming larger prey by sheer weight of numbers. Once common, but now IUCN listed as Endangered, it is most likely to be seen in Selous Game Reserve.

BLACK-BACKED JACKAL *(CANIS MESOMELAS)*

This jackal is a medium-sized canine, mostly tawny-brown, with a black 'saddle' flecked with white on its back. Unlike most dogs, jackals are not pack animals, and are usually seen alone or in pairs. They are efficient hunters of small mammals, but also scavenge from other predators' kills. Their characteristic call is a scream followed by three or four short yaps. In areas close to man (such as farmland), black-backed jackals hunt mainly at night, but they are commonly seen in daylight in the national parks.

SIDE-STRIPED JACKAL *(CANIS ADUSTUS)*

Slightly smaller and less common than the black-backed, the side-striped jackal looks uniform grey-brown from a distance. It has a faint pale stripe fringed with black on its flank, but the white-tipped tail is a better identifier. Usually seen alone, but sometimes in pairs or small family groups, it is most active at night and in the early evening. Unlike the black-backed, the side-striped jackal avoids open savannah, and prefers wooded areas. It is omnivorous, eating fruit as well as small prey and carrion.

BAT-EARED FOX *(OTOCYON MEGALOTIS)*

This small, silver-grey fox has black legs, a bushy tail, pale face, pointed black muzzle and enormous ears – the key to its success as an insect-eater. Its main food is harvester termites, which it can pinpoint up to 30cm (1ft) underground with acute directional hearing, before digging furiously to unearth them. A resident of dry scrub and grassland, it dens in burrows, which it sometimes digs itself but also colonises from other creatures. It hides during the heat of the day, emerging to feed in early evening.

SPOTTED HYENA *(CROCUTA CROCUTA)*

With its sloping hindquarters, coarse spotted coat, round face and broad black muzzle, the spotted hyena, Africa's second-largest member of the order Carnivora, is unmistakable. It is an opportunistic scavenger, but also an aggressive hunter – of antelope, zebra and even buffalo. It lives in clans of up to 15 animals, led by a dominant female. Most active at night, clan members communicate with an eerie whooping call. The **striped hyena** *(Hyaena hyaena)*, slightly smaller, with dark stripes on a grey coat, is much rarer but occasionally seen in northern Tanzania.

WHITE-TAILED MONGOOSE *(ICHNEUMIA ALBICAUDA)*

A very large mongoose, dark grey-brown with black legs, a rump that is higher than its shoulders, and a distinctive bushy white tail. Like most African mongooses, it is a solitary creature – though pairs are occasionally seen – and hunts mainly at night, feeding on a wide range of invertebrates, small mammals (up to the size of a hare) and wild fruits. By day, it lies in burrows dug by other animals, in rock crevices or amid dense vegetation. It is widespread in Tanzania, mainly in wooded areas and forest margins.

DWARF MONGOOSE *(HELOGALE PARVULA)*

One of the two social species of mongoose, the dwarf is also one of Africa's smallest carnivores, about 32cm (1ft) long including its tail, a sleek chestnut-brown creature with short legs and a pointed snout. A family of 10–20, led by a dominant male and female, will have up to 20 dens within its territory, often in old termite mounds. From here, they forage as a troop, hunting insects and other invertebrates, reptiles and birds. Usually only the dominant female breeds, but all the troop members care for the young.

BANDED MONGOOSE *(MUNGOS MUNGO)*

The most often seen of the mongoose family, and the most social, the banded is dark grey-brown with 10–12 dark stripes on its rump. It lives in family groups of between five and 40 individuals, and rarely ventures far from the troop. Sleeping at night in burrows, they spend most of the day foraging for food, occasionally pausing to stand upright to look around for danger. They are truly omnivorous, eating insects and other invertebrates, small rodents, lizards, birds, eggs and sometimes fruit and berries.

LARGE-SPOTTED GENET *(GENETTA TIGRINA)*

Genets are long, agile, feline creatures with short legs and a long ringed tail. The large-spotted species, which grows up to 105cm (41ins) overall, is creamy-yellow with distinct dark body spots and a black tip to its tail. Normally solitary and nocturnal, it hunts large invertebrates and small mammals, and is an agile climber. Its close relative, the slender **small-spotted genet** *(Genetta genetta)*, is greyer with very small spots and a white-tipped tail. Both species are sometimes seen scavenging round camps and lodges.

AFRICAN CIVET *(CIVETTICTIS CIVETTA)*

The height of a medium-sized dog, the civet is a stocky, powerful omnivore, its pale coat marked with dark blotches which merge into stripes nearer the head. It is a solitary hunter and may be seen at night (occasionally in the early evening) trotting with its head down in search of insects, rodents, reptiles – including venomous snakes – birds or carrion. It also eats fruit and can even digest poisonous plants. It is purely terrestrial, unlike its relative, the forest-dwelling **tree civet** *(Nandinia binotata)*, which rarely comes to ground.

RATEL *(MELLIVORA CAPENSIS)*

A powerful, low-slung carnivore, mostly black but with a silver-grey mantle from head to tail, the ratel is the same size as a badger (its other name is honey badger, after its habit of breaking into beehives to eat honeycomb and larvae). Hunting mainly at night, usually unaccompanied, the ratel uses its massive claws to dig out scorpions, rodents and other burrowing animals. It frequently scavenges round rubbish dumps and camps in parks and reserves, and will attack humans aggressively if threatened.

CAPE CLAWLESS OTTER *(AONYX CAPENSIS)*

Weighing as much as 35kg (77lbs) in exceptional cases, this fish-eating carnivore is dark brown with a bold white collar. Generally associated with freshwater habitats, it is sometimes seen in estuaries and mangroves, being most common in waters where it can easily avoid crocodiles. The smaller **spotted-necked otter**, which typically weighs around 5kg (11lbs), is absent from aquatic habitats that are alkaline, saline or offer poor visibility, but is quite common on islands and rocky stretches of shore on Lake Victoria.

ELEPHANT (*LOXODONTA AFRICANA*)

The largest of all land mammals, the African elephant can grow to 3.4 metres (11ft) at the shoulder and weigh 6,300kg (over 6 tons). Females live in loose-knit herds, in which the oldest cow plays matriarch. Males usually leave the family at around the age of 12, to drift between herds, roam singly or form bachelor groups. Elephants are active 16–20 hours a day, eating, drinking, bathing or travelling in search of food – they can eat up to 150kg (330lbs) of vegetation in 24 hours. For more information, see page 97.

HIPPOPOTAMUS (*HIPPOPOTAMUS AMPHIBIUS*)

This huge mammal (up to 2,000kg/2 tons) is found in most of Tanzania's large rivers and lakes, in herds of 10 or more presided over by a dominant male, who defends his territory fiercely. Hippos' skin is very thin and has no sweat glands – which means they can easily dehydrate and overheat, so they spend the day submerged in water, often with only their eyes, ears and nostrils showing. Evenings and early mornings are the time to see them on land, when they follow well-worn trails to and from their nocturnal grazing.

HOOK-LIPPED RHINO (*DICEROS BICORNIS*)

Also known as the black rhino, this Critically Endangered giant has been poached for its horn of compressed hair, which is used as an aphrodisiac in Asia and as a dagger handle in Yemen. Associated with dense thickets, it browses on the foliage with its muscular hooked upper lip. Though solitary, it does sometimes gather in temporary groups, and a calf will stay with its mother for up to four years. It is now very rare in Tanzania, and most likely to be seen in Ngorongoro Crater, though it is also present in the Serengeti and Selous.

GIANT ELEPHANT SHREW (*RHYNCHOCYON SPP.*)

Elephant shrews or sangis are peculiar rodent-sized creatures that hop around like miniature kangaroos and possess bizarrely elongated and twitchy snouts. Several species are present in Tanzania, of which the two giant (for which read 'rabbit sized') species are most impressive. These are the **chequered elephant shrew** (*R. cirnei*), a widespread resident of forest undergrowth, and the **grey-faced elephant shrew** (*R. udzungwensis*), an Udzungwa endemic. Both are terrestrial feeders.

BUFFALO *(SYNCERUS CAFFER)*

Africa's only species of wild cattle, the buffalo is very heavily built (up to 1.5 metres/5ft at the shoulder), with relatively short, stocky legs. Large ears fringed with hair hang below massive curved horns that meet in a central boss. It is gregarious, living in herds from a few dozen to several thousand in number, though it is not unusual to encounter lone bulls (which can be dangerous). It most often grazes at night, and drinks in the early morning and late afternoon, spending the day resting or chewing the cud.

ELAND *(TAUROTRAGUS ORYX)*

Africa's largest antelope (up to 1.8 metres/6ft at the shoulder), the eland is cattle-like in build, with a large dewlap and relatively short spiral horns. Its fawn coat sometimes has fine white stripes on the sides. The eland is common in grassland habitats, living in nomadic herds of 20 or more, but it is shy and can be difficult to approach. It is active both diurnally and nocturnally, but spends more time feeding at night in the hottest months. A prodigious jumper, an eland can clear 2 metres (6.5ft) from a standing position.

GREATER KUDU *(TRAGELAPHUS STREPSICEROS)*

A large, elegant antelope with slender legs, big ears, a grey-brown coat and six to 10 white stripes on each side of the body. The male has a fringe of hair on his throat and chest, and magnificent spiralling horns. The greater kudu is found all over Tanzania in small herds, usually in woodland or thickets and never far away from cover. It browses mainly on seeds and shoots. The best place to see it is Ruaha National Park, though it is also quite common in drier parts of the northern Rift Valley.

LESSER KUDU *(TRAGELAPHUS IMBERBIS)*

Smaller and even shier than the greater kudu, this East African endemic is found in small groups east of the Rift Valley, usually in quite dry environments. The male is darker than the greater kudu, with significant but smaller single-spiralled horns, and both sexes typically have at least 10 stripes on their sides. Recent research suggests that the lesser kudu is among the oldest of African antelope species, and some scientists now place it in its own genus, *Ammelaphus*.

BUSHBUCK *(TRAGELAPHUS SCRIPTUS)*

A medium-sized antelope that appears in various hues: males are often dark brown and females paler chestnut, but there is much variation. Both sexes may have white spots and/or stripes, but this, too, is inconsistent. The male has straight, sturdy horns. The bushbuck is both a browser and a grazer, preferring woodland and bush, always near water. It is mainly nocturnal. The closely related and rather similar **sitatunga** *(Tragelaphus spekei)* is a splay-hoofed aquatic antelope most commonly found on Rubondo Island National Park.

SABLE ANTELOPE *(HIPPOTRAGUS NIGER)*

You could never confuse the sexes of this handsome large antelope: both have magnificent curved horns (particularly long and striking in the male) and distinctive black-and-white faces, but the male's body is jet black and the female's chestnut brown. The sable avoids dense woodland and the open plains, preferring to live in dry, open woodland, mainly in the south of Tanzania. A herd of 10–30 individuals will be controlled by one dominant bull. It is generally a grazer, but sometimes browses in the dry season.

ROAN ANTELOPE *(HIPPOTRAGUS EQUINUS)*

The second-largest antelope after the eland (1.5 metres/5ft at the shoulder), the roan has a stocky, horse-like build, a short neck and a distinct erect mane. Both sexes have backward-curving, ringed horns (shorter in the female) and black-and-white face markings. The roan is a grazer, but prefers long grass. It is rare in the Serengeti, and more commonly seen in the reserves of southern Tanzania, in herds of six to 12. Territory is defended by an adult bull, but the herd is actually led by a dominant female, who selects feeding areas.

EAST AFRICAN ORYX *(ORYX BEISA)*

The oryx or gemsbok is a statuesque antelope with a grey body, a striking black-and-white face and unmistakable long, straight horns (both sexes). Tanzania's only variety is the **fringe-eared oryx** *(O. b. callotis)*, which has curious long tufts of black hair growing from its ear tips. An oryx can live for months in dry open country without access to water. It is predominantly a grazer, but also browses and sometimes eats fruit and acacia seed pods. Oryx are uncommon, but live in Tarangire and the Lake Natron region in small herds led by a territorial bull.

WILDEBEEST *(CONNOCHAETES TAURINUS)*

East Africa's most abundant antelope, the blue wildebeest or white-bearded gnu is an ungainly creature, dun-grey with a straggly black mane, black face and buffalo-like horns. It generally congregates in herds of around 30, but huge concentrations take part in the annual migration round the Serengeti and north into the Maasai Mara, following the rains and the fresh, young, short grass that is their sole diet. Breeding is synchronised so that hundreds of thousands of calves are born in the Serengeti in February and March.

TOPI *(DAMALISCUS LUNATUS)*

The topi is a distinctive antelope: its shoulders are higher (1.25 metres/4ft) than its rump, and its glossy reddish coat has dark patches on the upper legs. Both sexes have a dark face and stout ridged horns that curve backwards and upwards. The topi is a grazer, found on open grassy plains all over Tanzania, usually in small herds of five or six individuals controlled by one dominant bull, who defends his territory against other males. It is one of the fastest antelopes, and uses its speed and endurance to outrun predators.

HARTEBEEST *(ALCELAPHUS BUSELAPHUS)*

Similar in build to the topi, Coke's hartebeest or kongoni *(A. b. cokei)* has a longer, pointed head, narrow ears and a white rump. Both sexes have smallish lyre-shaped horns set very close together at the base. Fleet of foot, hartebeest prefer open grassy plains and are often found in small family groups in the Serengeti and Ngorongoro, where they sometimes post sentinels on termite mounds to watch for predators. A close relative, **Jackson's hartebeest** *(A. b. jacksoni)*, lives in small numbers in western Tanzania.

IMPALA *(AEPYCEROS MELAMPUS)*

Common throughout Tanzania, this slender, elegant, chestnut-coloured antelope is distinguished by unique black-and-white stripes on the rump and tail. Males have impressive lyre-shaped horns. Impala prefer wooded savannah, where they feed on fruits, seed pods, leaves and sometimes grass. They live in two kinds of groups: 'bachelor herds' (all male) and 'harems' of females and young. In the breeding season, a ram will take over a harem – and then battle with challenging males to preserve his breeding rights.

GRANT'S GAZELLE *(GAZELLA GRANTI)*

Grant's gazelle is between the impala and a Thomson's gazelle in size. It has a white belly, a pale side-stripe and a chestnut back, with black lines flanking white buttocks. Both sexes have long, elegant horns, particularly striking in the male. It lives in herds of about 30, controlled by an adult ram which will perform elaborate displays when confronted by a rival. Herds are mostly nomadic and can last long periods without water, but when food is plentiful, they stay in a small territory, both browsing and grazing.

THOMSON'S GAZELLE *(GAZELLA THOMSONI)*

The most abundant gazelle in East Africa (with numbers approaching 1 million), the dainty 'Tommy' is distinguished by a broad black horizontal stripe on its flank, with chestnut above and white below. Both sexes have upright, almost parallel horns, shorter and slimmer on females, and short black tails. Tommies graze on open savannah, preferring short-cropped grass, and often follow the wildebeest herds around the Serengeti. When threatened, they bounce around stiff-legged (known as 'pronking').

GERENUK *(LITOCRANIUS WALLERI)*

An unusual gazelle, the gerenuk is unmistakable for its long legs, elongated neck and huge ears. Males have fairly short, lyre-shaped horns. Equally distinctive are its feeding habits: the gerenuk is the only antelope habitually to stand on its hind legs to browse on new leaf growth, buds and flowers high up on trees and bushes. It is often solitary, but is sometimes seen in small mixed groups with a single ram. It is present but uncommon in the arid country in the northeast of Tanzania, where it can live without drinking water (taking in enough moisture from the leaves it eats).

ORIBI *(OUREBIA OUREBI)*

A graceful, small, reddish-brown antelope with a long, thin neck and a short, black-tipped tail. Rams have short, straight horns. The oribi is usually seen in pairs or small groups of one ram (which is vigorously territorial) and several ewes. It occasionally browses but mainly grazes, preferring short grassland with longer grass patches to provide cover. When disturbed, it gives a sharp whistle or sneeze and runs off with stiff-legged jumps. Alternatively (and unusually for antelopes), it lies down to hide in the long grass.

COMMON WATERBUCK (KOBUS ELLIPSIPRYMNUS)

This large, robust antelope (up to 1.35 metres/4.5f at the shoulder) has a shaggy grey-brown coat and a pronounced white ring on its rump. By contrast, the **Defassa waterbuck** (K. e. defassa), a subspecies which is more common to the west of the Rift Valley, has a solid white circle on its behind. The male of both types has gently curving, lyre-shaped horns. The waterbuck is a grazer, generally seen in family groups of five to 10 individuals in grassy areas, always near water.

REEDBUCK (REDUNCA REDUNCA)

The bohor reedbuck is a fairly nondescript reddish-brown antelope, identified by bare patches behind the ears and (in the male) smallish horns that turn forward at the point. Reedbucks are mostly active at night, but may be seen during the day, singly or in small groups, grazing in open grassland, always near water. In the south of Tanzania, the bohor's place is taken by a close relative, the **southern reedbuck** (R. arundinum), which is less red in colour and more commonly seen in daylight.

GREY DUIKER (SYLVICAPRA GRIMMIA)

Also known as the common or bush duiker, this small antelope can be anything from grey to chestnut in colour, with a distinctive tuft of black hair between its ears. Rams have short, pointed horns. It is the most widespread of all the duiker species, found (singly or in pairs) in savannah woodland or open bush, and often close to human habitation. It has a remarkably wide diet, feeding on shoots, leaves, fruits and cultivated crops, digging for tubers and roots with its front hoofs, and even taking termites and other insects.

KIRK'S DIK-DIK (RHYNCHOTRAGUS KIRKII)

This tiny, delicate, grey-brown antelope is easily identified by a crest of dark hair on its head, large eyes and an elongated nose like a small trunk. The ram's short, spiky horns may be hidden by the head crest. Usually seen in pairs or small family groups, dik-diks favour dry bush country and scrub, where they browse on leaves and also feed on flowers and fruit knocked to the ground by larger animals. Pairs mate for life and live in permanent territories, with regular paths between resting and feeding sites.

GIRAFFE *(GIRAFFA CAMELOPARDALIS)*

The subspecies found in Tanzania is the Maasai (or Kenyan) giraffe *(G. c. tippelskirchi)*, characterised by ragged edges to its blotchy markings. The world's tallest animal, a male giraffe can grow to 5.5 metres (18ft); females are somewhat shorter. The giraffe prefers open country to woodland, although its main food is leaves, especially from the tops of acacia trees, which it grasps with its amazing 45cm (18-ins) tongue. Giraffes are non-territorial, roaming around in loose herds of up to 15, of both sexes.

ZEBRA *(EQUUS BURCHELLII)*

The plains or Burchell's zebra (the only species found in Tanzania) is an unmistakable striped horse with a long erect mane. A zebra's stripes are as individual as a human fingerprint, and serve to break up the animal's outline and so confuse predators. A typical zebra herd consists of one stallion and half a dozen mares with their foals. Zebra mingle happily with other herbivores, but can eat long, coarse grass that is unpalatable to other grazers, so they are often the first to arrive in grazing areas, followed by wildebeest.

WARTHOG *(PHACOCHOERUS AETHIOPICUS)*

The only African wild pig that's commonly seen by day, the warthog has a grey body sparsely covered with bristly hairs, a dark coarse mane and upward-curving tusks. It is named after the wart-like growths on its face (the male has four, the female two). Warthogs graze on a variety of grasses, and in the dry season also root for bulbs and tubers, kneeling down and digging with their tusks. They live in family groups of females and young with one dominant male, sleeping and hiding from predators in networks of burrows.

BUSHPIG *(POTAMOCHOERUS PORCUS)*

This hairy pig varies in colour from grey to reddish brown, and has a characteristic crest of hair along its spine, tufted ears and a 'beard'. Males are larger than females (up to 1.7 metres/5.5ft long). The bushpig is probably as widespread as the warthog in East Africa, but is seen much less often, as it prefers thick vegetation and is mainly active at night, snuffling around for roots, fruits and fungi. Bushpigs are a favourite prey of leopards and spotted hyenas; they are also hunted by humans for food.

CHIMPANZEE *(PAN TROGLODYTES)*

This agile, muscular ape, standing about 1.2 metres (4ft) tall, is covered in black hair except for its bare face, hands and backside. Chimps live in woodland areas, in large communities of up to 100 individuals, usually dividing themselves into smaller family groups of six to eight. Their diet is varied, including fruit, leaves, bark, insects, eggs and animals such as bushpigs, guinea fowl and monkeys, which they hunt ferociously through the trees. In Tanzania, chimps are found on the northeast shores of Lake Tanganyika.

BABOON *(PAPIO CYNOCEPHALUS)*

The baboon is Africa's largest monkey, in varying shades of grey-brown, with a distinctive doglike black muzzle and a permanently kinked tail. Baboons are active during the day and largely terrestrial. They climb trees to gather fruits, to take refuge from predators or to sleep at night; otherwise they are found on the ground in complex social groups of up to 100, foraging, fighting, playing, grooming, nursing or courting. They feed on all kinds of plants, including crops, and also take insects, eggs and small mammals. The yellow baboon and olive baboon both occur in Tanzania.

VERVET MONKEY *(CERCOPITHECUS AETHIOPS)*

The vervet or green monkey is small and slender, with a long tail, grey-green fur, a white belly and black face and hands. It is common throughout Tanzania, living mainly in savannah and sparse woodland rather than thick forest, in troops of up to 30. The vervet is agile in trees, where it eats fruits, leaves and flowers, but it is equally at home on the ground, foraging for seeds and insects. It is a very social creature, communicating with a wide variety of calls, gestures and facial expressions.

BLUE MONKEY *(CERCOPITHECUS MITIS)*

This medium-sized primate (also called Sykes' monkey) has a dark blue-grey coat, with darker patches on the crown and limbs, and sometimes a white throat patch. An inhabitant of riparian woodland and forest, it lives in troops of 10–20, controlled by a single adult male. It is active during the day and spends most of its time in the trees, where it feeds on leaves, fruits, seeds, gum and bark, and occasionally insects and birds. It has a wide range of calls, including a very loud, far-carrying bark to warn of danger.

BLACK-AND-WHITE COLOBUS *(COLOBUS GUEREZA)*

A distinctive medium-large monkey, entirely black except for a white brow and 'beard' round its face, long white frills on its flanks and a bushy white tail. You will rarely see one on the ground: it lives high in trees in forested areas, in family troops of 10–20. In the early morning, troops will often sun themselves in the upper tree canopy. Later, you may see them leaping athletically from tree to tree, where they feed almost exclusively on leaves.

RED COLOBUS *(PROCOLOBUS SPP.)*

A medium-large monkey with long legs and a small head, a red-brown back and pale underside. The red colobus is less commonly seen than its black-and-white cousin, but there are several species in Tanzania, all tree-dwelling leaf-eaters. The **Udzungwa red colobus** *(P. gordonorum)*, with a greyish 'cape', is endemic to the Udzungwa Mountains, and fairly conspicuous there. Jozani Park in Zanzibar is the last stronghold of the **Zanzibar red colobus** *(P. kirkii)*, which has bushy white 'eyebrows', black shoulders and a red back.

BROWN GREATER GALAGO/BUSHBABY *(OTOLEMUR CRASSICAUDATUS)*

Also known as bushbabies, galagos are small nocturnal prosimians ('primitive' primates), distantly related to the lemurs of Madagascar. The brown greater or thick-tailed galago is by far the largest species in Tanzania (80cm/ 2.5ft overall), silver grey-brown with a darker bushy tail and large leathery ears. It is omnivorous but prefers fruit, especially figs. It has a loud screaming call, like a human baby in distress. Some scientists regard the silver western form to be a separate species, *O. monteiri*.

LESSER GALAGO/BUSHBABY *(GALAGO SPP.)*

Regarded to be one species until the 1980s, subsequent research has discovered this group of tiny nocturnal prosimians to comprise at least a dozen species, which are differentiable by their calls and the shape of the male's genitals. At least five species are resident in Tanzania, including the endemic Uluguru and Rondo galagos. All have huge eyes and ears, and forage by night, usually alone, feeding on sap and insects. Like their greater cousins, their vociferous nocturnal calls are a feature of the African night.

SPRING HARE *(PEDETES CAPENSIS)*

Despite its name, this is not a member of the rabbit family; and, despite its appearance, it is not related to the kangaroo. The spring hare is a true rodent, around 80cm (2.5ft) long, yellowish-fawn above and paler below, with large ears and eyes, a long bushy tail and enormous hind legs. It propels itself with these, in a series of leaps or hops, and uses its tiny forelegs solely for feeding or digging. It is a solitary animal, living alone in a burrow, and largely nocturnal, feeding on roots, grass and other plants.

ROCK HYRAX *(PROCAVIA CAPENSIS)*

Hyraxes look like large rodents, brown, round and short-legged, but are in fact distant relatives of the elephant. Rock hyraxes live in small colonies on rocky hillsides or kopjes, where they are often seen basking in the early morning. They feed on leaves, flowers and fruits, never moving far from the shelter of rock. They often become tame when accustomed to people, for instance around lodges. Their relative, the **tree hyrax** *(Dendrohyax arboreus)*, is a solitary, nocturnal forest animal with an eerie shrieking call.

PORCUPINE *(HYSTRIX SPP.)*

Easily recognised by its covering of long, black-and-white-banded quills, the porcupine grows up to a metre (3ft) in length. Two species are found in Tanzania, both very similar in appearance and both sharing the same habits. They live in burrows (often several animals in the same network) in all types of habitat except thick forest, emerging only at night to forage for roots, bulbs, tubers and tree bark. A porcupine makes use of regular pathways: their quills are easily detached and often found along these trails.

AARDVARK *(ORYCTEROPUS AFER)*

An unmistakable creature, the aardvark is vaguely pig-like, but with a long tail, long, tubular snout and huge ears. Digging is its speciality, using its powerful forelegs and massive front claws to excavate extensive burrows where it hides during the day. The aardvark is a solitary animal, and active only at night, when it may wander for several kilometres in search of termites, ants or larvae. When it finds a colony, it digs into it vigorously, lapping up insects with its long, sticky tongue.

THE ELEPHANT CLAN

Strictly matriarchal and highly gregarious, the African elephant usually moves in herds of up to 30 females and youngsters.

African elephants display intriguingly complex social behaviour. The typical herd consists of a core family group, led by the oldest female, whose wisdom and memory of landmarks is vital in lean times, and her offspring. The family group, including the matriarch's sisters and their young, and ranging to about 10 elephants, in turn then expands to the bond groups of the extended family, with up to 30 elephants or more. Bond groups spend up to 50 percent of their time together. The large herds formed by five to 15 bond groups joining together are called clans, while unrelated elephants using the same area are known as a sub-population.

During the wet season, elephants can gather in herds of up to 500. Great excitement is displayed when two families meet. Trumpeting, growling, rumbling, defecating and urinating accompany the greeting ceremony. Trunks are entwined, with much touching and caressing as the elephants renew their acquaintance. As the water dries up and food resources shrink, the group splits up, but will stay in touch.

Elephants can communicate over remarkably long distances using very low frequency infrasound, below the level of human hearing. This low-frequency sound enables elephants to maintain contact over a distance of 10km (6 miles). Elephants use their trunk to produce the classic trumpeting sound, both in anger and exultation.

It is particularly moving to see the gentleness with which elephants nurture their young. Calves are born at night, weighing about 100kg (220lbs), and can fit under their mother's bellies until they are six months old. A mother will use her trunk and feet to guide her baby under her tummy to shelter from the sun, or to her teats between her front legs. When on the move, she'll hold the baby's tail, guiding it forwards, crook her trunk around its rump to help it in steep places, lift it out of a wallow and spray it to keep it cool. As the baby grows, its older sisters help to look after it, preparing themselves for motherhood.

When a baby elephant is in trouble, its core family rallies around immediately, encircling the baby protectively. Similar concern is also seen if an elephant is injured, its companions using their tusks to support or lift it. When an elephant dies, it is mourned by family members, who display evidence of distress and sometimes will even cover the body with branches.

African elephants, Serengeti National Park.

Adolescent males, driven from the matriarch's herd when they become too boisterous, find companionship and safety in loosely knit bachelor herds of up to 20 males, who might move together for a day, a week or a season. When bond groups join in the rainy season, the matriarchal herds are often joined by a dominant breeding bull in musth, his readiness to mate recognised by a copious, pungent secretion from the temporal gland, the dribbling of urine and bouts of aggressive behaviour. Young bulls come into musth in their late teens for a few days; in a prime breeding bull, it can last four to five months.

Females come into oestrus for two to six days, every three to five years. The bull chases the cow briefly, lays his trunk along her back and rears up on his hind legs. Penetration only lasts 45 seconds. Immediately after mating, the cow will scream, with her family group gathering around and trumpeting loudly, as if sounding their approval.

:camera: ENDANGERED AND ENDEMIC WILDLIFE

From the ancient forests of Udzungwa to the open Serengeti Plains and tangled bush of Selous, Tanzania ranks among the world's most important strongholds for endangered wildlife.

The importance of Tanzania's national parks and reserves to Africa's beleaguered wildlife is underlined by recent reports on the alarming numerical decline of wild lions. An estimated 14,000 of these charismatic cats live in Tanzania – four times more than in the nearest runner-up (South Africa, with 3,500), and quite possibly as much as 40 percent of the global total.

It isn't just lions. Tanzania supports around 300,000 African buffalo, six times more than any other country, and about one third of the global tally. Its 51,000 elephants and 30,000 giraffes both account for more than 20 percent of the total wild population. The estimated number of hippos in Tanzania, around 30,000, amounts to one in five of the total African population of 150,000.

When it comes to antelope, around 85 percent of the world's Thomson's gazelle are more-or-less resident in Tanzania, as are 75 percent of blue wildebeest and 70 percent of puku – not to mention every last surviving individual of the endangered Abbott's duiker.

If any one of Tanzania's savannah ecosystems stands out in terms of global conservation significance, it is probably the Selous. Home to more lions, buffalo, elephants, hippos and sable antelope than any other reserve, Selous is also of singular importance to the endangered African wild dog, supporting a population of at least 1,000 – more than are found in any other country, let alone individual reserve.

Young male lion, Selous Game Reserve.

Superb starlings, Serengeti National Park.

The rare red colobus monkey, Zanzibar.

Hippo pod in the Grumeti River, Serengeti National Park.

Tanzania's endemics

Tanzania boasts an unusually high level of endemism, which means it supports a large number of species found nowhere else in the world. Ironically, however, it is not the country's celebrated savannah reserves that host most of these endemics, but the less well-known Eastern Arc and Southern Highlands, whose montane forests are among the most ancient on the continent.

The best-known Eastern Arc endemics are a couple of dozen bird species that attract twitchers from all around the world. However, Tanzania is also home to an astonishing total of 14 endemic chameleons – that's about 10 percent of the world's species – most of which are associated with isolated mountain forests. And while endemism is less notable among mammals, the Udzungwa Mountains and environs alone have five primate species found nowhere else.

Several endemics are associated with more popular sites. The dramatic Zanzibar red colobus monkey is easily seen in Jozani Forest, and at least half a dozen endemic birds – from the stunning black-collared lovebird to the quirky rufous-tailed weaver – are common along the ever-popular northern safari circuit.

...rican wild dog.

...e Western Usambara two-horned chameleon is ...demic to the Usambara Mountains.

Eastern Arc scenery.

BIRDS

Birdwatching in Tanzania offers the opportunity to spot more than 1,100 species, from mighty ostriches to tiny iridescent sunbirds.

Tanzania is one of the most exciting birdwatching destinations in Africa – indeed, anywhere in the world. The national checklist now stands at more than 1,100 species, including 30-plus that are unique to the country. New species are still being discovered with surprising regularity. To place this national tally in some perspective, around 250 species are regularly recorded in Britain, while the combined total for Canada, Mexico and the United States is around 850. Little wonder that Tanzania is regarded to be an ornithologist's delight.

You don't need to be a dedicated birdwatcher to appreciate Tanzania's birdlife. Casual visitors are routinely stunned at the abundance and variety of birdlife seen on safari. Brilliantly coloured lilac-breasted rollers, little bee-eaters and superb starlings perch on the trees, alongside bizarre beak-heavy hornbills and industrious nest-making weavers. The open savannah is home to the magnificent crowned crane and mincing secretary bird, as well as the flightless ostrich and showy kori bustard (the latter, it is claimed, is the world's heaviest flying creature). And everywhere the sky is alive with birds of prey, ranging from the shrike-sized pygmy falcon and dapper black-shouldered kite to the immense martial eagle and lappet-faced vulture.

Some of Tanzania's birds are so rare that it is many years since they have been positively sighted. Others, such as the Udzungwa forest partridge and Pemba green pigeon, are found only in specific small areas. Even so, the birds you are likely to spot on even a short safari holiday are far too numerous to describe in a book like this, and they include some spectacularly beautiful species. In many areas, a

Lilac-breasted roller.

reasonably competent novice to East Africa could hope to see between 50 and 100 species in a day, while dedicated ornithological safaris frequently locate more than 400 species in two weeks.

AGE-OLD MIGRATIONS

The vast majority of Tanzania's birds are breeding residents – that is, they live there all year round – but a significant proportion are non-breeding or breeding migrants. Some are intra-African migrants, for instance dividing their year between the Congo Basin and East Africa, but a far greater number are Palaearctic migrants, spending the northern summer in Europe, Asia or the Arctic, but heading south to Africa when the harsh northern winter depletes their food sources. This means the best time for ornithological tours of Tanzania is from October to March.

An estimated 6 billion individual birds – including many species of wader, raptor, waterfowl and warbler – undertake the annual migration to East Africa, from as far afield as the Bering Straits and northern Scandinavia. Some birds fly on to the southern tip of the continent. Those that survive make the return journey each spring to breed in their chosen latitudes.

Lesser flamingos in Lake Natron in front of Ol Doinyo Lengai.

Bird migration is not learned behaviour, but largely instinctive. Many species that breed in the northern latitudes and migrate to Africa each year actually leave their young to find their own way south, or perish in the attempt. A perfect example of this is the Eurasian cuckoo *(Cuculus canorus)*, which lays its eggs in the nests of foster parents. The young cuckoo, even when totally blind, instinctively and forcibly ejects any other egg or even young chick from its nest. Foster parents spend the next 20 or so days feeding this voracious monster until it can fly and feed itself. By now, its parents have long since left for Africa, often weeks before the European weather turns

miserable. The young cuckoo starts the long journey south with no guidance, following its instinct to fly or die.

Many ducks and geese exhibit similar behaviour. Once breeding is over, adult birds go into 'eclipse', when they moult their flight feathers and cannot fly until new feathers have grown. In the meantime, their new brood has learned to fly very well and they disappear south, well ahead of their parents.

Those that survive the long journey over harsh deserts, flying mostly at night, find rest and feeding grounds in the amenable climate of East Africa. There is a sudden influx of birds almost overnight as huge numbers appear in the bush country, forests and even suburban gardens.

The ability of migrant birds to navigate several thousand miles unaided by technology, and to return repeatedly to the same breeding site, is a remarkable phenomenon, and ornithologists have cooperated to study ringed birds in order to build up a picture of migration patterns. Nevertheless, though we know why birds migrate, and where, much research needs to be done before we fully understand the complexity of their highly tuned navigation systems.

MARINE BIRDS

The coastal climate is hot all year round, and the beaches, with wide tide differentials, provide massive food supplies for waders. At low tide, thousands of these birds can be seen feeding along the beaches, coral pools and mud flats, particularly from September to April, when numbers are boosted by migrants.

Resident birds are also much in evidence. The grey heron (*Ardea cinerea*) and Western reef heron (*Egretta gularis*) feed in the shallow pools, several species of gull are ever-present, and in the evening large flocks of tern come to roost on the coral cliffs.

In shallow water without coral cliffs, mangrove swamps develop. Here the mud attracts the handsome habitat-specific mangrove kingfisher (*Halcyon senegaloides*) and black-crowned night heron (*Nycticorax nycticorax*). Muddy shallows are the preferred habitat of the black heron (*Egretta ardesiaca*), nicknamed the umbrella bird for its unique method of hunting. It paddles in the mud with bright yellow feet and then brings its wings up over its head in umbrella fashion to shade the water underneath.

RIVERS AND LAKES

These (mostly) freshwater habitats support a huge number and variety of birds. Particularly rewarding for birdwatching are the stretch of the Rufiji that runs through Selous Game Reserve, and the Rift Valley lakes of the north, particularly Manyara.

Among the best-represented groups are shore birds such as waders, plovers (lapwings), herons and ibises. One bird you may see in this habitat is the African jacana (*Actophilornis africana*), whose chestnut and blue plumage is less striking perhaps than the long toes that enable it to trot swiftly across water lilies and other floating vegetation in search of insects, crustaceans and molluscs – from a distance, it can look like it is walking on water.

The hamerkop (*Scopus umbretta*) is a brown water bird 60cm (2ft) long, with a heavy black bill, and a thick square crest that earned it the Afrikaans name for 'hammerhead'. It is usually seen wading in the shallows of lakes or slow-moving rivers, searching for frogs, tadpoles, fish or mussels. For unknown reasons, pairs build an enormous nest (up to 2 metres/6.5ft in diameter) from twigs, sticks and even bones, usually in the fork of a tree. The brood chamber within is accessible only through a narrow tunnel.

Greater and lesser flamingos (*Phoenicopterus roseus* and *P. minor*) gather in their thousands in East Africa's shallow soda lakes, in particular Tanzania's Lake Natron, their only known breeding site in East Africa. They have a unique method of feeding: with their head upside-down and submerged, they sweep their angular bill from side to side, filtering out tiny water creatures and algae.

Another striking water bird is the great white pelican (*Pelecanus onocrotalus*), which can be up to 180cm (6ft) long, with an even greater wingspan, and an unmistakable huge yellow bill and pouch. Unusually for birds, they feed communally: up to 30 pelicans form a straight line or horseshoe and, plunging their bills into the water simultaneously, drive fish into the shallows where they can be easily caught.

There is also the yellow-billed stork (*Mycteria ibis*) and African spoonbill (*Platalea alba*), a long-legged and mostly white bird that feeds by sweeping its partially opened bill into

shallow water, and snapping it shut the moment it touches something edible.

The African fish eagle (*Haliaetus vocifer* – sometimes called 'the voice of Africa' after its loud, high-pitched cry) is commonly seen on rivers and lakes. Closely related to the North American bald eagle, it has a white head, breast and tail, yellow-and-black bill, chestnut belly and shoulders, and black wings. It preys on surface-feeding fish, seizing them in flight with its huge talons and carrying them off to a favourite perch to eat.

Yellow-billed stork in the Rufiji River, Selous Game Reserve.

⊘ ENDEMIC BIRDS

In Africa, Tanzania is second only to South Africa for avian endemics – bird species unique to one country. Up to 34 Tanzanian endemics are recognised by some authorities, and while most are restricted to remote forests in the Eastern Arc Mountains, several are readily observed on the northern safari circuit. These include grey-breasted spurfowl (*Pternistes rufopictus*), yellow-collared lovebird (*Agapornis personatus*), Ashy starling (*Cosmopsarus unicolor*) and Rufous-tailed weaver (*Histurgops ruficauda*). Also noteworthy is the Tanzanian red-billed hornbill (*Tockus ruahae*), common in Ruaha National Park.

BIRDS OF THE MOUNTAINS

The immense equatorial mountains of the Tanzanian interior – most famously Kilimanjaro but also Mount Meru, the Crater Highlands dividing the Serengeti from the eastern Rift Valley, and a dozen or so ranges that comprise the endemic-rich Eastern Arc – support a series of isolated habitats determined by altitude. These range from evergreen montane forests to Afro-alpine grassland and moorland.

Although the number of species associated with Afro-alpine grassland and moorland is limited, many are specific to it, notably the beautiful scarlet-tufted malachite sunbird (*Nectarinia johnstoni*), the somewhat drabber alpine chat (*Pinarochroa sordida*) and the utterly magnificent lammergeyer, or bearded vulture (*Gypaetus barbatus*). Despite the harshness of this alpine zone, the birds confined here probably could not survive elsewhere, but they are sometimes joined by more wide-ranging species.

The lower slopes of Tanzania's mountains are generally covered with dense evergreen forest, which thrives best on east-facing slopes, since they tend to have a higher rainfall and more morning mist. The forests grow all year round so they are always green, lush and cool, and provide a permanent home for birdlife.

At lower levels, nearer the moist, cool earth, plant and insect life are abundant. Robin-chats (*Cossypha spp.*) and thrushes (*Turdus spp.*) of several kinds find this perfect. So does a confusing array of similar-looking and closely related greenbuls (*Pycnonotidae*). Overhead, the crowned eagle (*Stephanoaetus coronatus*), possibly Africa's most powerful bird of prey, soars in display – sometimes appearing as only a speck in the sky, its piercing call drawing attention long before it is seen – before swooping down on its favoured prey of forest monkeys.

This is a place to sit quietly and watch. If the wild fig trees are fruiting, sit under one for a while and wait, because the ripe fruit may well attract Hartlaub's turacos (*Tauraco hartlaubi*), African green pigeons (*Treron calvus*) and silvery-cheeked hornbills (*Bycanistes brevis*), along with colourful starlings and barbets of many kinds. When the fruit becomes overripe, it attracts insects, which are followed by a huge influx of insect-eating birds.

Some of these forests, such as those on the volcanic massifs of Kilimanjaro and Ngorongoro, are ecologically modern. Others, particularly on the Eastern Arc ranges, are among the most ancient forests in Africa. Levels of endemism are high in these forests, with several species – the Uluguru bush-shrike (*Malaconotus alius*), Udzungwa forest partridge (*Xenoperdix udzungwensis*) and Usambara weaver (*Ploceus nicolli*), for instance – being restricted to the range for which they are named.

Secretary bird, Serengeti National Park.

⊘ A GROWING CHECKLIST

Tanzania's bird checklist stood at under 1,000 species in 1980. Today, a working checklist compiled by Neil and Liz Baker of the Tanzania Bird Atlas Project includes just over 1,100 species. This gain is exaggerated by the Bakers' admitted bias towards splitting controversial taxa. But it also reflects a huge volume of genuine new data. In 1987, one expedition to the Minziro Forest yielded 17 species previously unrecorded in Tanzania. Since then, 60 genuine new records have been added to the national checklist, leaving Tanzania poised to overtake Kenya as having Africa's second most varied avifauna, after the DR Congo.

THE GREAT SAVANNAHS

Although forests and other montane habitats are rich in unusual species, Tanzania's most rewarding habitat for novice birdwatchers is undoubtedly the vast tracts of savannah and woodland that also support most of the big game sought by safari-goers.

Large raptors such as tawny eagle (*Aquila rapax*), martial eagle (*Polemaetus bellicosus*), black-chested snake-eagle (*Circaetus pectoralis*), bateleur (*Terathopius ecaudatus*) and the migrant Wahlberg's eagle (*Aquila wahlbergi*) nest in the tree tops and feed off small mammals, game birds and snakes and lizards.

Characteristic of open grassland, the flightless ostrich (*Struthio camelus*) is the world's largest and heaviest bird, growing up to 2.8 metres (9ft) tall and weighing up to 90kg (200lbs). It is also the fastest running bird, reaching speeds of 50kmh (35mph). Males are jet black with white primary plumes in the wings; females and young are grey or dull brown.

Another striking resident of open country is the secretary bird (*Sagittarius serpentarius*), a terrestrial bird of prey with the body and head of an eagle, but stork-like legs that allow it to stalk through the open country, often in pairs, seeking prey, which it kills by stamping with strong feet. Although it hunts entirely on the ground, covering up to 20km (12 miles) a day, this 1.5 metre (5ft) tall bird can fly – albeit requiring an extraordinarily long run-up to launch itself into the air – and it roosts at night on the tops of thorn trees.

Abandoned kills in game reserves frequently attract up to six species of vulture. Most common is the white-backed vulture (*Gyps africanus*), distinguished from other vultures in flight by its white rump and a white band on the front underside of the wings. The similar Ruppell's vulture (*G. ruppellii*) has three narrow, pale bars on the underside of the wings and a distinctive bill. Neither is as spectacular as the lappet-faced vulture (*Torgos tracheliotos*), which can weigh up to 10kg (22lbs), is usually seen alone or in pairs, and can be distinguished by its rather hunched vampire-like stance.

Tanzania's most conspicuous game bird is the helmeted guineafowl (*Numida meleagris*), which is about the size of a well-fed chicken, and has white spots all over its grey body and wings, a bare blue neck and throat, a red face, and a bony yellow casque on top of the head.

Most savannah habitats are alive with smaller but eye-catchingly colourful birds. The nectar-eating sunbirds of the family *Nectariniidae* have slender curved bills, and the males of most species have brilliant metallic plumage, making them somewhat similar in appearance to hummingbirds (a classic example of convergent evolution). As an indication of their vibrant colouring, Tanzanian species include the scarlet-chested, green-throated, golden-winged, olive-bellied and amethyst sunbirds.

Other safari favourites include the bright-

Male red-billed hornbill looking for termites, Ruaha National Park.

red firefinches (*Lagonosticta spp.*), the closely related blue-grey cordon-bleus (*Uraeginthus spp.*), the aptly named superb starling (*Spreo superbus*) and paradise flycatcher (*Terpsiphone viridis*), the artful home-making weavers (*Ploceus spp.*), the comical cock-headed hornbills (*Tockus spp.*) and a rich variety of colourful and vociferous barbets (*Lybiidae* family). But if any one bird can be guaranteed to thrill every first-time safari-goer, it must be the lilac-breasted roller (*Coracias caudata*), whose vivid ultramarine rump and wing coverts, pink chest, blue head and elongated, pointed outer tail feathers are best displayed during the tumbling aerial routine that gives the family its name.

TANZANIA'S REPTILES

From ferocious giants that can kill and consume a zebra to tiny fly-eating lizards, Tanzania has a wild abundance of scaly, cold-blooded beasts.

The richness of Tanzania's reptile fauna compares favourably with any other part of the world. Since most species have no significant commercial value, poaching is not generally a problem, though crocodiles are sometimes killed for their skins. A far greater threat to many reptile species is habitat loss and the expanding human population, especially as it is customary for many locals to kill snakes and larger lizards on sight.

CROCODILES

The Nile crocodile *(Crocodylus niloticus)*, a ferocious inhabitant of rivers and lakes, grows to an average of 5 metres (16ft) in length, but can attain 7 metres (23ft) and weigh 900kg (2,000lbs). Though it rarely ventures far from water, its muscular legs can propel it across the ground at 45kmh (28mph). The world's largest crocodile, it feeds mainly on fish, but will also attack larger mammals that venture into the water, or close to its edge, and is responsible for many human deaths, particularly among local people using the rivers.

The Nile crocodile was once ubiquitous in suitable aquatic habitats, and while its range has been substantially reduced through uncontrolled trapping and shooting, it is still common in most larger rivers and other water bodies in protected areas. Good places to see large crocodiles include the Rufiji River as it runs though Selous Game Reserve, and the Serengeti's Grumeti and Mara rivers, where they gorge themselves annually during the crossings associated with the wildebeest migration.

SECRETIVE SNAKES

Visitors to Tanzania are often surprised at the apparent scarcity of snakes, which tend to be secretive creatures and are particularly shy of

Nile crocodile at the Rufiji River, Selous Game Reserve.

humans, whose approach they can sense through seismic vibrations along the ground. Despite this, snakes are by no means uncommon, though most species are harmless to humans.

Among the snakes that can be harmful are three species of mamba. The largest is the black mamba *(Dendroaspis polylepis)*, which can grow up to around 3.2 metres (10ft) long, and is not black but olive-brown in colour. It can inflict a lightning-fast bite, injecting immense quantities of exceedingly powerful venom, and it has a reputation for aggression when pursued or otherwise annoyed. In Tanzania this species is commonest in the east.

The coastal green mamba *(D. angusticeps)* and its more localised western counterpart Jameson's mamba *(D. jamesoni)* seldom reach over 2 metres

(6ft) in length. Both are brilliant green and deadly, but their venom is only about one-fifth as toxic as that of the black mamba.

The widespread puff adder (*Bitis arietans*) is considered the most dangerous of Tanzania's snakes. Relying on its mottled brown camouflage, it does not generally take evasive action but remains motionless, so a person walking through scrub or high grass can easily step close enough to be struck.

The black-necked spitting cobra (*Naja nigricollis*) is the most widespread of three cobra species that ejaculate their venom when cornered, aiming at the eyes. If the eyes are washed out quickly, the effect is only temporary but acutely painful; if neglected, permanent damage can result.

The largely arboreal boomslang (*Dispholidus typus*), though highly venomous, carries its poison fangs so far back in its jaws that a human being, in order to be bitten, would have to put a finger into its mouth.

The widespread southern rock python (*Python natalensis*) and more localised central African rock python (*P. sebae*) are heavy-bodied snakes that often attain a length of 5 metres (16ft). They are non-venomous and kill by strangulation, making them relatively harmless to adults, though they do very occasionally attack children. Although widely distributed, these impressive creatures are not often seen.

There are too many harmless snakes to mention in detail, including specialist feeders such as centipede-eaters, slug-eaters, egg-eaters and even a little shovel-nosed snake that lives off gecko eggs. Others are more general feeders, such as the sand snakes (*Psammophis*) which, despite their name, never live in sand.

Many snakes will take eggs opportunistically, for which reason large-scale agitation among birds in a tree is often a good indication that a snake (or small bird of prey) is around.

TORTOISES AND TURTLES

Only four species of tortoise are naturally found in Tanzania. The leopard tortoise (*Geochelone pardalis*), named for its distinctive yellow-on-black shell markings, is the largest, with some individuals weighing in at 40kg (88lbs). It is also the most common.

From the rocky areas of north-central Tanzania comes the strange pancake tortoise (*Malachochersus tornieri*), which is quite flat and has a flexible papery shell. Unlike most tortoises, which retire into their shells when threatened, these gallop off at speed to hide among the rocks, and wedge themselves in so tight that they are difficult to extricate.

The giant Aldabran tortoise (*Dipsochelys dussumieri*), the world's second-largest species, though not indigenous to Tanzania, has been introduced to Zanzibar and is most commonly seen on Prison Island or in the gardens of Livingstone House.

Green turtle at Mnarani aquarium, Zanzibar.

In addition to the land-dwelling tortoises, around seven species of freshwater terrapin occur in Tanzania, most being flattish with a rubbery shell and a narrow pointed head. The most widespread of these are the yellow-bellied hinged terrapin (*Pelusios castanoides*), which are mostly found along the coastal belt, and the helmeted

Seldom seen in the wild, snakes can be observed at close quarters at several zoo-like snake parks in Tanzania. The best is Meserani Snake Park (0754-440800; www.meseranisnakepark.com) on the road between Arusha and Lake Manyara.

terrapin *(Pelomedusa subrufa)* of the northern and central interior.

Five of the world's seven marine turtle species also occur off the East African coast, including breeding populations of hawksbill turtle *(Eretmochelys imbricata)* and green turtle *(Chelonia mydas)*.

LIZARDS

Almost 200 lizard species are found in East Africa. These vary in size from the giant monitors to the tiny cat-eyed coral-rag skink *(Ablepharus boutonii)* which lives on outcrops of coral rag (petrified coral

gecko species have adhesive toe pads that allow them to run up walls and walk on ceilings.

Giant plated lizards *(Gerrhosaurus major)*, named for their reddish-brown scaling, which looks like chain mail, are mainly fruit-eaters but will devour insects and mice if they get the chance.

Of Tanzania's multitude of lizards, there is one other that deserves a special mention: the blue-tailed gliding lizard *(Holaspis guentheri)*. These are small lizards of the high primary forest, conspicuously marked with bright yellow longitudinal bars, which can glide from tree to tree.

Flat-headed rock agama, Serengeti National Park.

in limestone) and maintains an osmotic balance by having very saline blood.

The 2-metre (6ft) Nile monitor *(Varanus niloticus)*, mainly found along rivers, is known to dig up crocodile's nests and to eat the eggs. The similarly proportioned but duller savannah monitor *(V. albigularis)* can be found in dry bush and savannah country, at a considerable distance from any water.

Many kinds of agama lizard, some with bright red, orange or purple heads, can be seen around lodges and camps, especially in rocky areas. It is the males that have the coloured heads, and the colours intensify when they are agitated.

Geckos are widespread, and often a welcome sight, due to their taste for household bugs. Though typically dull in colour, most of the country's 40-odd

CHAMELEONS

Notable for their prehistoric appearance, independently swivelling eyes, rapidly unleashed body-length tongues, and (sometimes overstated) capacity to change colour, chameleons come in many sizes and shapes. The smallish flap-necked chameleon *(Chamaeleo delepis)* is the commonest species of savannah and woodland chameleon, and can often be observed crossing roads. The giant chameleon *(C. melleri)*, a bulky dark-green creature with yellow stripes and a small horn, is mainly associated with the Eastern Arc forests. Also characteristic of montane forests are several types of three-horned chameleon, including the endemic *C. fuelleborni*, which is confined to Ngosi Volcano.

INSECTS AND ARACHNIDS

Tanzania's tens of thousands of insect species include a kaleidoscopic variety of brightly coloured butterflies, the tireless dung beetle, and enervating squadrons of disease-carrying mosquitoes.

Ants, beetles and locusts are among the better-known representatives of the class Insecta, members of which can be distinguished from other invertebrates by their combination of six legs, a pair of frontal antennae, and a body divided into a distinct head, thorax and abdomen. Insects are also the only invertebrates with wings, though some primitive orders have never evolved these appendages, and other more recently evolved orders have discarded them.

The tropical forests and savannahs of Tanzania are particularly rich in insects. These range from vividly coloured dung beetles that use their hind legs to push along the dung balls in which they lay their eggs, to fearsome columns of army ants that march single-mindedly along the forest floor, ready to attack anything that gets in their way.

This immense insect diversity is epitomised by the presence of more than 1,000 species of butterfly (as compared with roughly 650 in the whole of North America, and a mere 56 in the British Isles). Many individual forests in Tanzania harbour several hundred species; indeed, a visitor might easily see a greater variety of butterflies in the course of a few hours sitting quietly at a forest pool than one could in a lifetime of exploring the English countryside. Most spectacular are the large and colourful swallowtails (*Papilionoideae*), named for the streamers that trail from the base of their wings.

Not all flying insects are as benign as butterflies. Tanzania is home to numerous species of mosquito, including the genus *Anopheles*, which transmits malaria. Likewise, locusts, though strictly vegetarian, seasonally irrupt in numbers that can wreak total destruction on local crops.

Overall, however, the importance of insects in the food chain – they are the main source of nutrition to many bird and small mammal species – cannot be overstated. And many insects are not only harmless but truly fascinating to observe: take the intriguing praying mantises that are still held sacred by many African peoples, for instance, or the giant armoured rhinoceros beetles that march determinedly along forest verges.

PREDATORY ARACHNIDS

Distinguished from insects by having eight legs, arachnids are a class of mostly terrestrial and predatory invertebrates that include spiders, scorpions and ticks. Spiders are well represented in Tanzania, with some several thousand species identified to date, among them the spectacular golden orbs whose huge webs

Baboon spider walking over a rock.

are often seen in game reserves, and the scarily hairy baboon spiders.

Few African spider species are dangerous to humans, and bites fatal to adults are almost unheard of. However, the oddball jumping spider *Evarcha culicivora*, first discovered in the Lake Victoria region in 2005, is evidently partial to feeding on human blood – though fortunately it doesn't prey directly on people, but instead hunts down and kills blood-sucking mosquitoes, making it more of an ally than a foe from a human perspective.

Of the other arachnids, certain tick species transmit tick-bite fever, while scorpions, though seldom seen unless actively sought by turning over rocks or dead logs, are known for their painful and, in some cases, strongly venomous sting.

Palm-lined beach, Pangani.

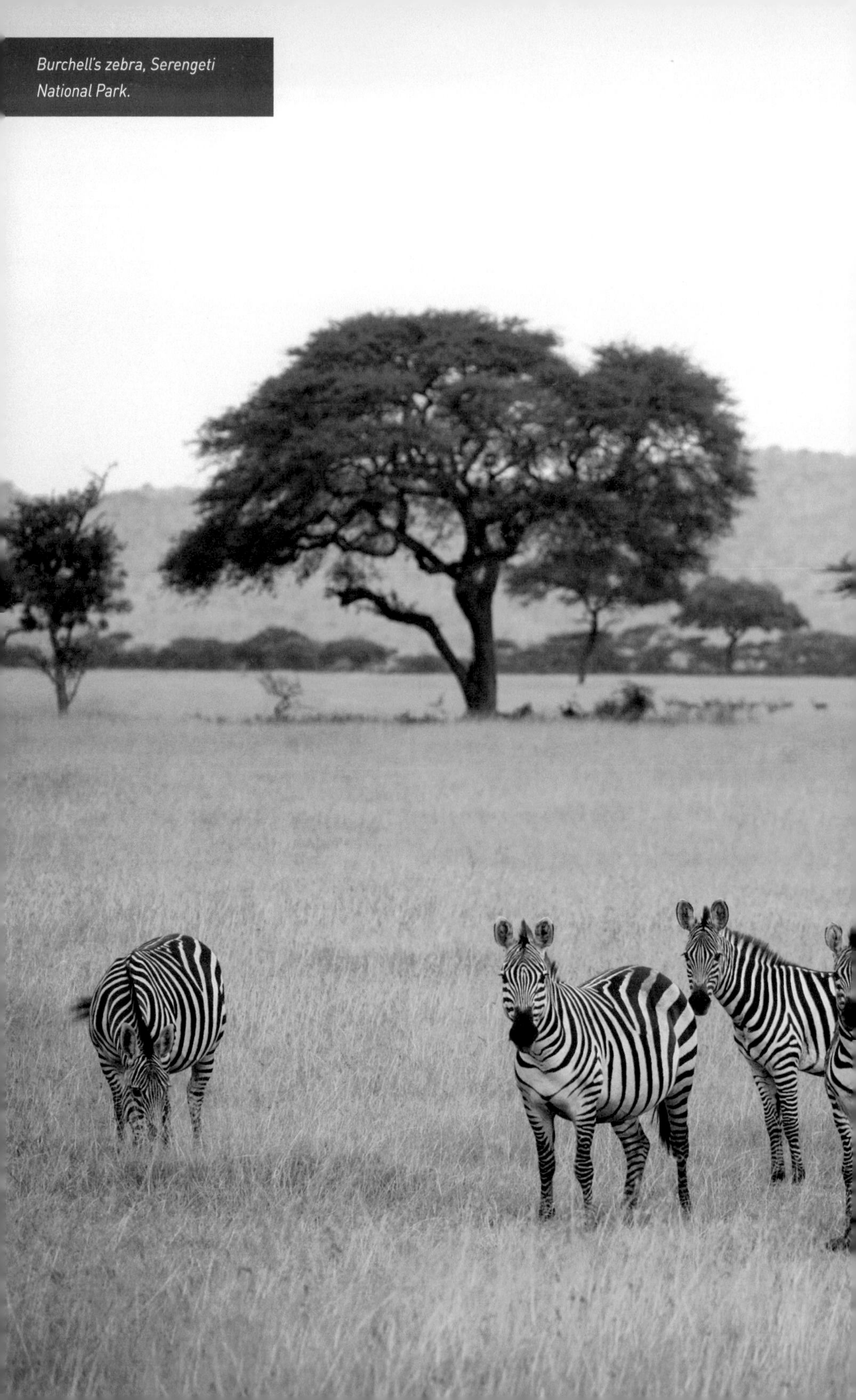

Burchell's zebra, Serengeti National Park.

Clocktower in Arusha.

INTRODUCTION

A detailed guide to the entire country, with principal
sights clearly cross-referenced by number to the maps.

*Tippu Tip's House,
Stone Town.*

You are at the top of a 600-metre (1,970ft) cliff, surrounded by
dense montane forest. Butterflies dance in the sunlight while
monkeys crash through the canopy. Laid out in front of you is a
vast volcanic caldera, with shadows of clouds chasing across
the short-cropped golden grassland on its flat floor. Near the
centre, a cloud of pink overlaps the blue of a small lake; and
here and there are dots of white, grey or black. Use binoculars
and the pink turns into a flock of flamingos; the white dots are
safari vehicles; the grey and black, the rocky bulk of elephants and buffalos.

This is the Ngorongoro Crater, one of the world's most beautiful and bountiful wildlife sanctuaries. A few hours' drive to the west and you reach the
broad Serengeti plains, home to the great migration of some 2 million wildebeest, zebra and antelope. A few hours' drive east and you
are at the foot of Mount Kilimanjaro, its rounded top, iced with
streaming glaciers, peering out from a shroud of clouds. Head
south to Tarangire, where lions loll in the shade of the trees
and giant fleshy baobabs stand like sentinels above the rolling
red dust. Further south still, you pass the ancient and mysterious rock paintings of Kondoa, as you head towards the great
Rufiji River that slices through the Selous Game Reserve.

In the west, you reach the great lakes – the clear, deep
waters of Lake Tanganyika, home to hundreds of species of
brightly decorative fish. Along the shoreline, the primeval forests of Gombe Stream and Mahale Mountains protect some
of the world's last thriving colonies of chimpanzees. By contrast, the steel-grey waters of Lake Victoria, shrouded in an
almost perpetual haze, are less forgiving and more mysterious – fitting for
the source of the Nile.

*Southern Ground Hornbill,
Tarangire National Park.*

Perhaps, instead, you choose to explore the magnificent coastline. Here
you will find the bustling city of Dar es Salaam, the brooding ruins of the
medieval city of Kilwa, and characterful Swahili backwaters such as Bagamoyo and Pangani. A short plane ride takes you to Zanzibar, the offshore
paradise with its dazzling white-sand beaches, turquoise seas, fragrant clove
forests, full-bellied fishing dhows and coral reefs teeming with colourful fish.
Whichever direction you take, Tanzania offers inspiration. It could take a lifetime to explore.

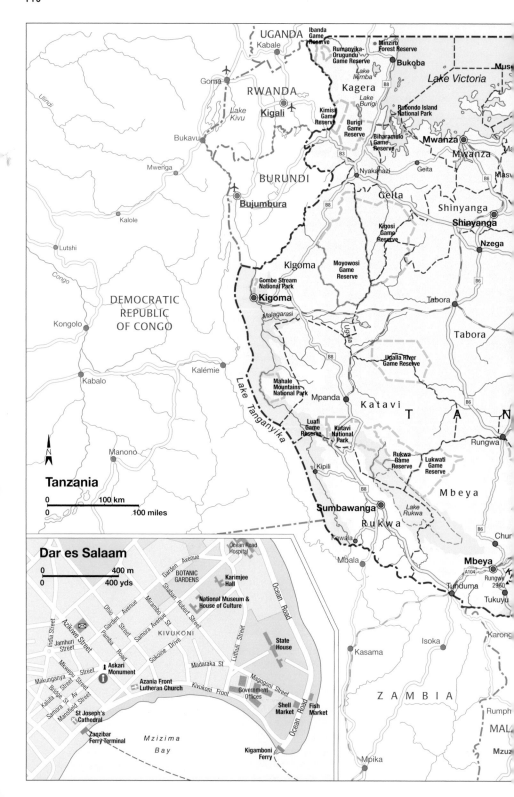

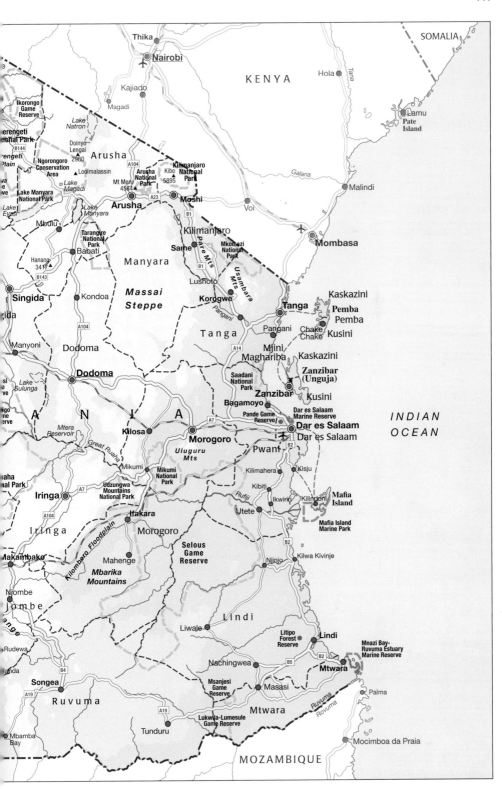

Azania Front Lutheran Church.

DAR ES SALAAM

If not technically the capital, Dar is the unchallenged economic and administrative hub of Tanzania and a vibrant, entertaining city.

Dar es Salaam is like the curate's egg – good in parts. British explorer and diplomat Frederic Elton, who went there in 1873, wrote: 'The site is a beautiful one and the surrounding countryside green and well-wooded'. Sixty years later, the writer Roald Dahl found it little changed: 'A vast rippling blue lagoon and all around the rim of the lagoon there were pale yellow sandy beaches, almost white, and breakers running up onto the sand, and coconut palms with their little green leafy hats were growing on the beaches.'

Time has moved on. The rippling blue lagoon is now a sullen mass of water sludgily washing a dirty beach. Dahl's paradise beaches are still there but you need to look for them. Even so, it's worth lingering to discover some of Dar's less obvious charms – its architecture, its people, its markets and its museums.

HOUSE OF PEACE

In 1862, Dar, one of many small fishing villages along the coast, was called Mzizima. Sultan Majid of Zanzibar was so impressed with its natural harbour and scenery that he established a trading centre there. In 1886, he built a two-storey palace of coral which he named *Dari Salaam* (House of Peace).

The Arab settlement developed into a sophisticated town, but Majid died in 1870 after a fall in his palace, and his successor, his half-brother Barghash,

had no interest in the town. Dar was forgotten, and the more northerly port of Bagamoyo, the coastal terminus for slave caravans from the interior, and an important dhow-building centre, gained ascendancy (see page 131).

In the 1880s, a station for Christian missionaries was established, followed by a seat for the German colonial government in 1891. The Germans felt that Dar's deeper and better-protected harbour was a safer bet for steamships than Bagamoyo, and Dar es Salaam became Tanzania's undisputed capital.

Main Attractions
National Museum and
  House of Culture
Azania Front Lutheran
  Church
Kunduchi Beach & Ruins
Ras Kutani

Map on page 124

Kivukoni fish market.

By 1914, when the Germans finished building the central railway line, the city was flourishing. Relics of the German architecture and their acacia-lined streets survive today. However, the Germans were forced out in 1916, and the British moved in, staying until Tanganyika gained its independence in 1961.

Under these colonial influences, the city developed a fine harbour, lovely parklands, tree-lined avenues and a good commercial centre. After independence, however, the nationalisation of many industries resulted in economic free fall, and the city slid into decline. In 1973, the legislature and official government transferred to Dodoma. By the 1980s, Dar es Salaam was in a sorry state. Since then, however, its stock has risen greatly, mirroring the economic recovery of the country as a whole.

Today, Dar es Salaam is the largest city in Tanzania, covering over 1,590 sq km (614 sq miles), with a population of nearly 4.3 million. Although technically no longer the capital of Tanzania, it remains the commercial, social and – for now at least – the political heart of the country, as well as its most important port. While many government offices have 'failed' to move to Dodoma, in spite of having 40 years to do so, the current administration under John Magufuli has finally kick-started the process, set for completion in 2020. At the same time, government plans will see Dar become an important regional trade hub, serving as a port for its land-locked central African neighbours.

The city centre has undergone something of a post-millennial facelift, exuding an aura of economic recovery that extends to the leafy suburbs running north of the city centre towards the Msasani Peninsula. Elsewhere, much of suburban Dar es Salaam – as with most other cities in the Global South – is run-down and riddled with poverty.

Most tourists bypass Dar because it is so easy to get to the main centres by air, but its people and architecture offer an interesting cultural mix of British, German, Asian and Arab influences in a city which is still unmistakably Swahili. Although most residents live a hard life, crowded on buses and *dala dalas* and

Bird's eye view of the roundabout holding the Askari Monument.

scratching a living from the streets, the people of Dar are friendly and helpful, and there is little of the hassle factor. They are proud of being Tanzanian and want to welcome visitors and show their country to people from overseas.

GETTING AROUND

Getting about in Dar is easy. The city centre is relatively small and easily explored on foot, during the day. Don't walk anywhere in the city at night. The cheapest way to get around is to catch a *dala dala* (minibuses that serve as public transport), but these are often overcrowded, and have a reputation for pickpockets and bag-snatchers, so watch your luggage carefully. Taxis are easy to locate and very inexpensive, especially if you are prepared to bargain (drivers will frequently ask tourists up to double the going rate). Local tour operators will provide a seat on a scheduled tour or offer a car and driver/ guide for the day, and take you round all the sights if you want to do things the easy, but more expensive way.

SAMORA AVENUE

The main thoroughfare through the city centre, **Samora Avenue** Ⓐ runs for about 1.5km (1 mile) northeast from the small (and decidedly uninteresting) **Clock Tower**, built in 1961 to commemorate independence, to the beach-front Ocean Road Hospital. An important landmark, situated at the junction with Azikiwe Street, is the **Askari Monument** Ⓑ, a small bronze statue dedicated to the many indigenous Tanzanians who lost their lives during World War I, when the country was the site of a little-known theatre of war (see page 51).

Samora Avenue has shops with clothing and electrical goods. Everything from food and newspapers to boots and brightly coloured tie-dye fabrics can be bought from the decrepit street stands lining the road. Many of the city's most useful offices and banks lie along, or within a block or two, of Samora Avenue.

The names of the surrounding streets are a tour of African nationalist history. Samora Machel was independent Mozambique's first president; Albert Luthuli was the former president of South Africa's African National Congress; Shaaban Robert was one of Tanzania's best-known writers; and Edward Sokoine was a former prime minister.

To the northeast of the Askari Monument, in a shady, tree-lined area, are the fragmentary remains of the **Botanic Gardens** Ⓒ, first planted in 1893, more recently a run-down and dusty haven in the middle of this very busy, noisy African city, and now the site of the Southern Sun Hotel, one of several conspicuously modern buildings in the vicinity.

The **National Museum and House of Culture** Ⓓ (Shaaban Robert Street; tel 022-211 7508; daily 9.30am–6pm) is only moderately inspiring by European standards, but has one of the best collections in East Africa. Highlights include some of the Leakeys' key fossil discoveries from Oldupai Gorge (see page 169), some interesting old photographs and traditional craft items, plus displays on

Erected by the British in 1927, the Askari Monument remembers the African soldiers who fought in World War I.

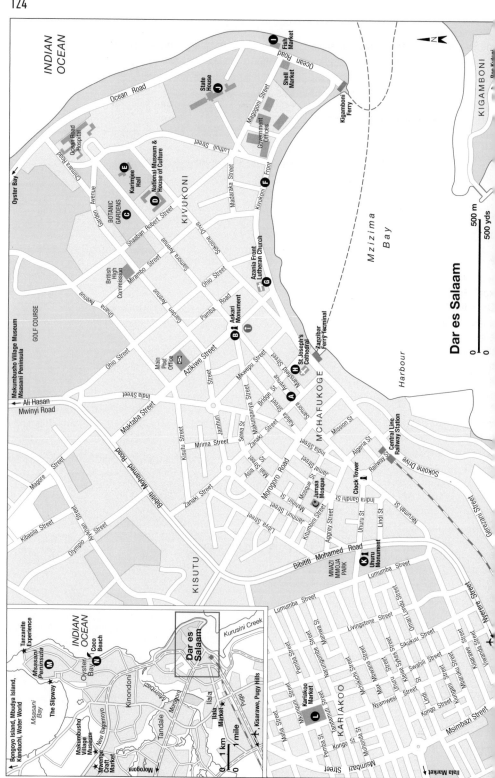

Dar es Salaam

the Shirazi civilisation of Kilwa, the slave trade, and the German and British colonial periods. There are also temporary exhibitions and theatre, dance and art performances.

On the other side of Samora Avenue, the **Karimjee Hall** 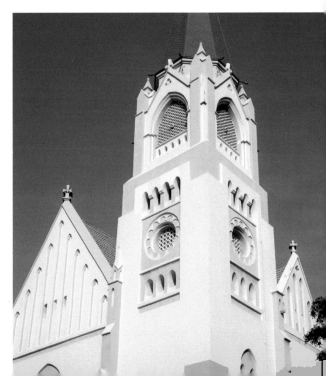, built by the British in 1916, is where Julius Nyerere was sworn in as independent Tanganyika's first president. This was the House of Parliament before the legislature was relocated to Dodoma, and it's now used for parliamentary committee meetings and political functions.

KIVUKONI WATERFRONT

A block south of Samora Avenue, **Kivukoni Front** lines the north side of Dar's impressively busy harbour, where dugout canoes, dhows and container ships jostle for space in a fascinating trip through the history of Indian Ocean shipping. Many of the government offices overlooking the harbour, including the Ministry of Justice and Constitutional Affairs and the Bureau of Statistics, are elegant colonial buildings, dating back to the short-lived German era. However, with current plans afoot to shift the government's seat to Dodoma, the future of these offices is unclear.

One of the most imposing buildings in the city, the **Azania Front Lutheran Church** (www.azaniafront.org), was built in the Bavarian style by German missionaries in 1898 and is still in use. Almost as grand, a couple of blocks west, is the Catholic **St Joseph's Cathedral** (www.daressalaamarchdiocese.or.tz), which was built between 1897 and 1902 and still contains many of the original German inscriptions and artwork. There are two other buildings worth taking a look at on Sokoine Drive: **Old Boma**, possibly the city's oldest building, founded by Majid of Zanzibar in the 1860s, and the **White Fathers' House**, also known as Altiman House, dating from the same period.

Opposite the Lutheran Church is the huge headquarters of the National Bank of Commerce, while opposite the

Catholic Cathedral is the **Zanzibar Ferry Terminal**. Several ferries make the journey every day, the faster services taking less than two hours. Further west, the **Central Line Railway Station** stands on the corner of Sokoine Drive and Railway Street. (The Tazara Railway Station, where trains leave for Zambia, lies a few kilometres west of the city centre.)

OCEAN ROAD

The east end of Kivukoni Front joins up with Ocean Road at the **Kigamboni Ferry Terminal**. The surrounding area is a good place to experience local life (including a small but real risk of being mugged, so take care), with a ragged street market offering piles of fruit and snacks such as corn on the cob grilled over an open brazier. Crows with vicious black beaks pick up anything from old fruit skins to fish heads, and here and there are lime-kilns – burning cairns of coal. The ferry that scurries across the unbridged harbour entrance to the south bank village of Kigamboni is the easiest way to get to the stretch of coast running south from Dar es Salaam as far as Ras Kutani. It

St Joseph's Cathedral, one of Dar's surviving colonial buildings.

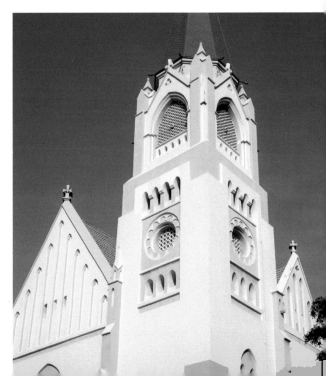

also, incidentally, offers a reasonable and inexpensive harbour tour.

Almost next door is the **Fish Market** ❶, located in hygienic, Japanese-built quarters. The fish is wonderful, fresh from the Indian Ocean. There are huge prawns and lobsters, and masses of colourful local fish. It is busiest in the early morning, and usually all but over by 9am.

Across the road are the drying and frying vats, an area of leaping flames and bubbling cauldrons, where thousands of tiny kapenta fish are preserved for future use.

Keep heading north along Ocean Road and you come to the vast, palatial **State House** ❶ (www.ikulu.go.tz), built by the Germans in the 1890s and restored by the British in 1922, after World War I damage. It is now the official home and office of the president, although current plans to move the administration to Dodoma will also see the president relocated. Beyond that is the **Ocean Road Cancer Hospital**, an interesting building combining Arab domes and windows with iron spikes and corrugated-iron roofing, built by the Germans in 1897. Restored

Fried fresh fish at the market.

again by the Germans in 2000, it is now a specialist cancer treatment centre. General treatment has been taken over by the shiny Aga Khan Hospital, almost next door. The beach along Ocean Road may look inviting from a distance, but is polluted and dirty and not good for swimming. To the north, there are the smarter areas of Upanga, Oyster Bay and Msasani.

KARIAKOO

Northwest of Samora Avenue, around India and Jamhuri streets, is the Asian quarter, while west of Mnazi Mmoja Park are the colourful areas of Kariakoo and Ilala. This is an essentially African part of Dar, named when African porters of the Carrier Corps were billeted there. The houses are typical Swahili *bandas* with corrugated-iron roofs, ornately carved front doors and often a small veranda or a stone slab in the front, shaped like a sofa for sitting outside.

In the Kariakoo area, the **Uhuru Monument** ❸ is a white obelisk with a flame called the Freedom Torch, dedicated to Tanzania's independence. **Kariakoo**

Market **❶** is the city's biggest and busiest, held daily. It sells everything, with trolleys filled with great pyramids of fruit and vegetables beautifully laid out in the sunshine. There are woven baskets full of maize, spices and lentils. Nothing is genetically engineered; everything is misshapen, blotchy and beautiful. The crowds are huge, and you may well be the only tourist, but it's quite safe as long as you watch your pockets. **Ilala Market** is similar.

THE MSASANI PENINSULA

The **Msasani Peninsula ⓜ**, 8km (5 miles) north of the city centre, is the local diplomatic enclave and Millionaire's Row, lined by high-security walls over which peep the tops of lavishly manicured gardens and crisp white villas. It is also the home of several of the city's best hotels. On the western side of the peninsula, Msasani is a delightful fishing village and the site of one of the oldest Arabic settlements along the Swahili coast. **The Slipway** is a waterfront complex with cafés, bars, art shops, Dar es Salaam's best bookshop, and an ATM machine. It also

has a lively but distinctly touristy market and wonderful sea views.

From here, you can catch boats out to **Bongoyo Island** (tel: 022-260 0893 or mob: 0713-328126; departure every two hours from 9.30am–3.30pm, returning an hour later) and you can also charter boats for fishing. The island has good diving and snorkelling, as does **Mbudya Island**, 4km (2.5 miles) further north, which can be reached from the beach hotels north of Dar. Good diving is also available from Dar. There are a couple of good dive centres just south of the Msasani Slipway; other dive centres can be found at the northern beach hotels.

NORTHERN BEACHES

Between the city centre and Msasani Peninsula, **Oyster Bay ⓝ**, better known as Coco Beach, is a popular place for expats to hang out on weekend afternoons (avoid it at other times as thieves operate in this area, and always keep a close eye on your belongings). The prettier beaches to the north of Dar are several kilometres away, which means using public transport or a taxi for the

Fishing boats at dawn.

⊘ PUGU HILLS

The **Pugu Hills Forest Reserve**, set aside in 1954 to protect the closest swathe of evergreen forest to Dar, is of considerable interest to wildlife enthusiasts. Even though much of the original forest has been cleared, the tracts that remain harbour a varied fauna, including blue monkeys, suni antelope, chequered elephant-shrews and rondo dwarf galagos, among the world's most endangered primates. Over 100 bird species have been recorded, notably the spotted ground thrush and East Coast akalat. The abandoned **Pugu Kaolin Mine** houses hundreds of thousands of bats, a dramatic spectacle when they exit at dusk. Situated on the outskirts of **Kisarawe,** a former hill station 25km (15 miles) southwest of Dar, the reserve has two excellent natural trails for hikers.

day. There are several interesting stops en route. The **Makumbusho Village Museum** (New Bagamoyo Road, about 10km/6 miles from the city centre; tel: 022-270 0437; daily 9.30am–6.30pm) is a well-presented open-air museum comprising a collection of 20 different styles of tribal huts from all over Tanzania. There are artists and craftsmen at work producing ebony signs, paintings, postcards, clay figures and games. Souvenir prices are good here, and there are music and dance performances many afternoons (additional charge).

For more concentrated souvenir shopping, the **Mwenge Craft Market**, off the New Bagamoyo Road, about 3km (2 miles) further along, is one of the best places in Tanzania for shopping. Craftspeople from all over the country sell spears, masks, woodcarvings – anything from a tiny malachite hippo to a full-sized African lady – some of it in highly polished ebony, some of it purporting to be ebony (spot the tin of black boot polish under the counter). You can watch them at work under the trees. Friendly, leisurely bargaining is expected here.

Makonde carver at work in Mwenge Craft Market.

Mbezi Beach and **Kunduchi Beach**, separated by a lagoon, lie about 35km (22 miles) from the city centre along the Bagamoyo Road. The beaches are lined with resorts and hotels, and offer a variety of excursions to nearby islands, plus diving, windsurfing and snorkelling. Next to the Kunduchi Beach Hotel, and under the same management, **Kunduchi Wet 'n' Wild** (tel: 0688 058 365; www.wetnwild.co.tz; daily 9.30am–6pm) is East Africa's largest water park, with more than 29 slides and seven pools, shops, restaurants, and a go-kart centre.

The **Kunduchi Ruins** (daily 9am–4pm), just up the beach from the Kunduchi Beach Hotel, include the remains of a 16th-century mosque and several 18th-century pillar tombs, many decorated with Chinese porcelain plates. Further along to the north, 5km (3 miles) inland from the main road, are more Arab graves at Mbweni.

SOUTH OF THE CITY

The best beaches are to the south, with white sands, palm trees and clear water. They can be reached by driving round the river inlet or catching the motor ferry to Kigamboni, which itself has a reasonable beach. If you have transport, take the road to Mjamema and head further south. Some 7km (4 miles) along, **Mikadi** is an attractive beach with backpackers' *bandas*. Seven kilometres further on, **Kipepeo Beach Village** is a popular expats' escape hatch with *bandas*, a bar and food. The beach is beautiful and you can swim at high and low tide. Both places are extremely cheap.

A further 15km (9 miles) south, the crown jewels of the Dar area, **Ras Kutani** and the **Amani Beach Club**, are both very upmarket and very different. Ras Kutani has luxury beach houses made of natural materials which blend with the area, and a superb outdoor restaurant overlooking the beach. Amani Beach Club has plush bungalows and a good swimming pool.

Soni Falls in the Usambara Mountains.

THE NORTH COAST AND USAMBARA

Brave the bumps and you will discover a tantalisingly beautiful corner of Tanzania, with fine beaches, a fascinating history, spectacular mountain scenery and superb birdlife.

Tanzania's north coast, though almost entirely undiscovered by tourists, is rich in off-the-beaten-track gems. The undeveloped coastline of Saadani National Park is one of the few places where you can go on safari before breakfast, and swim in the warm waters of the Indian Ocean afterwards. Relics of the slave trade abound at Bagamoyo, also the site of the country's oldest mainland Christian mission, while the dilapidated port of Pangani and medieval ruins such as Tongoni and Kaole evoke the ancient Swahili mercantile culture. Further inland, the Usambara Mountains offer wonderful walking, with the Amani Nature Reserve, in particular, showcasing the rich biodiversity that has led to Tanzania's Eastern Arc Mountains being described as an African Galápagos.

BAGAMOYO

A good 70km (43-mile) surfaced road runs north from Dar es Salaam to the timeworn port of **Bagamoyo ❶**, which was the most important port along this stretch of coast for much of the 19th century. This was largely due to its role as an embarkation point for slaves being taken from the interior across to Zanzibar. Today, the town looks set to benefit from a host of ongoing investment projects, including the extension of the port (in Mbegani) and its transformation into a Special Economic Zone supported by Chinese investors.

Bagamoyo was also an important town in the early era of European settlement. Indeed, the Catholic mission established there in 1868 is the oldest on the Tanzanian mainland. The missionaries bought slaves, liberated them and settled them in a Christian Freedom Village. In an unusual cooperation between the French and German missionaries and the British authorities, it was also here that the Catholics built East Africa's first primary school, secondary school and hospital.

Map on page 132

Main Attractions

Bagamoyo
Saadani National Park
Ushongo Beach
Tanga
Amani Nature Reserve
Western Usambara

Unloading the fish catch at Tanga.

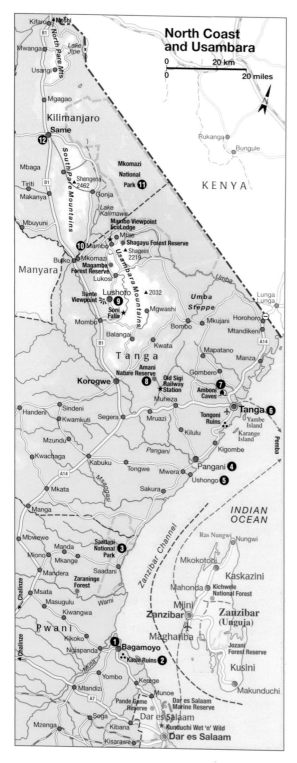

North Coast and Usambara

0   20 km

0   20 miles

N

Moshi
Kifaru
B1
Mwanga
Lake Jipe
Usangi
North Pare Mts
Mgagao

Kilimanjaro
Same
⑫

Rukanga
Bungule
KENYA

Mbaga
South Pare Mountains
Tiriti   B1   Shengena ▲2462
Makanya   Gonja
Mkomazi National Park ⑪

Mbuyuni
Lake Kalimawe
Mambo Viewpoint EcoLodge
Mtae
⑩ Mambo   Shagayu Forest Reserve
Bulko   Mkomazi   ▲ Shagein 2219
Manyara   Magamba
             Forest Reserve
             Lukosi
                            Umba

Irente Viewpoint   ▲2032
Lushoto ⑨   Mgwashi   Umba Steppe
Soni Falls   Lunga Lunga
Mombo   Bombo   Mkujani   Horohoro
Balangai   Mtandikeni
             Kwata   A14
B1   Mapatano   Manza

Tanga
Amani Nature Reserve
Korogwe   Old Sigi Railway Station   Gombero
⑧   Amboni Caves ⑦
             Muheza
Sindeni   Tongoni Ruins   Tanga ⑥
Handeni   Kwamkuti   Segera   Mruazi   Yambe Island
                              Kilulu   Karange Island
Mzundu   Kigombe
Kwachaga   Kabuku   Tongwe   Mwera   Pangani ④
             A14   Ushongo ⑤
Mkata   Msangasi

Manga   INDIAN OCEAN

Mbwewe   Ras Nungwi   Nungwi
Manda   Saadani National Park   Mkokotoni
Miono   Mkange
Mandera   Saadani   Kaskazini
Msata   Zaraninge Forest   Mahonda Kichwele National Forest
Masugulu   Wami
Kiwangwa   Mjini
Pwani   Zanzibar   Zanzibar (Unguja)
Kikoko   Magharibi
Ngiapanda ① Bagamoyo   Jozani Forest Reserve
           •• Kaole Ruins ②
Yombo   Kerege   Kusini
Mlandizi   Munoe   Makunduchi
         A7   Pande Game   Dar es Salaam
                 Reserve   Marine Reserve
Mzenga   Soga   Kibana   Dar es Salaam
                Kisarawe Kunduchi Wet 'n' Wild
                          Dar es Salaam

Chalinze
North Pare Mts
Usambara Mountains
Pemba
Zanzibar Channel

Nowadays, the **Holy Ghost Catholic Mission** (daily 10am–5pm), a few hundred metres north of the small town centre, houses a museum which tells the story of German colonisation and slavery, graphically illustrated with gruesome artefacts such as slave collars and whips, as well as a German letter of liberation of the last slave. At the oceanic end of the mango-lined avenue, the modest Livingstone Church is where the sun-dried body of the explorer David Livingstone was interred in 1874 before it was shipped to Zanzibar and eventually to England.

Bagamoyo's fortunes, hit by disease and the end of the slave trade, rose again in 1887 when it became the first capital of German East Africa. In 1897, however, the Germans realised that the harbour was too shallow and moved down to Dar. The town's potholed streets are flanked by once imposing, now decaying dwellings, but it's worth visiting for its history, its former grandeur, its ancient ruins and beaches, and also for one or two latter-day initiatives aimed at women and children. Although dilapidated, many of the old buildings in Bagamoyo are still lovely; their doorways may be covered in graffiti and falling off their ancient hinges, but they are also magnificent monuments, finely carved with intricate Arab and Swahili decorations.

The oldest building is the restored **Old Fort** (daily 9am–5pm), on the Kaole Road, on the outskirts of town. Expanded from a slave prison built by an Arab trader in 1860, it is entered via a wooden Zanzibari-style door fitted by Sultan Barghash in 1874. It was used as a jail and then a police post until 1992, when restoration work began.

Liku House, on India Street, was the German headquarters from 1888; it has a metal-columned awning and a large door. The Germans later moved to the **German Boma,** a crenellated two storey-building which has been undergoing restoration for some years.

The **Old Bagamoyo Tea House** is an Arabic building with attractive columns, a veranda and arched windows, restored in 2009–10 and now the seat of the local government. Further north, the **Jama'at Khana** is the Ismaili mosque, with a veranda and the double-fronted carved doors which once gave the town its air of grand prosperity.

The Old Caravanserai (daily 9am–5pm), close to the modern market and bus station, is where caravan parties used to assemble prior to trekking into the interior. Partially restored, it now houses the official town museum, as well as an information centre and internet café.

Bagamoyo was, over many years, the most important dhow-building port along the East African coast. Ocean-going dhows are still built here, on a beach 1km (half a mile) south of the town.

On the Dar es Salaam road, about 500 metres/yards south of town, the Bagamoyo Institute of Arts and Culture (www. tasuba.ac.tz), in an interesting modern building made entirely with traditional material, often stages performances of dancing and drumming.

Most of the hotels are on a 2km (1-mile) stretch of road that leads down to the gorgeous beach just north of Bagamoyo. They start at basic backpackers' rates and move up the range to luxurious accommodation. The most luxurious option in the area is Lazy Lagoon (www.lazylagoonisland.com), on an island-like spit facing the old town, and reachable only by boat.

A half-day boat trip available from most beach hotels takes visitors round the lagoon, islands and mangrove swamps. There is also the opportunity to swim among the coral reefs. Prices for these excursions vary hugely, so shop around.

KAOLE

About 4km (2.5 miles) south of Bagamoyo, the **Kaole Ruins** ❷ (daily 8am–4pm) are all that remains of a Shirazi trading centre founded in the 13th century. Resting in a secluded palm grove are two mosques, some 15th-century gravestones and around 30 tombs. There is also a small room with a selection of artefacts that have been found in the area. Kaole means in KiSwahili 'Go and see for yourself'. Many people go there to pray at particular tombs. Some of the Arab traders buried there have fascinating histories, such as Sher Ali, who had eight wives. There are pillars, some of which have collapsed, marking the wives' graves. Sher Ali's pillar is the biggest. Another grave, called the Love Grave, belonged to an Arab travelling from Zanzibar. He fell sick and died, and his wife was so grief stricken that she too died and was buried in the same grave. Other graves have superstitions attached; one tells the story of a young lady who died a virgin. Locals now climb into the grave to pray for something they desire.

The 15th-century well is also a place of pilgrimage where people come to take the water and pray.

Pagani residents.

⊙ LINKS TO THE SLAVE TRADE

The name Bagamoyo is a corruption of the KiSwahili phrase *bwaga moyo*, which can be translated as 'lose heart' or 'lay down your burden', or several variants thereof. The name dates to the 18th century, when Bagamoyo was the coastal terminus of the main caravan route from Lake Tanganyika. It was here that the exhausted porters, having carried ivory and other trade goods more than 1,000km (620 miles) from the interior, could finally unload their cargo and rest.

However, while Bagamoyo's name may have been coined by porters, it is now more widely associated with the slave trade. During the mid-19th century, Bagamoyo was the end of the road for an estimated 1.5 million East Africans captured in raids deep in the interior, then marched to the coast chained neck-to-neck. The march took three to six months, and captives too weak to accomplish the journey were killed. Once in Bagamoyo, the survivors – up to 50,000 annually – were hoarded in dingy dungeons before being shipped to Zanzibar, where they were sold at the infamous slave market and exported to Mauritius, Persia, Arabia and India. Only in 1873 was the trade officially abolished. Even so, despite the efforts of the British ships that patrolled the waters between Bagamoyo and Zanzibar to look for smugglers, a clandestine trade continued for several years after that.

Politicians frequently come to Kaole to pray before an election.

There is a popular crocodile farm located near Kaole – ask at your accommodation about arranging a visit.

SAADANI

Saadani National Park 3 (255 689 062 346; www.tanzaniaparks.go.tz; daily 6am–7pm) is geographically the closest reserve to Dar es Salaam, and a similar journey in terms of time to Mikumi National Park. (Both parks are accessible destinations for weekend mini-safaris.) Saadani is a four-hour, 200km (124-mile) drive from Dar via Chalinze and Miono, the first half of it on a good, surfaced road, the rest on dirt. However, until plans to construct a surfaced coastal road from Bagamoyo materialise, the easiest way to get to Saadani is by air. There is a decent airstrip close to Saadani village, and a flight from Dar es Salaam takes just 25 minutes. Saadani lies almost directly opposite Zanzibar's Stone Town, just 27km (17 miles) across the channel, and flights between the two take just

The 13th-century Kaole Ruins include the oldest mosque on the East African mainland.

15 minutes. Travel by boat from the island is not an option for visitors.

Situated along the coast in the centre of the historic triangle of Bagamoyo, Pangani and Zanzibar, Saadani encompasses over 1,000 sq km (386 sq miles) of diverse landscape and is the only national park that borders the sea. For a park that receives so few visitors, which is part of its appeal, there is a surprisingly wide variety of safari options available – game drives, boat safaris, fly-camping, walking safaris and birdwatching, all providing a different perspective on this unique area.

The range of different ecosystems sets Saadani apart from all other National Parks in Tanzania. Coastal forests, acacia woodlands, open grasslands and mangroves host large numbers of giraffe, zebra and hippos and increasing numbers of lions and elephants. The landscape in Saadani is diverse and constantly changing, from the high grasses and rolling hills in the north to the mangrove forests and acacia plains in the south. The southern areas of

Saadani are home to a wide range of plains game, including giraffe, zebra, kudus, wildebeest, elands, waterbucks and warthogs, along with reedbucks, hartebeest and baboons. Elephants are quite often seen in these areas, and lions are also present, but rather secretive.

The highlight of any trip to Saadani is a boat safari along the lush **Wami River**; these can be arranged through any camp in the park. Beginning in the brackish waters that attract plentiful wading birds to the mouth of the river, the boat makes its way inland, under the watchful gaze of a spectacular variety of birdlife and the ever-present hippos. Egrets, woolly-necked storks and pelicans line the Wami's banks, tiny malachite kingfish peer out from the twisted mangroves, fish eagles soar overhead and bee-eaters dart in front of the boat. Large pods of hippos appear around every bend. Nile crocodiles and monitor lizards are also seen on the banks, while black-and-white colobus and blue monkeys play in the trees overhead. The delightful ecology-focused Kisampa Camp (www.afrikaafrikasafaris.com) is on the banks of the Wami River and is the perfect place for keen birdwatchers to stay.

The warm waters of the Indian Ocean account for the fantastic food available in Saadani. Prawns and lobster are fished from these waters and represent some of the freshest, tastiest seafood in Tanzania.

In the park itself, there are a multitude of tracks to be explored. Most visitors will go on game drives with one or other of the camps and lodges, but self-drivers are advised to take an experienced guide with them to assist in locating game and finding their way around.

PANGANI

It's an 85km (53-mile) drive from Saadani to Pangani, following a dirt coastal road that is likely to be surfaced in the not-too-distant future. As things stand, however, the journey is a real adventure, through river beds, villages and sisal fields. Take

Ferry crossing at the Pagani river mouth.

Mangrove knees, the strange knobbly roots of the swamp-dwelling mangrove tree, are a vital part of the East African coastal ecology.

Selling fish in Tanga.

it at your peril, but don't attempt it in the rainy season (March–May): you will never get there. The safer but less exciting alternative, around three sides of a rectangle, heads away from the coast, back onto the main A14 north towards Segera, and then eastwards to the coast again. Either way, you eventually reach Pangani, which lies on the north bank of the eponymous river, and is connected to the south bank by a regular motor-ferry service.

Pangani ➍ is a small town, once a dhow port, about 290km (180 miles) from Dar. It enjoyed affluence during the Shiraz era, when the Pangani River became a transport route to the interior, and in the late 19th century when it was the terminus of the caravan route from Lake Tanganyika. From here, slaves, ivory, sisal and copra were exported.

Today, it still has a strong Arab feel. Relics of its prosperous past can be seen in the carved doorways and colonial buildings, two dilapidated Omani mansions and a German castle (now a coconut market). But it is really a place to seek the sun and relax. It is seen as one of the up-and-coming resorts in Tanzania. A string of low-key resorts lie along the main road towards Tanga, where a narrow tidal beach offers limited swimming. By contrast, a cluster of resorts at **Ushongo** ➎, about 15km (9 miles) south of town, and reached via the ferry, have particularly good beaches. The pick of these is The Tides, an ever-popular resort located on a glorious cliché of a beach with brightly coloured luxurious bungalows and superb food.

TANGA

Tanga ➏, 46km (28 miles) north of Pangani, is Tanzania's second-largest seaport. This quiet but substantial town can be reached by road, and there is a daily flight from Dar es Salaam. Like Pangani, it was once a springboard for trade caravans to the interior, and was further developed in the late 19th century during the German era, together with the railway line that linked Moshi and

Kilimanjaro with the sea. Today, its main industry is exporting sisal from the plantations, which stretch from Tanga westwards to the Usambara Mountains. There are regular flights from Dar and Zanzibar with Coastal Aviation (see page 243).

Today, Tanga is a pleasant waterfront town with a population of over 270,000 and a compact centre endowed with several attractive colonial buildings, notably the Usambara Courthouse on Usambara Street and partially disused Cliff Block on Hospital Road. The only formal tourist attraction in town is the waterfront **Urithi Tanga Museum** (mob: 0784-440068; Mon–Fri 9am–5pm), housed in the so-called 'Second Boma', a handsome administrative building constructed by the Germans in 1890. Displays include photographs of Tanga in the early 20th century, and historical artefacts unearthed in the harbour and town centre.

The upper-class area of Ras Kazone lies to the northeast of the town centre, while 'on the other side of the track' is the dusty and rather busier Ngamiani quarter. There are no truly upmarket hotels (for that, you're better off at Pangani or Ushongo), but several decent mid-range options line the Ras Kazone beach front, while the old town centre has a few adequate budget hotels.

The **Amboni Caves** ❼ (guided tours daily 8am–5pm) are 8km (5 miles) northwest of Tanga, off the surfaced road towards the Horohoro border post and Kenyan port of Mombasa. Often claimed to be the largest cave system in East Africa, it comprises 10 entrance caverns leading to a network of limestone tunnels, rumoured to be up to 200km (125 miles) long. Only about 1km (half a mile) is generally open to the public, but even this is not for the claustrophobic; in parts you have to crawl, sometimes in procession, through to a stalactite-clad cave. Locals believe the main cave is

the home of a fertility god and leave their offerings there.

AMANI AND THE EASTERN USAMBARA

For wildlife enthusiasts, Tanga District's main attraction is not the coastline, but the less-publicised **Amani Nature Reserve** ❽ (tel: 027-254 0313; open daily), which lies further inland, in the heart of the Eastern Usambara Mountains.

The centrepiece of the reserve is the Amani Botanical Gardens, set up as part of a German agricultural research station in 1901. In 1997, the gardens were incorporated into a 10,000-hectare (24,700-acre) **nature reserve** that also includes the Nilo Forest Reserve, and a trek romantically called a 'Climb into the Clouds' (a 1,360-metre/4,460ft climb up Lutindi Peak). The guided trails through the montane forest offer a wonderful collection of woodland vegetation, black-and-white colobus monkeys and magnificent birdlife, with some 340 species identified, including 12 that are globally threatened

The Amboni caves, the most extensive limestone cave complex in East Africa.

and 19 that are either endemic to the Eastern Arc Mountains or to the East African coastal biome. These include the green-headed oriole, long-billed tailorbird, Usambara eagle owl and Amani sunbird.

Ideally suited to keen walkers, the reserve also offers accommodation in a simple but clean and good-value resthouse, in the Amani Botanical Gardens. The gateway town is Muheza, which lies 40km (24 miles) from Tanga along the main surfaced road to Segera and Arusha. From Muheza, it's about an hour's drive to the entrance gate at Sigi, and another 30 minutes or so to the botanical gardens. The journey requires four-wheel drive at all times, and it may be impassable in the rainy season.

WESTERN USAMBARA AND MKOMAZI

Divided from its eastern namesake by the 4km (2.5-mile) wide Lwengera Valley, the Western Usambara also makes up part of the Eastern Arc formation, though it is more densely populated,

Mtae village, western Usambara Mountains.

and thus less biodiverse. The main town, **Lushoto** ❾, is 123km (76 miles) from Tanga, via **Segera**, **Korogwe** and finally **Mombo**. There are a number of hotels in the town, which is perched in a pretty valley, and offers plentiful opportunities for walking.

Probably the most popular hike around Lushoto, taking perhaps an hour in either direction, leads to the spectacular **Irente Viewpoint**, which has a 1,000-metre (3,300ft) drop to the plains below and offers a panoramic view of the Maasai Steppe. Another worthwhile goal for a day trip is the **Soni Falls**, which can be accessed from the small town of Soni along the road back to Mombo.

About 15km (9 miles) north of Lushoto, **Magamba Forest Reserve** protects the most accessible indigenous forest in the Western Usambara, swathing the upper slopes of Mount Magamba, the highest peak in the range at 2,230 metres (7,316ft). The reserve is popular with birdwatchers, with the old sawmill in particular offering a good chance of seeing two

species that are endemic to the Western Usambara, namely the Usambara weaver and Usambara akalat, while reptile enthusiasts can look out for the endemic Western Usambara two-horned chameleon. For non-birdwatchers, a popular goal for a day walk is a pretty waterfall on the forest-fringed Mkuzu River about 2km (1.25 miles) from Migambo village.

While Lushoto is the main tourist focus in the Western Usambara, the northern part of the range is also well worth exploring, particularly the cliff-top villages of **Mtae** and **Mambo** , perched on a high escarpment offering stunning views across the plains below to Lake Kalimawe, the Pare Mountains, Mkomazi National Park and even Kilimanjaro. The main base for exploring this area is the **Mambo Viewpoint EcoLodge** (www.mambo-viewpoint.org), a superb Dutch-run community-oriented project whose spectacular setting is complemented by an exciting range of guided and unguided hikes, mountain-biking excursions and vehicle-based trips

organised through its in-house tour operator. It is a good base for exploring the **Shagayu Forest Reserve**, whose impressive birdlife includes several Eastern Arc endemics.

Mambo Viewpoint is also a good base for organised safaris to the under-used **Mkomazi National Park** ⑪ (tel: 027-250 3471; www.tanzania-parks.go.tz; daily 6am–7pm), whose 3,702 sq km (1,429 sq miles) lie on the border with Kenya and form part of the same ecosystem as Tsavo West National Park. Set aside as a game reserve in 1961 and upgraded to a national park in 2006, Mkomazi lacks the large mammal densities associated with better-known parks, but it benefits from a genuinely remote feel. Wildlife includes lions, cheetahs, elephants, giraffe and other game, as well as 400-plus species of bird. There is one tented camp in the park, and plenty of budget accommodation in the small town of **Same** ⑫, which flanks the B1 between Moshi and Segera a few minutes' drive from the park entrance gate.

Lushoto's market.

⊘ THE EASTERN ARC MOUNTAINS

Although less celebrated than the likes of the Serengeti, the ancient Eastern Arc Mountains – a series of 13 forested massifs that run in a rough crescent through eastern Tanzania from the Pare and Usambara in the north to Udzungwa and Mahenge in the south – is unquestionably of greater ecological significance.

Listed as one of the world's 20 most important biodiversity hot-spots, the forests of the Eastern Arc are the most ancient and stable in Africa, having flourished continuously for some 30 million years due to moisture blown in on winds from the Indian Ocean.

Isolated from other similar habitats by tracts of low-lying savannah, the Eastern Arc ranges possess something similar to an island ecology – they are sometimes referred to as Africa's Galápagos – and harbour an astonishing 16 plant genera, 75 vertebrate species and perhaps 1,000 invertebrates found nowhere else in the world.

Over the past century, however, five of the Eastern Arc ranges within Tanzania have lost more than 75 percent of their forest cover as a consequence of human activity. Fortunately, none has yet approached the perilous state of the Taita Hills in Kenya, the one Eastern Arc range situated outside Tanzania, where only 2 percent of the original forest remains.

Maize field beneath Kilimanjaro.

ARUSHA AND KILIMANJARO

With Africa's highest mountain, the gateway to the great game parks of the north, and the cultural delights of Arusha, this little district packs a big punch.

The hub of Tanzania's buoyant safari industry, **Arusha ❶** is a popular first stop on the northern circuit (see page 155), as well as being a useful base for exploring Arusha and Kilimanjaro National Parks. International flights arrive at **Kilimanjaro International Airport** (www.kilimanjaroairport.co.tz), 45km (28 miles) away, but there's also a busy domestic airport on the edge of town, with regular flights to the national parks, Zanzibar and Dar es Salaam.

ARUSHA TOWN

The Naura River Valley divides Arusha into two parts. The relatively sedate old town centre, east of the river, is liberally studded with upmarket hotels, classy restaurants, safari companies and craft shops, as well as hosting the Tanzania Tourist Board (TTB) information office. West of the river, the more colourful market area is the site of the main bus station, the stadium and a plethora of budget guesthouses and eateries.

The focal point of the old town centre, reputedly centred midway between Cape Town and Cairo, is the **Clock Tower ❹** on the Uhuru Road roundabout. The venerable Arusha Hotel also lies on this roundabout, while the Old Moshi Road running immediately east passes through the leafy suburb of Kijenge, with its cosmopolitan selection of around a dozen restaurants.

A dala dala (minibus taxi) in Arusha.

A few hundred metres north of the clock tower, the original German fort on Boma Road is now the **Natural History Museum ❸** (tel: 027-254 5540; Mon–Sat 9am–6pm, Sun until 5pm). It has a small exhibit explaining the evolution of man. Interestingly, at Laetoli, the site of the footprints at Oldupai, there were once giant warthogs as large as rhino.

A short walk north, the **Arusha International Conference Centre (AICC) Building ❹** (Simeon Road; tel: 027-2050 181; www.aicc.co.tz) was built

Main Attractions
Arusha National Park
Lakes Chala and Jipe
Marangu
Mount Kilimanjaro
  National Park

Maps on pages
142, 146, 151

in 1969 and expanded in 1991 to host more than 1,300 delegates. It contains offices in one wing; the other was occupied by the International Criminal Tribunal for Rwanda before it was closed in 2015.

Two private institutions in the old town centre merit a visit. Operated by the world's largest tanzanite mining company, the modern **Tanzanite Experience** **D** (India Rd; mob: 0767 600 990; www.tanzaniteexperience.com; Mon–Sat 8.30am–5.30pm, Sun 10am–3pm; free) boasts imaginative multimedia displays introducing the history of Tanzania's mauve trademark gemstone. It is also a safe place to buy certified jewels from source.

The **Warm Heart Gallery** **E** (mob: 0754-672256; www.warmheartart.com; Mon–Sat 10am–10pm, Sun from noon; free) not only showcases contemporary local art, but is also home to a popular coffee shop and the Rock Art Conservation Centre (www.racctz.org), an NGO dedicated to the preservation of the Kondoa Rock-Art World Heritage Site.

Heading west across the Naura River, the roundabout at the junction of Makongoro Road and Swahili Street is dominated by the **Uhuru Freedom Monument** **F**. Right next to it, the **Arusha Declaration Museum** **G** (daily 9am– 5pm), dedicated to the economic and political history of Tanzania, contains ethnological paraphernalia and a selection of photographs from the early 20th century.

Further west along Sokoine Road, the **TFA Centre** **H**, Arusha's best mall, houses the immense Shoprite Supermarket, a good bookshop, half a dozen restaurants and coffee shops, a good selection of clothing and craft shops, hairdressers, banks with ATMs, and internet cafés.

Travelling west along the Dodoma road, the **Cultural Heritage Centre** **I** (tel: 027-250 7496; www.culturalheritage.co.tz; Mon–Sat 9am–5pm, Sun until 2pm) stocks an impressive collection of local arts and crafts. The headquarters for **Tanapa** (Tanzania National Parks; www.tanzaniaparks.go.tz) lies a few hundred metres further out of town.

Continuing west to **Kisongo** **J**, venue of a large Maasai market every

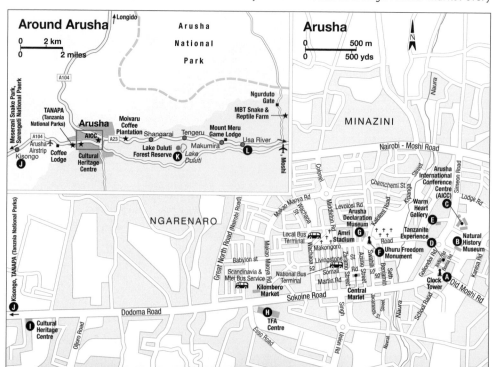

Tuesday, there's a **Maasai Gallery and Cultural Centre**, supporting disabled people and women's groups, and the **Meserani Snake Park** (www.meserani snakepark.com). Set in pleasant gardens, with a lively bar, it has an interesting selection of snakes, and knowledgeable guides on hand.

COMMUNITY TOURISM

Within the Arusha vicinity, a number of cultural tourism programmes have been organised by the Tanzania Tourist Board. Profits from tourist visits to local communities are used to fund educational projects, develop primary schools and provide bursaries. At **Ng'iresi**, **Ilkiding'a** and **Mulala**, on the slopes of Mount Meru, it is possible to experience the local Wa-Arusha culture, visiting homesteads, traditional healers and craftsmen. At **Monduli**, west of Arusha, there are walks with Maasai through the evergreen rainforest on the Monduli mountain range, with panoramic vistas across the Rift Valley to Ol Doinyo Lengai and Lake Natron, and visits to local herbalists and women making jewellery. At **Longido,** on the

Arusha–Nairobi road, similar activities are offered, together with guided walks on the Maasai plains or climbs up Mount Longido. There is a colourful Maasai cattle market each Wednesday.

On the outskirts of Arusha at **Tengeru**, 2km (1 mile) south of the Moshi road, is **Lake Duluti Forest Reserve** Ⓚ. A crater lake, Duluti is said to be 300 metres (980ft) deep and fed by an underground river. It takes an hour to walk around the lake, shaded by tall trees with straggling lianas. There's a good chance of seeing fish eagles and other birds. Further along the Moshi road, you can go horse riding through coffee farms and onto the Mount Meru foothills at **Usa River** Ⓛ, which is also where several of the most popular tourist lodges in the vicinity of Arusha are located.

ARUSHA NATIONAL PARK

The turn-off to Arusha National Park is a few kilometres east of Usa River. Near **Ngurdoto Gate,** the **MBT Snake and Reptile Farm** (daily 9am–5pm) has knowledgeable guides, a

Cultural Heritage Centre.

Ⓞ ARUSHA IN HISTORY

Arusha was founded in 1900 as a German garrison on the border of the lowland territory of the pastoralist Maasai and the southern Mount Meru foothills, inhabited by the Maasai's foes, the agricultural Wa-Arusha. Thanks to a fertile and well-watered location, it developed as an agricultural market centre, with coffee, wheat, maize, pyrethrum and flowers among the crops grown nearby. In 1967, the town gave its name to Nyerere's momentous Arusha Declaration (see page 56). Arusha was also the headquarters of the East African Community (EAC) between its foundation in 1967 and disbandment in 1977, a role it resumed when the EAC was revived in 2000. More recently, Arusha has become the main centre for exporting tanzanite, a unique blue gemstone mined in the nearby Mererani Hills.

comprehensive display of snakes and several types of chameleon, as well as tortoises and crocodiles. At Mkuru, 12km (7 miles) from the **Momela Gate**, at the northern base of Mount Meru, there are camel safaris on offer.

Covering 542 sq km (209 sq miles), **Arusha National Park ❷** has stunning scenery, ranging from the lofty peaks of Mount Meru and its magnificent montane forests, to craters, open glades and the alkaline Momela Lakes – from which both Meru and Kilimanjaro are visible on a clear day. Around 400 species of bird have been recorded in the park, along with a wide variety of butterflies and other wildlife. Only an hour's drive from Arusha, the park is often overlooked in the rush to head off on the Serengeti circuit, but it is well worth a visit.

To the left of the park boundary is the area known as little Serengeti – a large, open glade with giraffe, zebra, buffalo, warthogs and the occasional bushbuck on the woodland periphery. From the gate at Ngurdoto, the road winds up through the forest, where troops of black-and-white colobus and blue monkeys can be glimpsed in the high canopy, to **Ngurdoto Crater ❸**. From lookout points along the crater rim, you can see herds of buffalo, giraffe and warthogs grazing the grasslands on the crater floor, and listen to the less-than-musical cries of the silvery-cheeked hornbill and beautiful Hartlaub's turaco.

The road through the park to Momela Lakes descends from the Ngurdoto forest to the **Lokie swamp** and two small lakes, **Jembamba** and **Longil**, with hippos, waterbucks and reedbucks, saddle-billed storks, Egyptian geese and various heron species, before reaching the grassland and thornbush around the Momela Lakes. A mixture of wildlife, from giraffe to warthogs, and a diverse range of birds are commonly seen, including large seasonal concentrations of flamingos. Here you can really appreciate the scale of **Mount Meru**, which, when clear of cloud, looms, dark and threatening.

Lake Duluti.

MOUNT MERU

Known as *Oldonyo Orok* (Back Mountain) by the Maasai, Meru stands at 4,566 metres (14,980ft), the fifth-highest mountain in Africa. Walks on the lower slopes, climbs to the summit, **Socialist Peak**, and to Little Meru can be arranged with the park headquarters at the Momela Gate. Allow three to four days for the tough hike to ascend the peak; the best time to go is between July and September. Park guides are well trained and informative. Walking gives a different perspective on viewing the wildlife. Skirting past breeding herds of buffalo, getting to within 50 metres (160ft) of a giraffe, listening to the raucous sounds of Hartlaub's turaco, and searching for colobus monkeys in the trees, is guaranteed to sharpen the senses. Natural attractions include the giant fig-tree arch, the buttress roots of a strangler fig through which an elephant can pass, and the **Tululusia Waterfall**. Tululusia means 'sentinel', and the top of Tululusia Hill was used as a lookout point by the Maasai during the 19th-century war with the Wa-Arusha.

Interestingly, the volcanic rocks give the water a high mineral and fluoride content, staining teeth a dirty brown, as can be seen among the Wa-Arusha living on the slopes of the mountain.

THE ROUTE UP THE MOUNTAIN

The track up Mount Meru begins at the **Momela Gate**, at 1,500 metres (4,920ft). There are two routes to the first hut, **Miriakamba**, at 2,600 metres (8,530ft). The northern route takes three to four hours, and can also be driven. The southern route takes a couple of hours longer, but is more interesting and scenic, crossing streams and open grassland before climbing up through the forest, passing through the fig-tree arch, crossing the Jekukumia River to the Njeku viewpoint, with expansive views to Momela Lakes and across the park, before continuing to Miriakamba. On the way, there's a good chance of seeing giraffe, bushbucks, duiker, buffalo and various monkey species.

From Miriakamba, it's a four-hour hike to **Saddle Hut**, at 3,600 metres

A typical African food market in Moshi.

(11,810ft), passing through glades and forest to **Mgongo wa Tembo** (Elephant Ridge). From here, it's a pleasant afternoon's excursion to the summit of **Little Meru** (3,820 metres/12,530ft), from which there are impressive views of the crater, the ash cone and the sheer cliffs of the crater's inner wall towering some 1,500 metres (4,920ft) high. Look out, along the way, for the agile klipspringer, a small antelope which has adapted to steep and rocky terrain, and the imposing lammergeyer (bearded vulture) soaring on the updrafts.

From Saddle Hut, you can hike to the summit in about six hours, traversing a knife-edge ridge. Start early to watch the sun rising behind Kilimanjaro. Descending from the summit, you can stay at Saddle or Miriakamba Hut before the final descent to Momela Gate.

MOSHI AND MARANGU

Founded in 1911 as the terminus of the Tanga railway line, the sprawling town of **Moshi ❹** lies some 75km (45 miles) west of Arusha, at the foot of Kilimanjaro, where it serves as a staging post

for those inspired to conquer Africa's tallest mountain.

Moshi's main shopping and business area has a useful assortment of safari companies, exchange bureaux, internet cafés, hotels and coffee houses, along with a colourful vegetable market and a few interesting shops. Situated east of the railway line about 10 minutes from the town centre, **Shah Industries** (tel: 0754 851 393) specialises in quality leatherwear, while the more central **One Heritage** has the most varied stock of several general craft shops. Of architectural interest are the Hindu temple and colonial railway station.

Several worthwhile distractions surround Moshi. Day trips can be arranged to the **Rau Forest**, visiting the Materuni waterfalls. At **Mweka**, there's a small wildlife museum attached to the College of Wildlife Management (http://mwekawildlife.ac.tz). **Lake Chala ❺** is a small but scenic crater lake, about 1km (half a mile) wide, on the Kenyan border. Skirting the eastern slopes of Kilimanjaro, take the road to Taveta, from where a rough road to the lake passes

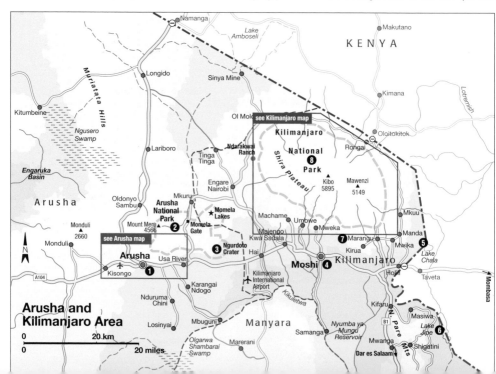

through farmland, west of Holili. There's a steep path down the 100-metre (330ft) crater wall, but crocodiles lurk here so don't be tempted to swim. Less visited is **Lake Jipe** ⑥, a shallow alkaline lake some 16km (10 miles) long. Bordering Tsavo West National Park in Kenya, Jipe is accessible from Kifaru on the Tanga road, and it offers excellent birdwatching, as well as the chance of seeing larger wildlife.

The main gate of **Kilimanjaro National Park** borders **Marangu** ⑦, a scenic small town set amid the coffee and banana plantations of the prosperous Chagga people, 40km (24 miles) by road from Moshi. Surrounded by babbling mountain streams and lush highland forest, Marangu is an agreeable place to overnight prior to a Kilimanjaro climb, with the added attraction of two impressive waterfalls – Kinukamori and Kilasia – close to the town centre.

KILIMANJARO

Kilimanjaro National Park ⑧ (www.tanzaniaparks.go.tz) covers an area of 760 sq km (293 sq miles). It was gazetted in 1977 to protect the mountain above the 2,700-metre (8,858ft) contour and includes the two main peaks: **Kibo** (5,895 metres/19,340ft) and **Mawenzi** (5,149 metres/16,893ft). Below this is a buffer zone of Forest Reserve to the 1,800-metre (5,905ft) contour. The summit of Kilimanjaro was first climbed in 1889 by Dr Hans Meyer and Ludwig Purtscheller (see page 153). Today, almost 40,000 people a year make a bid for Africa's highest mountain. Increasing numbers have made a considerable environmental impact on the park's trails. Efforts are being made to counteract the erosion, and the Marangu and Mweka routes have been upgraded.

Climbing Kilimanjaro can be arranged through tour operators in Moshi and Arusha and at the park headquarters at Marangu. The best months to climb the mountain are January, February and September. July and August are also good, but colder. Prices vary, but it pays to go with a reputable tour operator, as scrimping on price usually equates to poor equipment. If you book a tour from the UK or the US, the tour operator will

Night falls over Moshi, Mount Kilimanjaro and Mawenzi.

Make sure you budget for tipping the porters.

Walking through rainforest on the first day of climbing Kilimanjaro.

put together an itinerary tailored to your needs. (See page 259).

CLIMBING COSTS

Climbing the mountain is not cheap. National park fees, used to conserve the environment, include a daily entrance fee of US$70 per person, a hut/camping fee of US$50/60 per night, and a rescue fee of US$20 per climb. Allow for costs relating to porters, guides, food and transport, and you must expect a budget climb for two to four people to cost at least US$2,200 per person.

Climbing costs differ widely, according to the route taken, the number of days spent on the mountain and the number of people in the party. Camping is more expensive than staying in huts as more equipment needs to be carried. In addition to the amount paid for the climb itself, it is important to budget for tipping the guides and porters. Approximate figures per day are US$25 for the guide, $15 for the cook and $10 for each porter, but be sure to ascertain the going rate from tour operators before departing.

Climbing Mount Kilimanjaro is marketed as an easy trek to the roof of Africa, attracting many people who have little experience of hill-walking, let alone climbing – and who arrive ill-prepared. Kilimanjaro should not be underestimated: it claims several lives a year. Although walking on the easy routes – Marangu and Rongai – may not be taxing, few take into account the effects of altitude (headaches and nausea), which can be pronounced and debilitating. Being super-fit does not guarantee scaling the summit. You can double your chances of reaching the top by spending several days acclimatising and preferably walking at altitude, before the climb.

Many routes give a number of options for the days taken. It pays to spend an extra day on the mountain if time allows.

WHICH ROUTE?

There are six routes up the mountain – Marangu, Umbwe, Machame, Shira, Lemosho and Rongai; the Mweka route is used only for the descent. Some companies also offer a Northern Circuit

route, which is essentially a linking of the Lemosho and Rongai trails via some splendid isolated scenery on Kilimanjaro's northern slopes. Research thoroughly before you decide which of these to take. Note that hiking companies frequently offer variations of these routes (across different time-frames), so don't be surprised if the routes described here aren't identical to what is on offer. Some routes are more challenging, more scenic and less well-worn than others.

The easiest and cheapest (and therefore one of the most crowded), staying in mountain huts, is the **Marangu route Ⓐ**, commonly called the 'Coca-Cola route'. About 65 climbers a day can depart on the Marangu trail, which, since the path was renovated, is the best on the mountain. A typical five-day trek is to stay at the Mandara, Horombo and Kibo Huts. Be aware that due to the short acclimatisation time, the five-day treks have the lowest success rates of all the routes. The first day is a gentle four-hour climb through the rainforest from the Marangu Gate to **Mandara**, at 2,750 metres (9,020ft). On the second day, you emerge from the rainforest onto an alpine meadow to **Horombo Hut** (3,820 metres/12,530ft), with superb views of the peaks and the plains below on a clear day. It's here that the effects of altitude begin to kick in, with a shortness of breath. The third day brings spectacular views of Mawenzi before ascending to **The Saddle** across a lava desert, and crossing to **Kibo Hut** (4,730 metres/15,520ft).

The quest for the summit begins in the early hours of the morning in the dark, first climbing to Hans Meyer Cave, after which the scree slope becomes extremely steep. It takes six hours to cover 6km (4 miles) from Kibo Hut to **Gillman's Point** on the crater rim. This is acknowledged to be the top, but if time permits you can continue around the crater rim for two hours to **Uhuru Peak.**

A quotation by Julius Nyerere is engraved on a plaque at the top of Uhuru Peak. He had the idea of the Uhuru Torch in 1959, when he said: 'We, the people of Tanganyika, would like to light a candle and put it on top of Mount Kilimanjaro which would shine beyond our borders, giving hope where there was despair,

Camping at Shira Hut.

love where there was hate, and dignity where there before was only humiliation.'

On 9 December 1961, Tanganyika won its independence, and a symbolic torch, together with the flag of the new nation, was hoisted on the summit of Mount Kilimanjaro.

The descent is equally arduous, returning to Kibo Hut for a short rest and continuing down to Horombo Hut, descending to Marangu on the final day. In the 1990s, the management plan for the Park talked of 16 people a day on Kilimanjaro's other routes, which were considered to be wilderness trails. These days, a maximum of 60 climbers a day are taken on each route.

THE WHISKY ROUTE

After Marangu, the **Machame route** Ⓑ, labelled the 'whisky route', is another popular route and one of the most scenic. It's considerably harder going than the Marangu route and involves camping out, but is good for acclimatisation and has high success rates. From **Machame Gate**, it is a six-hour walk up a well-worn path, crossing tangled tree

Photo stop on the quest to reach Uhuru Peak.

roots, through rainforest to **Machame Hut**, at 3,000 metres (9,840ft). On the second day, there's a steady four-hour climb up a steep ridge, like a giant's staircase, before the path flattens out into a gorge, with a gentle two-hour ascent onto the moorland of the Shira plateau to **Shira Hut** (3,840 metres/12,600ft), which offers dramatic views of mist swirling around the Shira cone and across to Mount Meru.

From here, with the effects of altitude kicking in, you are faced by a long, steady climb, with views of the glaciers on Kibo, before making a steep descent into the Barranco Valley, eventually reaching **Barranco Hut** (3,950 metres/12,960ft) after about eight hours. The next day begins with a tough two-hour climb in single file up the rock face of the Barranco Wall. Although not technical climbing, at one point you must shuffle around a narrow ledge with a drop of 600 metres (1,970ft), before following the southern circuit across scree and ridges to Karanga and **Barafu Hut** at 4,600 metres (15,090ft).

Ⓞ CLIMBING IN COMFORT

It may be exciting, but climbing Kili is rarely easy or comfortable. The biggest danger to watch out for is altitude-related pulmonary oedema, a dangerous illness caused by ascending too rapidly, resulting in fluid build-up in the lungs. Most susceptible are fit young men. Symptoms include laboured breathing, shortness of breath at rest and coughing up frothy spit or blood. This can be fatal. If these symptoms exist, descend immediately and get medical attention. Useful equipment includes:

Two adjustable climbing poles – one for going up and two for the steep descent

A water pouch with a tube, carried in a daypack

High-energy snacks

Gloves

Strong sunglasses, a hat and suncream

Layers of clothes

Comfortable and sturdy walking boots

Gaiters

Windproof jacket and trousers

Head-torch

Medication pack with headache and diarrhoea tablets, plasters and rehydration sachets

The slow, final ascent begins at 1am, crossing the Ratzel and Rebmamm glaciers and continuing up to **Uhuru Peak**, in time for sunrise, before descending to Mweka Hut, and continuing down to the Mweka Gate the following day.

An alternative route from Shira Hut is to ascend to Lava Tower Hut (4,600 metres/15,090ft), climbing up the ridge towards Kibo, which takes about five hours. With an early start, there's a steady nine-hour climb through rocky cliffs – part of the Arrow Glacier – before reaching a ridge-like staircase with a point of no return, and continuing the scramble up to the crater floor. From here, it's about an hour and a half to Uhuru Peak. The descent is from Stella Point to Barafu Hut, with the option of continuing to Mweka Hut.

THE MWEKA AND UMBWE ROUTES

The **Mweka route ⒸG** is the quickest and steepest route to the summit, but is now used for descent. The less-steep **Kidia route** (Old Moshi) is used when Mweka is closed for maintenance.

From Barafu to the Mweka Hut takes around four hours, and it's another hour's walk along a logging track to the gate.

The **Umbwe route ⒹD** runs along a ridge parallel to the Umbwe and Lonzo rivers and starts from the mission near the park boundary. It's a six-hour climb up through the rainforest to the campsite at 2,800 metres (9,190ft). The next day's climb to **Barranco Hut** is extremely steep, and involves hauling yourself up rock faces via tree roots, with little remission. However, the scenery is beautiful, walking through feathery heather forests with views into steeply wooded valleys, the lobelia forest and moorland of the Barranco Valley. The route is little used, as there is no water at the campsite, and is best appreciated if descending the mountain. Walking poles are an invaluable aid.

THE SHIRA, LEMOSHO AND RONGAI ROUTES

The **Shira route ⒺE** starts from the western **Londorossi Gate** (1,800 metres/5,905ft). The first part of the

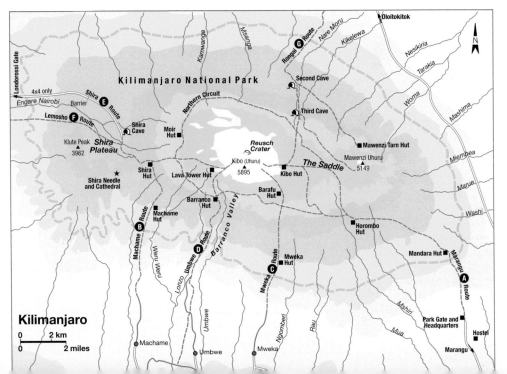

Kilimanjaro

trail is completed by car, which deposits you at 3,600 metres/11,800ft below the Shira plateau. From here, a six-hour hike to Shira Cave, via a detour around a hill on the northern edge of the plateau, gives views to Amboseli in Kenya. The track continues to Shira Cave, with views across the plateau to Kibo.

Next, it's a three-hour climb to Shira Hut, giving the opportunity to branch off the trail, climb the Shira Needle and Cathedral, look down onto the Machame ridge or visit the cone, the centre of the extinct Shira volcano, looking onto Johnsell Point and Klute Peak, the highest points on the Shira ridge. From Shira Hut, the options to ascend the summit are the same as for other routes.

The **Lemosho route** ❻, one of the newest, is essentially a variation of the Shira route (the first two days are different). Leaving from **Londorossi Gate** itself, the route follows a narrow trail from the outset (the Shira route makes use of a road on day one) through remote rainforest areas, before crossing the Shira plateau, merging with

the Shira route and then climbing the summit. There are good chances of wildlife encounters, with plenty of acclimatisation time and high success rates. With several steep sections, it is fairly demanding, but offers some stunning views to compensate – it is deemed to be one of the most beautiful routes on Kilimanjaro.

The **Rongai route** ❼ is one of the least used in Tanzania, with ascents normally made from Loitokitok in Kenya. It's a two-hour drive from Marangu to the **Rongai Gate** (1,800 metres/5,900ft), from where it's a four-hour walk through the forest to the **Rongai Cave** (3,000 metres/9,840ft). The next day, it's a steady climb through alpine moorland, with views across the Kenyan plains, to the **Third Cave** (3,800 metres/12,470ft). The third day gives an interesting climb through the lunar landscape of **The Saddle** to Kibo Hut. The final ascent is challenging and begins around midnight, making it possible to take in sunrise at **Gilman's Point** before reaching **Uhuru Peak**.

On the summit of Africa's highest mountain and the world's tallest free-standing mountain.

CLIMBING KILI

From ancient Ethiopian emperors to modern US presidents, Kilimanjaro's majestic snowcapped peak attracts adventurers from all over the world.

According to legend, the first person to ascend Mount Kilimanjaro was King Menelik I, supposedly the son of King Solomon and the Queen of Sheba. He ruled the Axumite Empire in what is now northern Ethiopia in the 10th century BC, and fought battles in present-day Ethiopia, Somalia, Kenya and Tanzania. As an old man, returning with the spoils of war, he camped between the peaks of Kibo and Mawenzi, at a height of 4,500 metres (14,760ft). Feeling that death was drawing near, he told his followers that he wished to die as a king. He, his warlords and slaves, laden with jewels and treasure, climbed to the crater, where he died.

The legend relates that one of Menelik's offspring will return to the mountain, climb Kibo and find the king and his jewels. Among these will be the Seal of Solomon, a ring which will empower the wearer with the wisdom of Solomon. The legend was so firmly believed by the Abyssinian Christians that when The Revd Dr Reusch (a missionary who spent many years in the Kilimanjaro area, and who later became president of the Mountain Club of East Africa) reached the summit in 1926, many were deeply sceptical that he had reached the top as he found no trace of the long-dead king.

Although news of a snowcapped mountain was first mentioned in European literature in 1848 by another missionary, Johannes Rebmann, no serious attempts at exploring Kilimanjaro were made until 1861, when it was attempted by Baron von der Decken and Richard Thornton. The first successful ascent of the mountain was eventually made by Hans Meyer and Ludwig Purtscheller on 5 October 1889.

Since then, many have reached the summit. Africa's highest mountain has attracted the rich and famous, and adventurers, including such unlikely people as the former US president Jimmy Carter and Australian supermodel Elle Macpherson.

Remarkably, wildlife can survive at this high altitude – John Reader, filming on the mountain in 1983, saw elands, buffalo, jackals and wild dogs on the Shira plateau. The explorer Wilfred Thesiger describes being tracked by five wild dogs at a height of 5,750 metres (18,865ft). Perhaps the most famous was the frozen specimen of a leopard discovered by Dr Donald Latham on his 1926 ascent. This gave its name to Leopard's Point on the crater rim.

For some, just climbing Africa's highest mountain hasn't been enough. In 1962, three French parachutists beat the record for the highest parachute drop by landing in the crater. Others have successfully reached the top on a motorbike or bicycle. Several people have paraglided from the summit – on one occasion, a paraglider was blown off course, and was promptly arrested as a spy. In 2014, 30 cricket players and officials went to the summit of Kilimanjaro to play the world's highest cricket match in the flat crater below Uhuru Peak. Such wacky feats are no longer permitted by the park authorities, but there are now regular expeditions to the summit by wheelchair users and people with various disabilities.

Trekkers negotiating scree and barren Alpine terrain.

Maasai children herding goats at Ol Doinyo Lengai.

THE NORTHERN SAFARI CIRCUIT

The world's finest safari circuit incorporates the legendary
Serengeti and Ngorongoro Crater, as well as the lovely
Lake Manyara, Oldupai Gorge and the rock art of Kondoa.

Running westwards from Arusha towards the eastern shores of Lake Victoria, the well-established safari circuit through northern Tanzania is explored by almost all first-time visitors to the country. Some will cherry-pick the most famous bits over the course of a few days. Others will cover more ground on a longer safari that might be anything from one to three weeks in duration. But however you choose to do it, just make sure that you do. This is simply one of the most compelling destinations in Africa: comprising the world-famous Ngorongoro Crater, a trio of superb national parks (Serengeti, Tarangire and Lake Manyara) and several intriguing lesser-known sites, it offers a superb blend of wildlife viewing, stupendous scenery, traditional cultures and outdoor activities.

The jumping-off point for the circuit is **Arusha** ❶ (see page 141), with flights coming into Arusha or Kilimanjaro international airports. From then on, you have two broad choices when it comes to getting to the different reserves. The first (and generally costlier) option is to use the scheduled light-aircraft flights that connect the region's plentiful airstrips, and to book into small exclusive camps and lodges that provide guided game drives as part of the accommodation package. Alternatively, you can do the whole

Elephant in Tarangire National Park.

thing by road, travelling with a four-wheel drive and driver/guide supplied by one of numerous Arusha-based safari companies. This may seem like a luxury, but you need good ground clearance and height for game viewing, four-wheel drive is necessary in some areas, and a driver costs very little more than self-drive hire.

Don't expect to do this without spending money. The area has a variety of lodges, from small tented camps to large hotels. Most are comfortable, some extraordinarily luxurious, but few

Main Attractions
Tarangire National Park
Kondoa Rock-Art Site
Lake Manyara National
Park
Lake Natron and Ol Doinyo
Lengai
Ngorongoro Crater
Serengeti National Park

**Maps on pages
158, 166, 174**

are cheap. You could bring costs down by taking a camping safari but you still have to pay the steep National Park entrance and camping fees (see www.tanzaniaparks.go.tz), unless you never enter the parks – which rather defeats the purpose of going.

TARANGIRE NATIONAL PARK

From Arusha, head west on the Dodoma road, through **Makuyuni** , 80km (50 miles) away. This is part of the Great North Road, the Pan-African 'highway' that runs from Cairo to Cape Town. The entrance to **Tarangire National Park** is 115km (71 miles) south of Arusha, with good tarred roads all the way.

Tarangire is a long, thin park covering 1,360 sq km (525 sq miles), roughly running north–south along the line of the Tarangire River. It is made up chiefly of low-lying, rolling hills on the Rift floor, and the dominant cover is savannah, acacia woodland and giant baobabs. These are interspersed with huge areas of swamp that form a magnet for wildlife (including mosquitoes

Elephants crossing the Tarangire river.

and tsetse flies, so take precautions). The swamps of black cotton mud produce rich grasslands, while the watercourses are lined by huge trees, including sycamore fig, tamarind and sausage trees.

Although it is relatively small, Tarangire has huge benefits, including its easy access to the seasonal concentrations of game that peak in the second half of the year. In theory, it also supports several rather localised dry-country antelope species, including the lesser kudu, oryx and gerenuk, but these are all quite thinly distributed and unlikely to be seen on a short visit. Black rhino, once a speciality of the area, have vanished, shot out by poachers in the dark days of the 1970s and 1980s.

BABY ELEPHANT BOOM

Tarangire's elephants also suffered badly from poaching prior to the late 1990s. They have recovered with a vengeance, following the CITES ban on ivory trading, and hundreds now roam the hills, though it is rumoured that poaching has been on the increase in

the surrounding Maasai Steppes since 2009. There are few tuskers akin to those that roam the Ngorongoro Crater floor, but this is definitely the place to come for family herds containing cute elephant babies.

The park lies at the southern end of a vast migration area which stretches north towards the Kenyan border. As the land dries and the smaller rivers cease to flow, the herds head south towards the permanent water in the Tarangire River and its surrounding swamps. June to October is the best time to visit, but the herds remain in the area until March, when thousands of calves are born.

The main lodges are all near the gate, overlooking the Tarangire River and baobab-clad hills, although there are a couple of smaller luxury camps in the centre of the park. There is little accommodation in the south, and few visitors ever get there. Do try and make it at least as far as the **Silale Swamp**, the most northerly of several large swamps in the park. Fuelled by natural springs, they are year-round oases of lush green grass. Many of the animals you see nearby are coated in black cotton mud, having waded in waist-deep to reach the best shoots. There are also masses of birds, including tawny, steppe and fish eagles, marabou storks, goliath herons, white pelicans, spur-winged geese and sacred ibis.

Tarangire is known for its prolific birdlife. Some 550 species have been recorded, including a number of Palaearctic migrants that fly here to escape the northern hemisphere's winter. Typical residents of acacia woodland include the orange-bellied parrot, bare-faced go-away bird, red-and-yellow barbet, and silverbird. This is also the easiest place to observe two species endemic to central Tanzania: the lovely yellow-collared lovebird, which is often seen in the vicinity of the baobabs where it nests, and the drabber ashy starling.

Upon leaving Tarangire, most tourists head back north to Makuyuni, from where a surfaced 90km (54-mile) road heads west to the main gate of the Ngorongoro Conservation Area via Lake Manyara and Karatu. But for those seeking a more off-the-beaten-track adventure, it is possible to continue south along the Pan-African 'highway' to Babati, Hanang or the Kondoa Rock-Art World Heritage Site near Kolo.

BABATI AND HANANG

Situated on the outskirts of the eponymous small market town, **Lake Babati** ❹ practically laps the western verge of the main road 70km (42 miles) south of the main gate to Tarangire. The papyrus-fringed lake shore, encircled by low mountains, attracts a fair variety of water birds – orderly flotillas of white pelicans, eagle-eyed herons and egrets, and sweeping spoonbills and yellow-billed storks. Birds are easily seen on foot, but the best way to locate a few of the lake's prodigious hippos is to pay a small fee to be taken out on a boat by one of the local fishermen. This

White-headed buffalo weaver, native to East Africa.

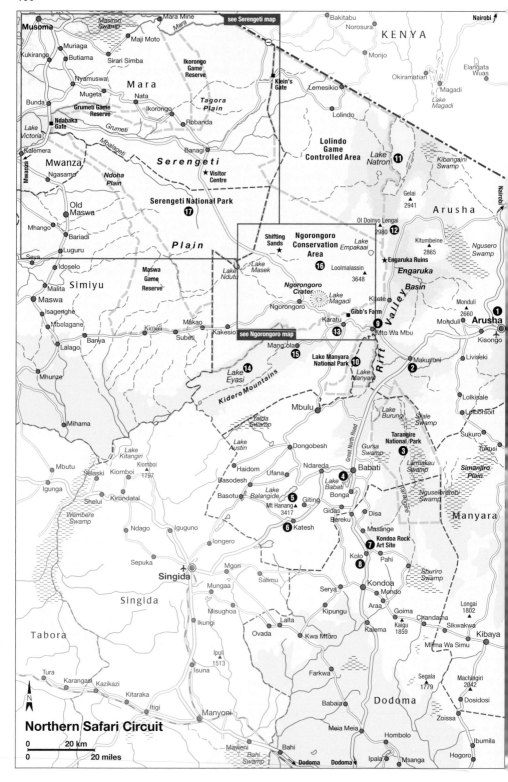

Northern Safari Circuit

0   20 km
0   20 miles

can be arranged through the offices of Kahembe Trekking and Cultural Safaris (mob: 0784-397477; www.kahembeculturalsafaris.com), a Babati-based company that also sets up overnight trips to the rustic bomas of the various nomadic pastoralist cultures that inhabit this part of the ridge.

The focal point of the Babati ecotourism project is the 3,417-metre (11,211ft) high **Mount Hanang** ❺, an extinct volcano that towers like a miniature, snow-free Kilimanjaro above the surrounding flat plains, visible from hundreds of kilometres away on a clear day. The third-tallest mountain in Tanzania, Hanang can be climbed over a very long day – fit hikers will need a minimum of 12 hours for the round trip – or, more realistically, as an overnight hike, sleeping in caves or a tent. Experienced and properly equipped independent travellers could arrange a hike from the small town of **Katesh** ❻, which lies at the southern base of the mountain, 50km (30 miles) from Babati along the Singida road. It is safer, however, to arrange a package through Kahembe Enterprises, whose guides all speak English and have vast experience of the mountain. Either way, because Hanang lies outside the national park system, hikes are light on the pocket in comparison with the Kilimanjaro and Meru climbs.

ANCIENT ART

Dusty **Kondoa**, located on the north bank of a river with the same name, lies roughly 100km (60 miles) south of Babati. The town also shares its name with the **Kondoa Rock-Art Site** ❼, a fascinating central treasury of prehistoric rock art that decorates the granite faces and overhangs of north-central Tanzania, and was inscribed as a Unesco World Heritage Site in 2006. Although many hundreds of these ancient panels are scattered throughout the Kondoa region, all that is known about the artists is what can be deduced from their fading visual legacy. No credible local tradition relates to the paintings – not surprising when they predate the arrival of Bantu-speakers in East Africa by a

Manyara and Tarangire are famous for their tree-climbing lions.

thousand-plus years – but they do display inescapable stylistic links with the rock art executed by southern Africa's Khoisan-speaking hunter-gatherers in historic times.

Coming from the north, you don't need to travel as far as Kondoa to see the rock art. This is because the main concentration of rock art is found along the ridges running east of the main road between **Kolo** ❽ and **Bereku**, about halfway between Babati and Kondoa. Starting at the Department of Antiquities office in Kolo (tel: 0784 948 858) 30km (19 miles) north of Kondoa, knowledgeable guides will direct visitors along the 12km (7-mile) back route to the most famous of the region's sites.

This is **Mungomi Wa Kolo** (The Dancers of Kolo), where three separate panels, easily visited over the space of one or two hours, depict the eponymous dancers, numerous other diagrammatic stick figures with characteristically woolly hairstyles, and a menagerie of wild animals. The final approach (15 minutes on foot) to

Lesser flamingos at sunrise, Lake Natron.

Mungomi is gaspingly steep, so less fit travellers might prefer to visit a separate cluster of panels at the base of the ridge near **Lusangi** village, a similar distance away from Kolo. Less impressive overall than the finely realised paintings at Mungomi Wa Kolo, Lusangi does display two features not found at that site, namely petroglyphs (engravings) and a number of paintings of the so-called 'late white' period. Another good and relatively accessible site is **Fenga Hill**, overlooking the Bubu River 10km (6 miles) west of Kolo.

MTO WA MBU

Back on the main tourist circuit, the agricultural and market town of **Mto Wa Mbu** ❾ stands next to the entrance of Lake Manyara National Park, about 50km (30 miles) west of Makuyuni, at the foot of the **Gregory Escarpment**, the western wall of the eastern arm of the Great Rift Valley. Named after Scottish geologist John Walter Gregory, the first to map and name the East African Rift, this is one of the most dramatic points along its length, rising almost

sheer some 800 metres (2,625ft) from the valley floor.

The enormous amount of ground water pouring through the rocks of the escarpment has created a lush, green swamp here, and the locals are excellent farmers, growing everything from bananas and maize to citrus fruits, rice and vegetables. The road is lined with produce stalls, and the town has a self-satisfied feeling of wealth. The town is a useful stopping point, with several inexpensive lodges, campsites and guesthouses, but it is also very malarial – Mto Wa Mbu ominously and accurately means 'mosquito creek' – so lash on the repellent and cover up at night.

MANYARA

Many people pass by **Lake Manyara National Park ⑩** in their rush towards the Serengeti, but although small, this is one of the prettiest, most interesting and game-rich parks in the country. It is also home to Tanzania's first treetop walkway. Pending the planned incorporation of the Marang Forest

above the escarpment, the park is only 330 sq km (127 sq miles) in size – tiny by Tanzanian standards – and about two-thirds of that is water. The rest is a long thin strip of land sandwiched between the lake and the cliff, served by a very few extremely rough roads. There is only one permanent lodge actually within the park, the exclusive **Lake Manyara Tree Lodge** (www. andbeyond.com/lake-manyara-tree-lodge/) at the far end of the park beyond the reach of most day-trippers. Most of the other lodges are built along the rim of the escarpment, with fabulous views across the lake, and safely out of the way of the mosquitoes.

The park and lake take their name from the manyara bush (*euphorbia tirucalli*) used by the Maasai to build their stockades. The Maasai actually use the same word, *emanyara*, for a kraal. There is a manyara bush at the park entrance. Once inside, the first part of the park is thick ground-water forest with huge trees, including Cape mahogany, croton, sycamore fig and several sorts of palm. Beneath these

⊘ **Fact**

The phenomenon of tree-climbing lions was first studied at Manyara, and is still associated with the park, though it is also seen in some other parts of Tanzania, particularly the Serengeti's Seronera Valley. It is thought it began as a way of avoiding biting flies, and has been imitated as individuals move across territories.

Hadzabe bushman family at Lake Eyasi.

soaring canopies, dense undergrowth provides a delightful array of wild flowers and butterflies, but this is not easy country for game viewing.

You should see troops of olive baboons and Sykes' monkeys playing beside the road. Bushbuck may emerge from the shade, and as you round a bend, you are quite likely to find an elephant in your path. They frequently choose to use the roads rather than having to struggle through the tangled undergrowth. Remember to keep looking up. The local lions frequently take to the trees, and there are also plenty of leopards, although you need luck to see them. Even if the cats elude you, there are many wonderful birds, including the giant silvery-cheeked hornbill.

The further you reach into the park, the drier it becomes, gradually opening out into forests of umbrella-topped fever trees and baobabs. As the vegetation changes, so does the wildlife, with plains animals such as buffalo, wildebeest, zebra and giraffe making an appearance. Above, martial and bateleur eagles circle idly on the thermals as they scan for prey. Near the southern end of the park, there are two groups of bubbling, steaming hot springs that have dyed the surrounding ground a rainbow of colours with their chemicals.

Like most other Rift Valley lakes, Manyara is a shallow soda lake, fed by ground water, and varying hugely in size according to the season. As it shrinks back, a broad floodplain opens up. Many animals choose to graze the new shoots and wallow in the muddy shallows. Among them paddle water birds such as pelicans, flamingos, cormorants and herons, while a little further out, pods of hippos grunt and puff their way through the heat of the day.

LAKE NATRON

From Mto Wa Mbu, a relatively little-used dirt road follows the base of the Rift Valley escarpment north towards **Lake Natron** , which extends for about 1,040 sq km (401 sq miles) in a shallow depression running up towards the border with Kenya. In keeping with its rather arid and hostile setting,

Growing coffee beans in Karatu.

⊘ THE DATOGA

Sharing the Eyasi Basin with the Hadza, the Datoga are a Nilotic-speaking people who arrived in Tanzania in the 1st millennium AD. They lived around Ngorongoro until 200 years ago, when they were chased out of the area by the Maasai. As a result of this altercation, the Maasai refer to the Datoga as 'Mangati' (feared enemies), and part of their territory, around Mount Hanang, is sometimes called the Mangati Plains.

The Datoga are pastoralists who herd cattle and goats, living in comfortable, thatched rectangular huts, with holes in the walls. Women usually wear skin robes with fringes and beadwork, which can take two months to make and last up to five years. Other decorations include huge earrings and holes in their ears, and quantities of brass and copper bangles.

Natron is a hypersaline lake whose viscous water has an average pH of 9–11, making it almost as caustic as ammonia when the level is low. Aside from one endemic species of fish, which congregates near a few spring inlets, the only aquatic life supported by Natron is halophytic (salt-loving) organisms such as Spirulina. This form of algae feeds East Africa's 2.5 million lesser flamingos, for whom the inaccessible central flats of Natron are the only known breeding site.

Serviced by two rather austere tented camps, Natron is the best base for hikes up **Ol Doinyo Lengai** ⑫, an active volcano that last erupted in 2010. It stands at 2,980 metres (9,777ft) and is sacred to several tribes, including the Maasai, who call it the 'Mountain of the Gods' and believe it to be the home of Engai, a single deity with both benevolent and vengeful characteristics. The climb to the summit takes a very long day (most operators start at midnight to avoid the baking heat on the shadeless slopes) and you need to be very physically fit: be prepared for sheer, slippery slopes, icy winds near the summit, and an exhausting descent that places huge strain on the knees.

KARATU HIGHLANDS

At the top of the Manyara Escarpment, you enter a lush area of richly fertile farmland and superb mountain scenery, with purple hills ringing rich red earth and neatly ordered fields of wheat, sweet potatoes, beans and coffee, carved up by high green hedges of spiky plants.

The roads along the edge of the escarpment lead to most of the Manyara hotels, perfectly positioned for the views. As you head towards Ngorongoro, several signs entice you towards 'cultural villages' – of mixed value – and some excellent souvenir shops, including one specialising in jazzy T-shirts. The largest town in the area is **Karatu** ⑬, a bustling market and business centre that is a useful stop for travellers, with several campsites, phones and internet cafés, as well as the only bank with an ATM between Arusha and the Serengeti.

Locals use Lake Eyasi to fish in.

The lush Karatu Highlands were once a great centre of white farming, colonised by the Germans in the mid-19th century. The plantations have long since been carved up again among the Mbulu and Iraqw peoples, Cushitic-speaking tribes who moved into the area about 3,000 years ago. The area is heavily populated, with villages scattered across the hillsides, buses groaning past with passengers on the roof and clinging to the fenders. It could not be a greater contrast to the remote, dusty world of Tarangire on the Rift floor.

Several former plantation homes around Karatu have been converted into plush lodges, including **Gibb's Farm**, **Plantation Lodge** and the **Manor at Ngorongoro**. Any one of them is worth an overnight stop, for the magnificent gardens, fine views and superb food, much of it grown on the premises. However, it should be noted that Karatu is less convenient for day safaris to Ngorongoro Crater than the lodges on the crater rim, at least if you are hoping to get to the crater floor as early in the morning as possible.

Datoga woman with traditional facial ornamentation.

LAKE EYASI

If you have time, spend a day detouring down to **Lake Eyasi** . Look for the turning to the left, 10km (6 miles) west of Karatu town. The 60km (37-mile) road is poor almost from the start and gets increasingly bad until, at times, it disappears on the rocks altogether. It is just passable without four-wheel drive in the dry season, as long as you have good ground clearance. As the road drops down from the plateau, the lush farms of the highlands give way to bare earth creviced by erosion canyons, and to acacias and baobabs powdered white by flying dust, and herds of goats and skeletal cows.

Lake Eyasi is a long, skinny soda lake that stretches up to 80km (50 miles) when the rains are good and virtually dries up at other times. Above it soars the 800-metre (2,625ft) **Eyasi Escarpment**, one of the more spectacular cliffs in the Tanzanian Rift Valley. At certain times of year, the water can be thick with clattering pink flamingos, while numerous other birds call from

⊘ THE HADZA

The Hadza represent a precious link with human prehistory. They are among the last adherents to the hunter-gatherer lifestyle that sustained the world's entire human population for perhaps 99 percent of its existence. Their tongue belongs to the dying Khoisan language group, distinguished by punctuating clicks that many linguists believe to be a preserved element of the first human language.

The Hadza refuse to adopt a settled lifestyle, so a tract of state land fringing Lake Eyasi has been set aside for their use. Here, small nomadic family bands, typically numbering about 20 adults and their children, construct temporary grass shelters, moving according to weather conditions, game movements, or the location of a kill. Anything from sparrows to giraffes is fair game, but the local delicacy is baboon flesh. Hunting with poisoned arrows and honey gathering are generally male activities. But meat accounts for only 20 percent of Hadza food intake; the remainder consists of vegetable matter gathered by women.

The Hadza philosophy of living for the moment is encapsulated in their favourite gambling game. A wooden disc, with rough and smooth faces, is thrown down together with one similar disc per participant. This action is repeated until only one person's disc lands same-face-up with the master, deciding the winner.

the shores. The locals fish in the lake, smoking their catch on the foreshore.

All activities in the area must be organised with guides from the **Lake Eyasi Cultural Tourism Programme** (mob: 0753-808601; email: eyasiculturaltourismprogramme@yahoo.com) in the village of **Mang'ola** ⑮, about 10km (6 miles) from the lake shore. This is also the only place where you can buy basic groceries and cold drinks, so take your own lunch and eat it at the campsite, an idyllic green glade near a hot spring (there are no facilities, other than a basic toilet).

As far as the locals are concerned, the freshwater springs are the real attraction of the area, supporting intensive farming of maize, beans, bananas, rice, wheat and, above all, onions. During the harvest, the whole village reeks of them. More and more people are moving in to rent farmland, putting huge pressure on traditional lifestyles. There is little grazing land left, and the game is all but shot out. Meanwhile, up to 60 tribes now live in the area, and the Maasai are also trying to move in their enormous herds of cattle and goats. The area is a political cal powder keg, but so far, the lid has stayed on.

THE HADZA

However, the real attraction for tourists lies in the original peoples. The Hadza (see page 164) are Tanzania's last remaining hunter-gatherers and are thought to have been in the area for at least 10,000 years. There are only around 2,000 of them left, living a nomadic lifestyle, using hollowed baobabs for storage and sleeping in the open, with a stockade of thorns or a grass enclosure to protect them from predators. They have few possessions – basic skin aprons, a few beads for decoration, bows, arrows and knives for hunting, and cooking pots, although many now wear T-shirts. Their lifestyle can seem shocking, but they have repeatedly refused attempts to bring them into the modern world. They are used to visitors, will welcome you warmly and may even take you out hunting with them.

Datoga couple at their homestead on Lake Eyasi.

NGORONGORO

The **Ngorongoro Conservation Area (NCA)** ⑯ stretches from the Karatu Highlands to the Serengeti and down to the northern tip of Lake Eyasi, covering some 8,300 sq km (3,205 sq miles). **Lodoare Gate** Ⓐ is 29km (18 miles) west of Karatu. Remember that you need to reach the gate before it shuts for the night.

The only road connecting Arusha and Karatu to Serengeti National Park runs through the NCA, so you have to pay that entrance fee at Lodoare Gate, even if only in transit. And be warned – the NCA entrance fee doesn't actually get you into the crater itself. If you wish to drive down, you need to pay an additional fee per car.

The tarred road ends at Lodoare; the rest of your circuit will be on gravel roads that range from bumpy to diabolical. From the entrance gate, the road climbs steeply up through the thick montane forest to a T-junction and **Heroes' Point** Ⓑ, from which you get your first, mind-blowing view of the crater itself. In the parking area is a memorial to rangers

Baobab trees can grow to an impressive 98ft (30 metres).

killed while protecting the crater from poachers. The right fork leads to Sopa Lodge, the only permanent lodge on the crater's eastern rim, while the left fork leads to all the other hotels, and the main access routes to the crater, Oldupai and the Serengeti.

MAASAI TERRITORY

Formed by the same immense geological upheavals as the Great Rift Valley, Ngorongoro was once a mountain as high as Kilimanjaro. About 3 million years ago, it blew itself to bits, covering the Serengeti in ash while the crater floor sank into the mountain. Today, the rim stands at 2,285 metres (7,497ft). The **Ngorongoro Crater** Ⓒ is the world's largest complete volcanic caldera, with a diameter of about 18km (11 miles) and an area of 260 sq km (100 sq miles). The sheer-sided rim is just over 600 metres (1,969ft) at its highest point. From the top, it is impossible to see the animals down on the plains without binoculars, but the ever-changing play of light across the flowing grasslands can be hypnotic.

Ngorongoro is a Maasai word; some say it mimics the clatter of cowbells, others that it is a traditional name for a type of bowl, similar in shape to the crater. The Maasai are the traditional owners of the area, although they are relative newcomers, having forced the Mbulu and Datoga out around 200 years ago. Two German brothers farmed the crater floor for a short while in the early 20th century, but when the area was first incorporated into the Serengeti National Park in 1951, around 12,000 Maasai lived in the crater.

A deal was struck that turned Ngorongoro into a Conservation Area, rather than a National Park, allowing the Maasai to continue to water their animals on the crater floor, in exchange for moving out and receiving a share of the profits from tourism. Today, with the populations of people, cattle and goats growing, and water and grazing land short in the surrounding area, some 40,000 Maasai are claiming rights over the crater and demanding a larger slice of the cake.

Even though Ngorongoro was declared a World Heritage Site in 1978, there is no room for complacency.

INTO THE CRATER

Perhaps the truest indication of how busy the crater can get is that the two main access roads operate as a one-way system (the third, close to the rather isolated Sopa Lodge, is a two-way road effectively used by that lodge only). The crater is open only between 7am and 6pm, and most people prefer to spend the whole day there. There are two picnic and toilet spots, in the Lerai Forest or at **Ngoitokitok Springs** in the southeast. At the latter, watch out for the dive-bombing black kites, who have discovered that chicken sandwiches taste better and are easier to catch than mice.

The main descent road twists down the western wall, near the **Seneto Springs**, used by the Maasai to water their cattle. The crater floor is a true Shangri-La, one of the most densely crowded game areas in the world, home to an estimated 30,000 animals.

> **Ⓣ Tip**
>
> Many Maasai boys spend their days hanging around on the roadside dressed in their full tribal finery, waiting for people to take their picture. This is technically illegal in the Conservation Area. If you want to take a photo, negotiate a fee first, or you may find yourself in trouble.

View from Heroes Point on the Ngorongoro crater rim to the crater floor.

Because it is enclosed and the flat crater floor is largely made up of open grassland, it is easy to police, with the result that this is a stronghold for endangered species including black rhino and, increasingly, cheetah. The only downside of the open vistas is that you can see other vehicles – although even they can be a useful way of helping you spot something of interest. The best vantage point is flat-topped **Engitati Hill** in the northeastern corner.

There are no giraffe, topis or impala in the crater – they find it too difficult to negotiate the cliffs, and there is insufficient grazing for large herds of antelope. The usual prey animals are wildebeest, zebra and buffalo. It is easy to spot and track a hunt across the open plain. The crater is thought to support the world's densest populations of lions and spotted hyenas, and it is here that researchers first realised that, contrary to popular perceptions, lions will scavenge hyena kills as often as theirs are scavenged by hyenas. Cheetahs are also quite commonly seen on the crater floor, but leopard

Burchell's zebra graze on the crater floor.

sightings are rare. The crater is also probably the best place in Tanzania to see the golden jackal, a close relative of its more common black-backed and side-striped cousins.

In the southwestern corner, **Lake Magadi** is a large, shallow soda lake, home to large populations of flamingos and other water birds as well as hippos, which can also be seen in the central **Mandusi Swamp**. The **Lerai Forest** of fever trees, in the south close to the start of the ascent road, is near here and is the best place in the park to see elephants. Presumably due to seasonal fluctuations in the food supply, the only elephants resident in the crater are old bulls, many of which have enormous tusks. The large breeding herds hang around in the dense forests on the rim, and only descend into the crater occasionally.

A common bird in the crater, the bulky kori bustard is truly spectacular if you catch it during a mating dance. Less prominent, but of great interest to dedicated birdwatchers, is the lovely rosy-throated longclaw. Two striking raptors often seen here are the augur

buzzard and long-crested eagle. The exquisite bar-tailed trogon is sometimes seen in forest patches along the ascent road.

EMPAKAAI AND OLMOTI CRATERS

To the north of Ngorongoro Crater, the NCA also protects two other immense calderas, both of which are worth a visit, and offer a welcome opportunity for a short but stiff, steep walk in lovely mountain scenery. The most alluring of the two craters is the **Empakaai Crater Ⓓ**, a 6km (4-mile) wide, 300-metre (980ft) deep volcanic crater whose rim offers spectacular views both to the crater floor and to the distinctive volcanic outline of Ol Doinyo Lengai.

Enclosed by sheer forested cliffs, Empakaai's floor is dominated by an emerald-green soda lake whose shallows are frequently tinged pink with thousands of flamingos. A well-maintained footpath from the rim to the lake shore takes about 45 minutes each away, with the possibility of seeing many forest birds and monkeys en route. Coming from Ngorongoro Crater, the drive to Empakaai takes around 90 minutes, leaving from close to the Sopa Lodge, and passes close to the 3,648 metre (11,970ft) Mount Lolmalasin, which is the highest point in the Crater Highlands, and the third-highest in Tanzania. A 4x4 is required, and if you want to hike to the crater floor, you need to pick up a mandatory armed ranger at Nainokanoka Ranger Post.

Smaller and less dramatic, the **Olmoti Crater Ⓔ** near Nainokanoka is also worth a stop. The crater rim is accessed on a footpath that passes through montane forest and takes 20 to 30 minutes in either direction. The crater offers good grazing for Maasai cattle and it also sometimes supports a few antelope. Raptors are much in evidence, cartwheeling the thermals, and you can follow a short footpath to a seasonal waterfall where the Munge River leaves the crater.

OLDUPAI AND NDUTU

Heading west from the crater rim towards the Serengeti Plains, a rough

An olive baboon eating berries.

Empakaai crater, Ngorongoro Conservation Area.

Maasai giraffes in Serengeti National Park.

Cheetah in the Ngorongoro Crater.

dirt road winds gently down the western flank of the crater highlands, through rolling grasslands and acacia woodland. It is here that you will find the many giraffe and antelope absent from the crater floor, mingling freely with the Maasai livestock. This is probably also your best opportunity to see the decorative Maasai people; several local *manyattas* (homesteads) offer expensive guided tours. Ask your driver to fix the price.

About 30km (18 miles) from the crater, a 3km (2-mile) side road on the right leads to the **Oldupai Gorge Museum** ⓕ (daily 8.30am–5pm). This is one of the most important palaeontological sites in East Africa (see page 33), and guides are on hand to give tours of the gorge and any current excavations. A cast of footprints made at Laetoli about 3.6 million years ago is just one of the fascinating items on display in the museum. The human-fossil exhibits are all copies (the originals are in Nairobi Museum, Kenya), but the explanations are fascinating. There are also plenty of animal remains, belonging to extinct species such as the pygmy giraffe.

About 40km (25 miles) further on, a left turn leads down to **Lake Ndutu** ⓖ, which is within the NCA, close to the border with Serengeti National Park. Too saline for human consumption, the lake's water is drunk by cattle and wildlife, and it also attracts many birds. Rather disconcertingly, the black cotton mud around the shores is littered by wildebeest and buffalo skulls belonging to animals trapped as they tried to cross the lake. The main reason for visiting is to stay at **Ndutu Lodge**, a charming small safari lodge used as a base by many wildlife film units. Every evening, a posse of genets invades the lodge, peering down at the dinner tables from the rafters.

THE SERENGETI

The **Serengeti National Park** ⓱ is quite probably the most famous game reserve in the world. It first achieved legendary status when Professor Bernard Grzimek wrote *Serengeti Shall Not Die*, the story of two men's quest to

⊘ OLDUPAI PREHISTORY

About 90 metres (295ft) deep, Oldupai Gorge is named after the spiky wild sisal plant that is known to the Maasai as *Oldupai*. It lies on the site of an ancient lake, and is covered by thick layers of volcanic ash which have carefully preserved some of the world's earliest records of mankind. About 100,000 years ago, seismic activity split the earth, creating the gorge and laying bare the fossil beds. These were discovered in 1911 by a German professor named Katwinkle while he was out hunting for butterflies. He carried out one small dig in 1913, but little else was done until Louis and Mary Leakey arrived a few decades later (see page 37). Palaeontologists have been working here ever since, and have made many famous and influential discoveries in the gorge.

document the Great Migration in a bid to help conserve the park's wildlife. The Serengeti is now a World Heritage Site.

The National Park covers 14,763 sq km (5,700 sq miles), an area roughly equivalent to Northern Ireland. The full Serengeti ecosystem is far larger still, incorporating the Maasai Mara in Kenya and the NCA to total a massive 25,000 sq km (9,653 sq miles). Animals wander freely throughout the system.

Only about a third of the park is made up of the flat grassy plains which gave the park its name – *Siringit* is Maasai for 'the place where the land runs on forever'. However, it is these plains and their role in the annual migration of some 2 million animals (see page 172) which have made the area so special.

About 3 to 4 million years ago, during the massive eruptions of the Ngorongoro, Sadiman and Kerimasi volcanoes, a thick rain of ash settled over the plains, creating a rock-hard topcoat, known as hard-pan. Although richly fertile, it is too tough to be broken by tree roots, leaving the landscape

to the shallow-rooted grasses, packed with nutritious minerals which act as a magnet to grazers such as wildebeest, zebra, impala and Thomson's gazelle. From **Naabi Hill Gate** Ⓐ, the grasslands stretch around you in all directions. There are animals here at any time of year, but from October to May the area is teeming with wildlife, including wildebeest, zebra, warthogs, topis, hartebeest, impala, Thomson's and Grant's gazelle, kori bustards, secretary birds and ostrich. Hyenas and jackals prowl nearby, while circling vultures may indicate the position of a kill.

Lions, almost the exact colour of the grass in the dry season, are more easily visible at some of the rocky kopjes, granite inselbergs scattered across the landscape. The **Moru Kopjes** Ⓑ are favourites among many cats, including lions, leopards, servals and caracals, and you may even find elephants in the area. The kopjes also host a rare and well-signposted Maasai rock-art site. **Simba Kopjes** Ⓒ are frequently used for sunbathing by the lions after which they are named. **Gol Kopjes** Ⓓ

Pod of hippos in the Grumeti River, Serengeti National Park.

THE GREAT MIGRATION

East Africa's greatest mammalian spectacle is the migration of millions of wildebeest and zebra through the greater Serengeti ecosystem.

Imagine a column of wildebeest 40km (24 miles) long and two or three abreast, patiently plodding across the plain for hour after hour. Now multiply that until you have about 1.5 million wildebeest, throw in some 300,000 zebras, another 300,000 Thomson's gazelles, and about 30,000 Grant's gazelles, all on the move in the search for fresh new grass. Imagine it taking more than two weeks for the column of animals to pass a single spot, and visualise them all bunching together into protective herds in the evenings or scrambling across each other's backs in their panic to cross the river and stay clear of the snapping jaws of the crocodiles. Imagine the

Wildebeest crossing the bed of the Mara River in the north of the Serengeti.

lions and hyenas roaring and cackling as they prowl the outskirts of the herds looking for weakened animals. Now you may just begin to have an idea of the awesome spectacle that is the Serengeti migration.

The various different species that make up the migration live amicably together, part of a carefully balanced cycle that allows them to get the maximum amount of food from any area. The cycle actually begins with the elephants who open up the woodlands, the heavy buffalo and hippos who rip up the coarse, long grass, and the antelope such as topis, elands and hartebeest who have their own much smaller migration cycle around the woodland fringes.

Wildebeest are the most dedicated travellers in their quest for the finest shoots. Zebras are less picky, going for quantity rather than quality, so they need to travel less far. Behind them come the smaller gazelles, nibbling the delicate new growth. The wildebeest's keen sense of smell, the zebras' fine eyesight and the gazelles' acute hearing together create a formidable early warning system, while the huge herds make it easier to stay alive. These defences are absolutely necessary – such a smorgasbord attracts the predators in droves.

The Serengeti migration is actually a year-round phenomenon, a broad, slow clockwise route march covering a total of around 3,000km (1,870 miles). The cycle begins in May, when the grass on the southern plains is exhausted and the herds begin to move slowly northwards through the Western Corridor. This is the time of the rut, the wildebeest bulls working to the point of exhaustion to build and protect their harems.

The migration reaches the Northern Serengeti and Maasai Mara by late June, remaining there until September, when it returns south through the Lobo area, following the scent of the small rains. It reaches the southern plains by November, remaining there to feed on the nutrient-rich grass during the breeding season. In three weeks from February to March, over 90 percent of the female wildebeest (around 500,000 animals) give birth. Calves can stand within seven minutes and within two days can outrun a lion, but even so, the predators grow fat. The herds remain in the south, allowing their young time to build strength, before heading north as the grass runs out and the cycle begins again.

are popular with cheetahs, while the **Maasai Kopjes ⓔ** again attract lions and formidably large cobras.

SERONERA

In the centre of the park, the **Seronera River Valley ⓕ** is one of the richest wildlife habitats in the region, not only providing a valuable water source, but also marking the boundary between the grassy plains and the wooded hills to the north, attracting animals and birds belonging to both environments. Site of the park headquarters, its oldest lodge, a visitor centre, and several public campsites, Seronera is also the busiest part of the park in terms of tourist traffic, and so it tends to be avoided by more exclusive safaris. It is the base for **Serengeti Balloon Safaris**, and there can be few experiences more magical than drifting over this endless scenery at dawn, sometimes low enough to skim the trees, at others, soaring to see the true scale of this vast wilderness.

Despite the heavy tourist traffic, Seronera offers reliable, superb game viewing throughout the year. In addition to typical plains grazers, the woodland is favoured by olive baboons and vervet monkeys, as well as buffalo, giraffe, elands, bushbucks and dik-diks. Waterbucks and reedbucks hang out along the river banks, and many of the park's 500-plus bird species can be found in the area. About 15km (9 miles) north of the park headquarters, the **Retima Hippo Pool ⓖ**, near the confluence of the Seronera and Grumeti rivers, usually supports several dozen hippos basking in close proximity.

Seronera is the best place in Tanzania to see leopards, which habitually laze away the heat of the day in the shady sausage trees and acacias that line the river, revealing their presence only by an occasional flick of the tail. The area is also home to several indolent lion prides, which have taken to the trees with increasing regularity in recent years – indeed, you are now more likely to see lions in arboreal action at Seronera than in Lake Manyara, which was once famed for this unusual behaviour.

Hot-air balloon safari over the wildebeest migration in the Serengeti.

⊘ THE SERENGETI HIGHWAY

In 2010, the Tanzanian government controversially proposed the construction of an asphalt road linking Arusha to the Lake Victoria region. Intended to help isolated communities living in the Lake Victoria hinterland, the proposal was condemned by ecologists, since it would cross through the northern Serengeti for about 55km (33 miles).

The two main arguments against the road were that it would bisect the annual wildebeest migration routes, and that regular truck traffic would result in a huge number of road kills. Other concerns were that it would improve access for poachers, spread disease and invasive weeds, and jeopardise the Serengeti's status as a Unesco World Heritage Site.

In 2014, the East African Court of Justice ruled that a paved commercial highway through Serengeti National Park would have irreversible negative impacts on the park's fauna, and banned the construction of the proposed asphalt road. Important as the ruling was, implicit loopholes – an asphalt upgrade was banned, but upgrades of other sorts were not mentioned – left environmentalists discouraged. Indeed, shortly afterwards the government announced plans to upgrade the current track through the Serengeti National Park to an all-weather gravel road, with paved roads planned up to the park boundary. Many fear the consequences will be just as damaging as the asphalt road would have been.

LOBO AND THE MARA RIVER

Heading north from Seronera, tourist traffic decreases and you enter a more rugged landscape of craggy hills covered by scrubby bush and open woodland, bisected by the Grumeti River and an associated ribbon of lush riparian forest. The road leads to the **Lobo Hills** 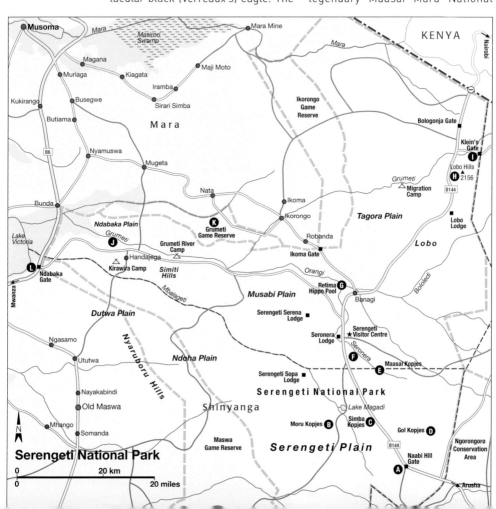, a cluster of spectacular granite outcrops close to the park's eastern border some 70km (42 miles) north of Seronera. The area is favoured by buffalo and elephants, and the hills host several large lion prides. Cheetahs and bat-eared foxes are also quite common, while the rocks provide refuge to the localised klipspringer antelope, and the spectacular black (Verreaux's) eagle. The wildebeest migration usually passes through in July.

Practically untouched by tourism until 2005, but now the site of several small exclusive bush camps, the far north of the Serengeti is incised by the Mara River as it flows between the Kenyan border and Lake Victoria. Game viewing here is good throughout the year, but it peaks from July to September, when the migration stalls in the vicinity of the Mara, and large herds of wildebeest regularly cross between the two banks of the river. North of the Mara, accessed via a concrete causeway near Kogatende Rangers Post, a wedge of sloping grassland – effectively a southern extension of Kenya's legendary Maasai Mara National

Reserve – supports large numbers of lions, elephants, elands, topis, buffalo and other grazers, as well as a small population of black rhino.

Klein's Gate ①, on the eastern border of the Serengeti 20km (12 miles) north of Lobo, is the main access point to the 4,000-sq-km (1,545-sq-mile) **Loliondo Game Controlled Area**, a patchwork of Maasai community land that forms an integral part of the wildebeest migration route. Several lodges lie on exclusive concessions in Loliondo, the largest and best being &Beyond Klein's Camp, where leopards and lions are often seen at close quarters on guided foot safaris and night drives.

THE WESTERN CORRIDOR

The **Western Corridor** sticks out like a panhandle, following the line of the **Grumeti River ①** and taking the borders of the Serengeti the whole way to Lake Victoria. A central range of hills is flanked on either side by large areas of plains, their sticky black cotton soil bursting into flower during the rains. It may look spectacular but is a nightmare for drivers, and the area is best visited in the dry months (June–Oct), when the non-migratory animals cluster along the river.

Elands and roan antelope both live in the area, and the river is home to some spectacularly large crocodiles (up to 6 metres/20ft in length), which spring into a feeding frenzy when the wildebeest come through, usually in May to June. The riparian woodland along the river is home to black-and-white colobus monkeys and several bird species more normally associated with sites further west, notably the eastern grey plantain-eater, Schalow's turaco and double-toothed barbet. The acacia woodland around the junction for Mbalageti Safari Lodge is the only place in Tanzania where the localised patas monkey – a spindly terrestrial primate whose

gingery coloration distinguishes it from the more common vervet – is regularly seen.

A northern extension of the Western Corridor, the 1,410-sq-km (545-sq-mile) **Grumeti Game Reserve ⓚ** is one of several buffer reserves created to protect the Greater Serengeti in the 1950s. Neglected by tourism until 2003, it now effectively functions as a private reserve serviced by a trio of lodges and camps – Sasakwa, Faru Faru and Sabora – operated by the highly regarded South African organisation Singita. Offering an exclusive safari experience, the reserve protects a similar range of wildlife to the Western Corridor, but off-road driving is permitted and the standard of guiding is superb.

The Western Corridor terminates a few kilometres east of Lake Victoria, where the **Ndabaka Gate ⓛ** provides access to the park from the surfaced eastern lake shore road. **Serengeti Stop Over**, situated right outside Ndabaka Gate, is the best contact for inexpensive day and overnight safaris into the western Serengeti.

Nile crocodile in the Serengeti.

📷 MAASAI: NOMADS OF THE PLAINS

The Maasai are a striking feature of the northern Tanzanian landscape, often to be seen herding cattle along the dusty plains in their dramatic red attire.

The Maasai arrived in East Africa about 500 years ago, migrating southwards from the lower Nile region into Kenya, then crossing into Tanzania in the late 18th century. Here, they soon established a reputation as ferocious warriors whose raiding parties would venture deep into neighbouring territories to steal cattle and demand tribute from the coastal trade caravans.

The Maasai of northern Tanzania still live a largely traditional lifestyle, grazing their cattle over vast areas, and living in semi-permanent villages (manyattas) of huts ringed by a thorn fence as defence against wild animals.

Maasai men dress in a distinctive manner. They are usually draped in toga-like red or purple blankets, and often style their red ochred hair in a shape reminiscent of a Roman helmet. They almost invariably carry a long fighting stick wherever they go, and are also often armed with spears. Beadwork, traditionally undertaken by women, is an important facet of Maasai body decoration, and is often used to indicate social status.

The central unit of Maasai society is the age-set. In their teens, Maasai males are initiated as a new age-set of *moran* (young warriors), and for the next 10 to 15 years their duty is to tend livestock and defend the clan. Strict taboos apply to this age-set, including a prohibition on marriage and alcohol until its members graduate to become *eunoto* (elders), usually around the age of 30.

Appearance is important to the moran, whose long hair is braided with animal fat and coloured red with ochre.

The Maasai's traditional ipid dance, which involves leaping high in the air, demonstrates the vigour and virility of a moran.

After serving his time as a moran, the young warrior has his head shaved and his body decorated for the ceremony of eunoto.

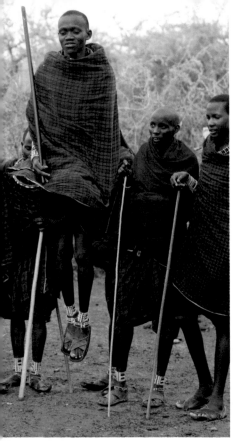

Maasai are skilled at drawing blood from cattle without killing the beast. An arrow is first shot at the cow's jugular vein – a disc on the arrowhead limits the depth it penetrates. Blood then spurts into a gourd before the wound is sealed with a mixture of dung and grass. Later, clotted blood is eaten from the gourd.

The currency of cattle

The Maasai are staunch pastoralists, and every aspect of their lifestyle is informed by their relationship with their beloved cattle. Even today, wealth is measured in terms of cattle rather than money: broadly speaking, a herd of 50 cattle would be considered respectable, but a man who has plenty of cattle and few children will be thought of as poorly off.

Traditionally, the Maasai will not eat vegetable matter or fish, and the flesh of wild beasts is forbidden, except for the cow-like eland and buffalo. However, because cows are more valuable alive than dead, they are seldom slaughtered, and then only for ceremonial purposes.

The traditional Maasai diet consists mainly of cow's milk and blood, the latter drained – it is said painlessly – from a strategic nick in the animal's jugular vein. The concoction is then allowed to curdle in a calabash before it is consumed. Meat and milk are never eaten on the same day, because it is regarded to be insulting to the cattle to feed off the living and the dead at the same time.

A colourful example of intricate Maasai beadwork.

It is the women's task to look after the manyatta. This woman is waterproofing the roof of a hut with mud and cow dung.

This ancient board game is played throughout Africa. The Maasai call it enkeshui.

Young Eastern Chimpanzee, Gombe Stream National Park.

WESTERN AND CENTRAL TANZANIA

Forest-fringed inland seas and vast semi-arid plains characterise this remote and little-visited area of Tanzania, whose main attraction is close encounters with chimpanzees.

For the intrepid traveller, this lonely part of the country boasts a scattering of worth-while stops. Two gargantuan freshwater lakes and their abutting national parks – two of which offer world-class chimp tracking – give way to Tanzania's dusty central plateau, home to the country's capital, Dodoma. Long regarded as a town with little – if official – importance, the promise to transfer the government headquarters to Dodoma by 2020 is aimed at encouraging investment in the district. However, with Dar long-established as the de-facto capital, rejuvenating Tanzania's small and overlooked official capital will not be an easy task.

LAKE VICTORIA

Bordering the western Serengeti, the 70,000-sq-km (27,027-sq-mile) **Lake Victoria ❶** is the world's second-largest freshwater body, set within a shallow elevated basin shared between Tanzania, Uganda and Kenya. Yet despite its proximity to the northern safari circuit, this shallow inland sea is perhaps notable more for its dimensions than for any great scenic qualities, and it has never featured prominently on tourist itineraries.

For nature lovers, its main attraction is the 240-sq-km (93-sq-mile) **Rubondo Island National Park ❷**, where jungle-swathed hills tumble down to a shore of lush papyrus swamps and sandy beaches, to create a bewitching freshwater tropical paradise. Among the least visited of Tanzania's parks, Rubondo forms a consummate post-safari retreat for those more interested in low-key wildlife viewing than lazing around at an Indian Ocean beach resort.

The island is best explored along a network of walking trails that lead through tangled jungle to rocky bays and rickety stilted hides overlooking the marshy shore. Here, the handsome sitatunga antelope, a localised

Map on page 180

Main Attractions
Rubondo Island National Park
Gombe Stream National Park
Mahale Mountains National Park
Katavi National Park

A fish market on Lake Victoria's shores.

and elsewhere-elusive swamp resident, is exceptionally easy to locate. It is no less rewarding to hang around the park's only lodge, where exquisite paradise flycatchers flutter their long orange tails through the trees, grey parrots maintain a perpetual mutter and squawk, and pairs of spot-necked otters climb over the offshore rocks. Further afield, the swampy **Mlaga Bay** – inhabited by scores of hippos and water birds – can be explored by motorboat.

THE FLOATING ZOO

Rubondo has an odd history. In 1966, it was earmarked as a 'floating zoo', to be used to breed introduced rainforest species such as okapi and bongo.

This plan was abandoned in 1973, but not before chimpanzees and black-and-white colobus monkeys had been settled on the island, together with several non-forest-specific species including elephant, giraffe, suni and roan antelope, and black rhinoceros. And while chimp-tracking excursions are not always successful, the scenery and other wildlife seen along the way are ample reward in themselves.

DEATH OF THE LAKE

Visited in isolation, Rubondo Island might give a misleading impression of Lake Victoria's ecological state. The Tanzanian littoral has been all but denuded of indigenous vegetation through overgrazing and agriculture.

Below the surface, the 200 endemic cichlid species are undergoing what one biologist describes as 'the greatest vertebrate mass extinction in recorded history', due to the introduction of the predatory Nile perch in the colonial era. Sixty years ago, cichlids constituted 80 percent of the lake's fish biomass; today they account for a mere 1 percent. This change in species composition has promoted a fivefold increase in algae levels and drop in oxygenation, reducing the lake's capability to sustain vertebrate life.

MWANZA

On a rocky peninsula on the southeastern lake shore, Tanzania's second-largest city, **Mwanza ❸**, is a pivotal regional transport hub, serviced by a good selection of flights, ferries, trains and buses. More, perhaps, than any other settlement in the Tanzanian interior, Mwanza feels like a proper city, reflected in its good selection of hotels and clutch of top-notch restaurants, whose menus typically reflect the prominent Indian community. The substantial city centre, with its washed-out colonial and Asian facades, has a strong sense of place, too.

Smooth granite outcrops stud the surrounding peninsula. Particularly striking is **Bismarck Rock,** a precarious balancing formation that stands sentinel over the open waters of the ferry harbour. The offshore **Saa Nane Island National Park** (daily 6am–6pm) is of interest mainly to birdwatchers, but it also has some outsized monitor lizards, which stalk the undergrowth like scaled-down dinosaurs.

Mwanza on Lake Victoria.

THE EASTERN LAKE SHORE

In Bujora Parish, 20km (12 miles) east of Mwanza, the **Sukuma Museum ❹** (daily 9am–5pm; http://sukumamuseum. org) preserves the traditions of the eponymous tribe. Displays include a Sukuma homestead, a blacksmith's house, a traditional healer's workshop and a collection of thrones and crowns. Try to visit on a Saturday afternoon, when the bizarre Sukuma Snake Dance is sometimes performed – complete

Marabou storks at Lake Victoria.

⦿ THE RIDDLE OF THE NILE

No geographical enigma was so hotly debated in Victorian times as the elusive source of the White Nile. It was a primary goal of Burton and Speke's 1857–8 expedition, which resulted in the 'discovery' of the continent's two largest lakes. The two men were together when they first sighted Lake Tanganyika, but Speke marched to Lake Victoria without Burton, who stayed in Tabora recuperating from illness.

The expedition left its protagonists at bitter odds. Speke was certain Lake Victoria was the source of the Nile. Burton regarded Lake Tanganyika as the most likely candidate. Scientific opinion in Europe tended to side with Burton. In 1863, Speke returned to Lake Victoria to discover a substantial north-flowing outlet near present-day Jinja. 'The Nile is settled,' he declared. His detractors sniggered. Speke died in 1864, hours before a scheduled public debate with Burton. The Nile question was finally resolved in 1874–7 by Stanley, who tested the various theories by circumnavigating lakes Tanganyika and Victoria, then following the Lualaba River – Livingstone's favoured candidate – to emerge at the mouth of the Congo.

The Nile did indeed flow out of Lake Victoria at Jinja; the oft-ridiculed Speke had, according to Stanley, 'understood the geography of the countries we travelled through far better than any of us who so persistently opposed his hypothesis'.

Bismarck Rock, Mwanza's famous landmark, on Lake Victoria's shores.

with live python. The Sukuma are renowned for their exuberant dance competitions. The main festival days are 7 July and 8 August, public holidays which occur shortly after the harvest season. The Bujora Cultural Centre organises *warshas* (workshops) in Sukuma culture, Swahili, dance, song and drumming – see the museum website for details.

Close to the Kenyan border about 220km (130 miles) from Mwanza, **Musoma ❺** is a very laid-back town, on a narrow green peninsula leading to a rocky outcrop, splattered with the guano of its resident cormorant colony. Inland, **Butiama ❻**, the birth and burial place of former president Julius Nyerere (see page 59), houses the somewhat rundown Mwalimu Julius Nyerere Museum (daily 9am–5pm).

THE WESTERN LAKE SHORE

The main port on the western shore, **Bukoba ❼** was founded by the Emin Pasha in 1890, and settled three years later by Catholic missionaries, who built the well-maintained cathedral

that stands out from the time-worn colonial buildings that otherwise characterise the town centre. The marshy lake shore below the town hosts large concentrations of water birds. At **Bwanjai**, 25km (15 miles) northwest of Bukoba, a mysterious rock-art shelter is daubed with ancient geometric patterns and stylised human figures, the sole surviving legacy of some long-forgotten Stone Age artists. Further north, nestled against the Ugandan border, the little-known **Minziro Forest Reserve ❽** supports an incredible 56 Guinea-Congo biome bird species recorded nowhere else in Tanzania.

LAKE TANGANYIKA

Southwest of Lake Victoria, **Lake Tanganyika ❾** is the longest freshwater body in the world, running for 675km (419 miles) from Burundi in the north to Zambia in the south, and the second-deepest, plummeting to almost 1,500 metres (4,910ft). Hemmed in by the mountainous western Rift Valley Escarpment, it is also immensely beautiful, lined by long sandy beaches,

rustic fishing villages, and patches of forest rattling with wildlife.

The aquamarine water – reputedly the world's least polluted – is so clear that you can wade in chin deep and still see your toes. It harbours several hundred fish species, most endemic to the lake. On the eastern lake shore, a pair of beautiful national parks offer the best chimpanzee-tracking in Africa. Countries have built a thriving tourist industry on less, and yet this lovely part of Tanzania remains resolutely off the beaten track.

KIGOMA AND UJIJI

Kigoma  is the largest town on Lake Tanganyika's Tanzanian shore, favoured by the Germans for its deep natural harbour, and since 1914 the lake-shore terminus of the central railway line. Historical landmarks include the stately German-era **Railway Station** and **Kaiser House**. The town is serviced by scheduled flights and trains from Dar es Salaam, as well as ferries to Zambia and the Democratic Republic of Congo (DRC),

A flameback African cichlid from Lake Tanganyika.

making it a useful springboard for extended travels around the lake. It is also an inherently agreeable place to spend a couple of days, its shady avenues leading down to a stretch of lake shore routinely lit up by spectacular sunsets.

Pre-colonial Kigoma was dwarfed in significance by the Arab trading post of **Ujiji** ⑪ , which lies only 8km (5 miles) to its southeast and has retained a distinct Muslim atmosphere, epitomised by the coastal-style dhows that billow out from the old fishing harbour. It was at Ujiji, in 1858, that Burton and Speke became the first Europeans to set eyes on Lake Tanganyika; here, too, that Stanley uttered perhaps the most famous – and most ridiculed – phrase ever spoken on the African continent: 'Doctor Livingstone, I presume.' A modest memorial marks the place where Stanley and Livingstone met in 1871. The adjacent **Livingstone Museum** (daily 9am–5pm; tel: 076 601 4335) houses little to justify the steep entrance fee.

Fresh catch arrives at Kigoma.

⟳ ABOARD THE *LIEMBA*

The MV *Liemba* is the weekly ferry that plies Lake Tanganyika from Kigoma south to Mpulungu in Zambia. Originally called the *Graf von Goetzen*, this boat was brought in pieces to Kigoma by the Germans, who assembled it but then decided to scupper it rather than let it fall into enemy hands. Salvaged by the Belgians in 1924, when it became the *Liemba*, it has since provided a vital lifeline to remote parts of the lake. In 2015, the ship transported thousands of Burundian refugees to safety in Kigoma. Although Kigoma and Kasanga have proper jetties, the *Liemba* is elsewhere met by a flotilla of rickety fishing boats that jostle aggressively for position – all part of an offbeat excursion that embodies the romance of African lake travel. Be aware that the *Liemba* is scheduled for renovations in summer 2017, so check before you travel.

JANE'S CHIMPS

Lake-shore Gombe Stream and Mahale Mountains national parks are undoubtedly the best places in the world to track chimpanzees in their natural environment.

Even so, Tanzania cannot be regarded as a major chimpanzee stronghold; its estimated total of 1,500–2,000 chimps – roughly half resident in Mahale, another 100 or so in Gombe – represents less than 1 percent of the global population. This only makes Lake Tanganyika's pre-eminence in almost every aspect of contemporary chimpanzee research and conservation more remarkable.

The reason can be summed up in one name: Jane Goodall. In July 1960, this academically unqualified young Englishwoman arrived at Gombe Stream to initiate what has become the world's longest-running – and arguably most ground-breaking – study of any wild animal population.

An old male chimpanzee in Gombe Stream National Park.

Goodall's pioneering research cannot be summarised in a few sentences; her absorbing books are requisite reading for anybody heading to Gombe or Mahale. Perhaps the most significant of her early observations, however, were modes of behaviour thought until then to distinguish *Homo sapiens* from other living creatures – the manipulation of twigs to 'fish' termites and ants from their burrows; inter-community warfare; the methodical hunting of other primates; and even an orchestrated campaign of cannibalism.

Goodall's work was enhanced by a parallel project in Mahale Mountains, instigated in 1965 by the Japanese primatologist Junichiro Itani. Comparative studies have revealed the fascinating cultural differences in chimp behaviour. The palm nut, for instance, forms a major part of the diet of the Gombe chimps, but is never eaten at Mahale. Up to 40 percent of plants available in both reserves are eaten by one population but not the other.

Chimpanzees are related more closely to humans than to any other living creature. They live in large territorial communities, within which different individuals move around in smaller sub-groups, which can change on a daily basis. Every community is headed by an alpha male, whose dominance is often achieved by the intelligent manipulation of his fellows rather than through brute strength. Male chimps seldom leave their ancestral community, but females regularly migrate outside them.

There are three communities at Gombe, with the largest being Kasekela, the focus of Goodall's studies. Of the 15 communities in Mahale Mountains, the 100-strong Mimikere community is the most habituated, and the one that tourists will normally encounter.

Chimp-tracking is available all year, but the late dry season – July to October – has several advantages: the steep slopes are less treacherous underfoot, and the chimps tend to stick to lower, more accessible altitudes. Of the two reserves, Mahale has better facilities for upmarket tourists, and offers a more holistic wilderness experience, while Gombe Stream is more accessible and more affordable to budget travellers. Whenever and wherever you go, it is an experience that you'll remember for a lifetime.

GOMBE STREAM NATIONAL PARK

Covering 52 sq km (20 sq miles), **Gombe Stream National Park** ⑫ protects a hilly stretch of lake shore bisected by forest-fringed streams. Gombe Stream's fame derives from its association with Jane Goodall's chimp research project (see page 184). Inevitably, it's the chimp community habituated by Goodall that forms the centre of tourist activities at Gombe, but there are numerous other reasons for visiting. Red colobus monkeys (which are hunted and eaten by the chimps) crash about in the canopy, while the olive baboons that comb the beach are relatively tame and easy to photograph. Birdlife is prolific, too.

Gombe Stream lies on the eastern lake shore, 25km (16 miles) north of Kigoma. Most visitors arrive from Kigoma by charter boat. A more affordable option is to use a public boat-taxi from **Kibirizi** (3 km/2 miles north of Kigoma). These leave in the afternoon, returning in the early morning, and take two hours in either direction. Guided forest walks can be arranged on the spot, with a near-certainty of encountering chimps in the morning.

MAHALE MOUNTAINS NATIONAL PARK

Mahale Mountains National Park ⑬ (www.mahalepark.org) extends for 1,613 sq km (623 sq miles) across a bulbous peninsula of forested mountains, roughly 120km (75 miles) south of Kigoma. The scenery alone is magnificent: rugged mountains rise sharply from sandy beaches, through tangled miombo woodland and montane forest and grassland, to the 2,462-metre (8,077ft) **Nkungwe Peak**.

Mahale is most famous for its chimpanzees, which are usually seen at close quarters on daily tracking expeditions. Smaller primates, such as red colobus monkeys, red-tailed monkeys, Sykes' monkeys, vervet monkeys and yellow baboons, should be encountered by casual visitors. Less often observed are a few West African rainforest species such as the brush-tailed porcupine and giant forest squirrel.

Hippos in Katavi National Park.

⊙ CENTRAL RAILWAY

Though not for the faint-hearted, the train journey between Dar es Salaam and Kigoma is one of Africa's greatest. A leisurely two-day chug through the country's barren heartland, it passes through torpid small towns that spring into life as the train pulls in, and hungry passengers spill out to mill around stalls serving fresh kebabs and hearty chicken stews with rice and *ugali* (maize porridge).

The journey follows a route pioneered by the first Swahili slave caravans on their months-long march to Lake Tanganyika. Burton and Speke followed this ancient trade route on their way to Lake Tanganyika. So did Livingstone in his misdirected and fatal quest to locate the source of the Nile, and Stanley on the expedition that led to his famous meeting with Livingstone at Ujiji.

There is no road access. Most visitors visit by charter flight from Arusha or Katavi. But hardy independent travellers can get as far as the village of **Lugosa** with the MV *Liemba*, then hike – or hire a local boat – to cover the remaining 15km (9 miles) to the park headquarters and rest camp. The trusty *Liemba* is expected to undergo renovation in summer 2017 (although nothing is confirmed), so look out for updates before making any concrete plans.

KATAVI NATIONAL PARK

Covering 4,471 sq km (1,726 sq miles), **Katavi National Park** (www.katavipark.org; gates are open daily 6am–7pm) is the most inaccessible of Tanzania's major savannah reserves. It is also inexplicably underrated, offering an undiluted bush experience that's increasingly precious in these days of package safaris and over-orchestrated private game lodges. During the latter part of the dry season, when the Kavuu River and associated tributaries form the only source of water for miles around, the game viewing can be little

The market area of Dodoma.

short of astounding. Thousand-strong herds of buffalo are a regular sight, elephants lurk round every other corner, and hundreds of hippos huddle tightly in any suitably deep pool. This is one of the few remaining game reserves anywhere in Africa where you can expect to encounter more lions that you will other visitors. Need more be said?

The only comfortable way to see Katavi – short of driving a private vehicle halfway across Tanzania – is by charter package to one of a handful of remote bush camps. Katavi is best avoided from November to April, when game disperses, roads are impassable, and the heat and insect activity are insufferable.

THE CENTRAL BADLANDS

Tanzania's vast and drought-prone central plateau is all red-dirt plains and mean acacia scrub studded with boulders the size of mountains. It does possess a certain austere beauty, but the poor roads, long distances and relatively meagre travel pickings

ensure that the very few tourists who pass this way are usually putting miles behind them en route between the coast and one of the great western lakes. With this goal in mind, the only land transport worth contemplating is the 1,500km (930-mile) German-built railway line connecting Dar es Salaam to Kigoma (and to Mwanza) via Tabora and Dodoma (see box page 185).

Strategically located at the junction of the lines to Kigoma and Mwanza, the workaday town of **Tabora** ⑮ has long been the most important transport hub in western Tanzania. Within the leafy confines of the modern town centre, the only physical evidence of Tabora's antiquity is a German railway station and fort. Only 6km (4 miles) outside Tabora, however, a house built by the slave trader Tippu Tip once provided shelter to both Livingstone and Stanley during their trans-African journeys. Known as **Livingstone's Tembe** (daily 9am–5pm), this fine example of coastal architecture, nestled in a grove of mango trees and complete with original carved Zanzibar doors, is now

a museum, housing some worthwhile displays on the Victorian explorers.

The other large town along the central railway, **Dodoma** ⑯, possesses some curiosity value as the official – albeit improbable – capital of Tanzania, though you'd be hard pushed to find a reason to spend more time here than transport logistics dictate. Dodoma was an established stop along the 19th-century caravan route, and it served as a regional administrative centre under the German colonials prior to being made designate capital in 1973. In 2016, President John Magufuli announced plans to move the government headquarters from Dar to Dodoma by 2020, hoping to stimulate investment in the area and to raise its profile. For now, political status aside, all that really distinguishes Dodoma from other moderately sized upcountry Tanzanian towns is a low-key local wine industry. Sightseeing in the immediate vicinity is limited to a large and climbable rock outcrop – vaguely lion-like in outline – which stands over the Arusha road less than 5km (3 miles) from the town centre.

Selling food through train windows during a stop.

Impala ram, Mikumi
National Park.

SOUTHERN PARKS AND TANZAM HIGHWAY

Tanzania's second safari circuit is, to aficionados, even better than the north, a magnificent wilderness teeming with game and virtually devoid of tourists.

The **Selous Game Reserve** ❶ exists on a barely comprehensible scale. Covering 47,500 sq km (18,340 sq miles), it is Tanzania's largest protected area: 50 percent larger than Switzerland, situated at the core of a 155,000-sq-km (59,800-sq-mile) cross-border ecosystem traversed by some of the world's greatest remaining herds of buffalo (150,000), hippopotamus (40,000) and sable antelope (8,000). And yet such statistics, thrown about glibly by tour operators, flatter Selous to the point of deceit. The life-sustaining waters of the **Rufiji River** divide this semi-arid wilderness into two wildly disproportionate sectors: an immense and practically impenetrable southern block used exclusively by commercial hunting concerns, and a more compact northern circuit – about 8 percent of Selous' total area – dedicated to less bloodthirsty forms of tourism. Selous is undeniably a fine game reserve, but the statistics are misleading. On top of this, its elephant population has sadly been decimated by poaching, falling from nearly 110,000 elephants to just 15,000 in 2016.

THE RUFIJI RIVER

The divisive Rufiji, its constantly mutating course spilling into a labyrinth of intimate, lushly vegetated channels and open lakes, defines the Selous experience. It is best explored on one of the motorboat trips offered by most of Selous' camps. Sandbanks lined with outsized crocodiles, menacing mouths agape, erupt into sinuous energy as a motorboat approaches and the prehistoric beasts slither with one loud splash beneath the river's surface.

Yellow-billed storks and spoonbills scoop methodically through the shallows, pied kingfishers hover overhead like fast-forward clockwork toys, African skimmers fly low across the surface dipping their bright-red beaks into the water, and carmine

⊘ Main Attractions
Selous Game Reserve
Ruaha National Park
Mikumi National Park
Udzungwa Mountains
  National Park

Map on page 190

Giraffe eating from a sausage tree, Ruaha National Park.

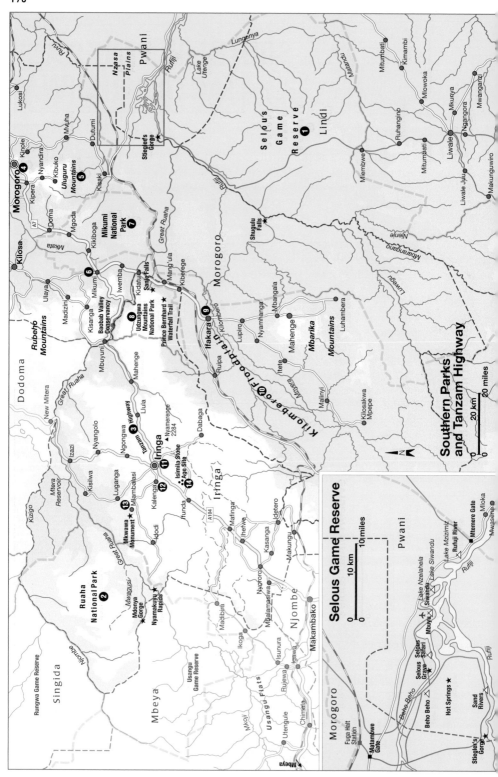

bee-eaters swirl in a crimson cloud around the exposed mud banks in which they breed. Becalmed channels flow northwards from the main river, past swampy islets where elephants browse and waterbucks graze. And, as the motorboat returns to the lodge, a light evening breeze wafts across the water to diffuse the still heat of the day, hippos enter into earnest grunting debate, and a red-coal sun sinks behind a neat row of borassus palms – the quintessential African river scene.

A network of game-viewing roads connects the lakes, where congregations of zebra, giraffe and various antelope slake their thirst during the dry season. The odds of seeing a kill here are unusually high: the lions of Selous seem disinclined to follow the time-honoured leonine strategy of stalking their dinner by night, but instead prefer to laze quietly in the lakeshore woodland waiting for lunch to venture within pouncing distance. Wild dogs snuggle below shady raffia palms in the heat of the day, emerging towards dusk to scamper and frolic at the water's edge. In recent decades, wild dog populations elsewhere in Africa have gone into rapid decline: the estimated 1,000-plus individuals that roam the Selous account for more than 20 percent of the free-ranging global population, exceeding that of any other African country.

TOURIST LODGES

The Selous (pronounced 'Seloo') is named after Captain Frederick Courteney Selous, the legendary game hunter and writer who was killed by German sniper fire near the Rufiji during World War I (see page 200). A year after the war ended, P.H. Lamb trekked to the 'wild inhospitable district' where a plain wooden cross marked Selous' grave, and predicted that 'the object of most people who have seen it will be to avoid it carefully in the future'. Inherently, the Selous remains as wild and inhospitable today as it was in 1919. By comparison to the more famous Serengeti, it is also remarkably free of safari traffic, visited by a mere 1 percent of tourists to Tanzania.

Tourists in a safari vehicle watching a lion on a kill, Selous Game Reserve.

Lamb would doubtless have revised his gloomy prediction had he been hosted by one of the dozen-or-so exclusive tourist lodges that scatter the Selous today. With a combined bed space less than that of some individual hotels along the northern circuit, these lodges are justifiably known for their luxurious accommodation, personalised service and integrated bush atmosphere. In addition to boat trips, guided game walks add vivid immediacy to exploring the Selous – the thrill of emerging from a riverine thicket onto a plain where a surprised elephant bull trumpets a warning, or a herd of buffalo stare down the oddly clad intruders.

Not exciting enough? Then take things one step further and arrange to spend a night or two at a private fly-camp, separated from the pristine night sky by a transparent drape of mosquito netting. As hippos and elephants tread gingerly past the makeshift tent, sleep might not come easily, but this primal African nocturnal experience will never be forgotten.

The buffalo looks placid but can be one of Africa's most dangerous animals when riled.

RUAHA

The Selous features prominently in many seasoned African travellers' top ten wilderness areas, but ask a Tanzania-based wildlife lover what their favourite game reserve is, and odds are that the reply will be **Ruaha National Park ❷**. This rugged tract of wilderness, expanded to 20,220 sq km (8,690 sq miles) by the addition of the vulnerable Usanga Floodplain in 2008, is now the largest national park in Tanzania, and one of the continent's five largest. Like the Selous, Ruaha forms the core of a much vaster ecosystem, extending into half a dozen other protected areas. Characterised by parched slopes covered in dense Brachystegia woodland, and wide open baobab-studded plains, Ruaha fulfils every expectation of untrammelled Africa, no less so because its 400km (250-mile) road circuit is accessed by only half-a-dozen small lodges and a few campsites – indeed, even the Selous seems crowded by comparison.

Game-viewing roads follow the perennial Great Ruaha River and

⊘ WILD DOGS IN DECLINE

In the early 20th century, an estimated 500,000 African wild dogs ranged across 40 countries. Today, thanks mainly to human persecution and canid disease borne by domestic dogs, the free-ranging population is estimated at fewer than 5,000. Quite why the Selous has escaped this precipitous decline is an open question. Perhaps it is because the low human population around the reserve has minimised exposure to domestic dogs and vengeful stock farmers. Perhaps it is because wild dogs here face less competition from other large predators. Quite possibly, it is simply a matter of good luck. Whatever the case, with an estimated population of 1,000 to 1,300 wild dogs, the Selous' importance to the future of this endangered species is difficult to overstate.

seasonal Mwagusi River through thick riparian forest frequented by what was once one of Africa's densest elephant populations – sadly, population estimates have fallen from around 35,000 in 2009 to around 16,000 in 2015. Still, cheetahs pace the open savannah, which is grazed upon by herds of buffalo stretching to the horizon, as well as the usual cast of ungulates: impala, waterbuck, zebra and Grant's gazelle. The woodland, transitional to the eastern savannah and southern miombo biomes, is the most southerly haunt of the shy striped hyena and delicate lesser kudu, as well as three endemic birds: the blackcollared lovebird, ashy starling and the recently described Ruaha red-billed hornbill. Ruaha also harbours a trio of lovely antelope that are rare in northern Tanzania: the imposingly horned greater kudu, sleekly handsome sable and roan antelope. Near the Mwagusi River, prides of 20-plus lions reduce a freshly killed buffalo or zebra to skin and bone in a couple of hours.

Fine game viewing indeed, and yet if Ruaha leaves one overwhelming impression, it is the sense of solitude associated with driving for hours through untamed Africa without encountering another human soul.

THE TANZAM HIGHWAY

Selous and Ruaha are linked to each other, and to Dar es Salaam, by a daily scheduled flight, and most tourists who visit one or both reserves fly in from Dar es Salaam. Yet the two reserves also form part of a looser road circuit connected by the **Tanzam Highway** ❸ – the endless strip of asphalt that runs southwest from Dar es Salaam, via Morogoro and Iringa, to the Zambian capital of Lusaka (Tanzam being an abbreviation of Tanzania–Zambia). The Selous can be reached from Morogoro along the rough 120km (75-mile) Matombo Road (named for a buxom pair of peaks known as *Matombo* – 'Breasts'), while a fair 100km (60-mile) dirt road runs west from Iringa to the main entrance gate of Ruaha.

Bat-eared fox in Ruaha National Park.

Yellow-billed storks in the Great Ruaha River at sunrise.

Bypassed by the Tanzam Highway, 200km (120 miles) out of Dar es Salaam, **Morogoro ④** is a lively town transformed into one of the prettiest cities in Tanzania by the **Uluguru Mountains ⑤**, which rise to a majestic 2,635 metres (8,645ft) on the southern horizon. Clear freshwater streams tumble down the forested slopes of the Uluguru to provide generous sustenance to the local agricultural community, a vital source of fresh produce for Dar es Salaam. Neat, compact and energetic, Morogoro makes for an agreeable, even relaxing, stopover, and yet it's somehow surprising to learn that this rapidly growing town is one of Tanzania's largest urban centres.

A German boma and railway station stand as isolated reminders of Morogoro's colonial roots, while the packed central market, stalls laden with succulent papayas, sweet pineapples and candelabras of bright yellow bananas, reflects its modern agricultural base. An undemanding 30-minute stroll out of town leads to the **Rock Garden** (www.facebook.com/RockGardenMorogoro), a botanical garden on the lower slopes of the Uluguru.

THE ULUGURU MOUNTAINS

For a more ambitious day walk, **Morningside Camp** is a disused German research station on the higher slopes, set amid patches of natural forest and pretty cascades. Morningside is difficult to locate without a local guide – best arranged through Chilunga Cultural Tourism (mob: 0754-477582; www.chilunga.or.tz), a highly regarded community-based organisation based in the town centre, opposite the hospital.

This is also the best place to enquire about travel deeper into the Uluguru Mountains, a vast Eastern Arc range inhabited by dedicated Luguru agriculturists who work their fertile, well-watered smallholdings throughout the year. Between the cultivated fields, approximately 500 sq km (200 sq miles) of indigenous forest harbours black-and-white colobus

Hiker crossing the Sanje River, Udzungwa Mountains National Park.

⦿ UDZUNGWA ENDEMICS

Arguably East Africa's most important biodiversity hotspot, Udzungwa yields new species with sensational regularity. In 1979, ecologists working in the mountains heard a whooping call similar to that of a mangabey (a West African monkey not known to occur within a 1,000km/620-mile radius). Initially, they thought they were victims of a prank, but their guide told them that an orphaned monkey of the type that made the call was being tended at Sanje village. It turned out to be a new species, Sanje crested mangabey, which occurs nowhere else in the world.

In 1991, biologists working in the Udzungwa noticed a pair of strange feet floating in their 'chicken stew'. Upon enquiry, they were shown a snared specimen of a wildfowl that more closely resembled the Asian hill partridge than any African bird. Subsequently named the Udzungwa forest partridge, this localised endemic – the sole living representative of a lineage dating back 15 million years to when a forest belt along the Arabian coastline linked Africa and Asia – underscores the antiquity of the Eastern Arc forests.

The list of Udzungwa endemics keeps growing. Prominent more-recent discoveries include a bushbaby species in 1996, and the grey-faced elephant shrew (the largest known species in the family), which was first photographed in 2005 and described in 2008.

monkeys and various small antelope – as well as 40 vascular plant species, 10 reptile and amphibian species, and more than 100 invertebrate species found nowhere else in the world. The secretive Uluguru bush-shrike, a striking canary-yellow bird with a jet-black cap, is one of three endemics to tantalise ornithologists. At present, the forests of the Uluguru are realistically explored only from **Nyandira**, a humble Luguru village situated 25km (16 miles) from the Tanzam Highway along a four-wheel-drive-only road that forks to the left, 20km (12 miles) south of Morogoro.

MIKUMI

Unprepared travellers driving southwest along the Tanzam Highway towards the town of **Mikumi ❻** (120km/75 miles from Morogoro) are frequently taken aback at the sight of an elephant emerging from the bush or a herd of buffalo masticating lazily on the verge. This is one of the few trunk routes in Africa to cut through the heart of a major game reserve. Indeed, **Mikumi National Park ❼** directly owes its protected status to the construction of the Tanzam Highway, which opened up the formerly remote area to poachers. Gazetted in 1964 and later expanded to share a border with the Selous, Mikumi is the fourth-largest national park in Tanzania, extending over 3,230 sq km (1,247 sq miles).

Popular with expatriate weekenders, Mikumi has never caught on among international visitors. It is, nevertheless, delightful. The extensive Mkata Floodplain, crossed by a 60km (37-mile) road loop running northwest of the Tanzam Highway, feels like a compressed replica of the Serengeti. Its seasonally inundated grassland hosts impressive herds of zebra, wildebeest, buffalo, elands and impala; hippos snort and grunt in the waterholes, and around 400 species of birds have been spotted here. Giraffes lope elegantly

through stands of flat-topped acacias, elephants stroll majestically across the grassland, and the majestic greater kudu and sable antelope skulk in the thick Brachystegia woodland. Handsome golden-maned lions are common, and hyenas are regularly heard serenading the night sky.

Mikumi town, on the western border of the national park, was founded in 1914 and named after the borassus palms that flourished in the vicinity. Sadly, no palm groves grace Mikumi today: this scruffy little town, whose shape is defined by the highway along which it seems to creep further with each passing year, has all the aesthetic appeal of an overgrown truck stop. However, it is a popular budget base from which to explore the national park, and it also lies at the junction of the approach road – signposted left – to the marvellous Udzungwa Mountains.

UDZUNGWA

The road to Udzungwa runs south from Mikumi for a surfaced 37km (23 miles), before crossing the white-water rush

Burchell's zebra, Mikumi National Park.

Trumpeter hornbill.

The Sanje Waterfalls.

of the Great Ruaha River to enter the lively, small town of **Kidatu**. Humid and low-lying, Kidatu has a naturally torpid atmosphere, overlaid with the heavy scent of molasses emanating from the adjacent Kilombero Sugar Estate – which, along with a hydroelectric scheme on the Great Ruaha, has stimulated rapid local population growth in the last decade. Unfortunately, neither the tropical riverside setting nor the Udzungwa Mountains on the western horizon are sufficient to justify a stop here. Certainly not when another 25km (16 miles) of rutted road leads south to the overgrown village of **Mang'ula**, at the entrance gate to **Udzungwa Mountains National Park** ❽.

The 1,900-sq-km (730-sq-mile) Udzungwa Mountains National Park protects the most extensive of the Eastern Arc ranges, a craggy, forest-swathed massif that erupted from the plains more than 100 million years ago. The undemanding self-guided **Prince Bernhard Waterfall Trail**, named after the Dutch royal who opened the park in 1992, provides a lovely introduction to the magic of Udzungwa's forests. Turkey-sized trumpeter hornbills flap heavily through the canopy, the exquisite green-headed oriole betrays its presence with a repetitive song, pairs of forest weavers flit restlessly through the mid-strata, and dozens of different butterfly species flutter above the shadowy forest floor.

Lucky visitors may catch a glimpse of a shy suni crossing the forest path, or a chequered elephant shrew rummaging its elongated nose through the litter. Common around the waterfall, the endangered Uhehe red colobus is distinguished from the ubiquitous blue monkey by its translucent orange fringe. A longer guided hike leads from the entrance gate to **Sanje Falls**, which plunge 300 metres (980ft) down the escarpment in three discrete stages.

KILOMBERO

Bisected by the Umena River some 40km (25 miles) south of Mang'ula, the small town of **Ifakara** ❾ wouldn't win any beauty contests. Continue 5km (3 miles) south of Ifakara along

the Mahenge road, and you'll reach the **Kilombero River**, a wide and muddy tributary of the Rufiji crossed by a regular motor ferry. The 4,000-sq-km (1,544-sq-mile) **Kilombero Floodplain** ❿, an unprotected extension of the Selous ecosystem, is East Africa's largest seasonal wetland, and has been listed as a Ramsar site since 2002. The area is home to 50,000 puku antelope (almost 75 percent of the global population), it attracts up to 5,000 elephants in the dry season (although numbers are in decline), and it has thrown up three previously undescribed bird species since 1986. Much of the floodplain is inaccessible to all but self-sufficient four-wheel-drive expeditions, but hippos, and, on occasion, the endemic birds can be observed near the ferry crossing. For a small fee, the dugout-canoe owners who hang around the ferry will carry travellers upstream in search of elephants and buffalo.

IRINGA

For 50km (30 miles) south of Mikumi, the Tanzam Highway runs through undistinguished acacia scrub, before abruptly giving way to a steep valley densely packed with haunted forests of ancient baobabs. This magnificently austere landscape is softened by the Great Ruaha River, which meanders along the valley floor flanked by a ribbon of lush riparian woodland. Within this valley, slopes studded with immense baobab abut the western border of Udzungwa Mountains National Park. Known as Baobab Valley, and situated on a migration route associated with Ruaha National Park, the area attracts a significant seasonal elephant population, and there is no better place to see the stately greater kudu, which regularly comes to drink at the river.

There's nothing about **Iringa** ⓫ to set pulses racing, but this substantial town, perched on a small plateau overlooking the Little Ruaha River, has an architectural and cultural cohesion lacking in many of its peers. The covered central market sells the rugs and basketwork for which the region is famed, while well-preserved German

The Isimila Stone Age Site, near Iringa.

Woman carrying firewood.

and Asian colonial-era buildings on Majumba Street house a miscellany of small shops. The local Hehe tribe, probably the most populous in southern Tanzania, arose as a powerful expansionist empire forged under Chief Munyigumba in about 1850 – their name derives from their 'hee-hee' battle cry.

The name Iringa is a corruption of the Hehe word *lilinga* (fort), a reference to **Kalenga ⑫**, the fortified capital of Chief Mkwawa, 15km (9 miles) from the modern town. Mkwawa, a merciless conquistador who profited greatly from the slave trade, has been transformed by posterity into a folk hero for his resistance to German colonisation. In 1891, Mkwawa's army ambushed a German war party in Hehe territory, killing three-quarters of the troops. German revenge came three years later, when Kalenga was destroyed by a hilltop bombardment. The remains of the fortified walls are still discernible today, and a touching museum houses several of Mkwawa's personal effects. Following the destruction of

Kalenga, Mkwawa inflicted a series of successful guerrilla attacks on German positions, but in 1898, with his encampment at Mlambalasi surrounded, the chief shot himself rather than face capture. Mkwawa's body – minus his head – was buried where it fell. An 11km (7-mile) road signposted off the road from Iringa to Ruaha leads to Mkwawa's tomb and centenary memorial at **Mlambalasi ⑬**.

Situated 22km (14 miles) southwest of Iringa along the Tanzam Highway, the **Isimila Stone Age Site ⑭** (daily 9am–4pm) is a dry watercourse incised through sequential layers of sediment deposited by a lake which dried up 60,000 years ago. The site museum displays tools and weapons used by Stone Age hunter-gatherers, as well as the fossilised remains of the creatures they preyed upon: buffalo-sized swine, giraffe-like ungulates with huge antlers, and gargantuan hippos with projecting eyes. Ten minutes' stroll from the museum, a deeper gorge is dotted with tall sandstone pillars carved by an extinct river.

SELOUS

Buried in the game reserve that now bears his name, Frederick Courteney Selous was both a voracious hunter and a visionary conservationist.

Born in London in 1851, the son of the chairman of the London Stock Exchange, Frederick Courteney Selous was even as a child an avid naturalist, inspired by David Livingstone and the hunting pursuits of Gordon Cumming and Charles Baldwin.

In 1871, he realised his boyhood dream, immigrating to southern Africa where he led a colourful existence as a hunter-explorer, killing hundreds of elephants and other animals, and acting as a guide for Cecil Rhodes in opening up Zimbabwe to European settlers. Writing about his exploits – in *A Hunter's Wanderings in Africa* and *African Nature Notes and Reminiscences* – earned him international fame, and he was hired as a hunting guide for American president Theodore Roosevelt, with whom he became friends, staying at the White House on several occasions.

Selous showed the hunter's passion for his quarry, possessing a remarkable skill for observing the wildlife he shot, and for debating wildlife issues. He also developed a deep respect for the San and Matabele, who taught him bushcraft. His writing gives a valuable insight into the state of African wildlife at the end of the 19th century, and led the way to modern methods of conserving wildlife.

On noticing that black rhinoceros were extinct in many areas where they had previously been plentiful, he suggested that certain species be protected – today there is a major rhino conservation project running in the Selous. He also envisaged national parks, believing that it would be possible to establish large sanctuaries in uninhabited parts of the country to preserve considerable numbers of wildlife.

After his hunting career, Selous retired to England. At the outbreak of World War I, he volunteered for duty, only to be told that at 63 he was too old. He reapplied, was appointed as an intelligence officer in the 25th Royal Fusiliers and sent back to East Africa. Here he pitched his cunning against the legendary skills of the German commander, Colonel Paul von Lettow-Vorbeck (see page 51).

Climate and disease took their toll on his company – of the original 1,166-strong force, only 60 remained by the time they drove the Germans out of the fortified village of Kisiki in 1916. For his action and bravery in the field, Captain Selous was awarded the DSO.

Remarkably, even during the war, Selous still found time to pursue his interests as a hunter and naturalist. After battle, he took out his butterfly net to collect specimens, and also went out hunting, bagging a kudu trophy. But his glory was to be short-lived.

In January 1917, the company was involved in a series of skirmishes near the Rufiji River, and, while out scouting, Selous was shot dead by a German sniper. His grave can be seen north of the Rufiji River near the Selous Safari Camp, not far from Beho Beho.

A simple concrete slab is marked by a small plaque, which reads: 'Captain F.C. Selous, DSO, 25th Royal Fusiliers, Killed in Action 4.1.1917'. The Selous Game Reserve was named after him in recognition of his contribution to wildlife as a naturalist and conservationist.

Frederick Selous, greatest of the great white hunters.

The Kipengere Range, also known as the Livingstone Mountains, lies in southwest Tanzania at the northern end of Lake Malawi.

MBEYA AND LAKE NYASA

Virtually unknown, southeastern Tanzania is a glorious landscape of lakes and mountains, rich in wildlife, birds and flowers.

Tanzania's remote southern highlands climb steeply from the sultry northern shore of Lake Nyasa in a spectacular montane crescent, shaped by the same ongoing tectonic violence that wrenched open the Rift Valley around Nyasa many millions of years ago. Studded with dormant volcanic peaks, mysterious crater lakes, wild tracts of indigenous forest, pretty waterfalls and haunting volcanic rock formations, the southern highlands, seldom visited by tourists, are rich in offbeat pickings for devoted hikers and keen natural historians.

MBEYA

The urban pulse of this lovely region is **Mbeya ❶**, Tanzania's fifth-largest city, a neat, bustling, well-equipped and climactically pleasing base from which to explore the highlands, yet curiously unmemorable in itself. The **Sisi Kwa Sisi Tourism Office** (corner of School Street and Mbalizi Road; mob: 0754-463471; www.sisi-kwa-sisi.com) offers inexpensive guided tours to all accessible sites of interest in the southern highlands. Its services are virtually essential for hikes on Ngosi, Rungwe and the Kitulo Plateau. Make arrangements directly through the office, since several impostors hang around the bus station and streets of Mbeya.

The Mbeya mountain range, noted for its wet-season floral displays of

orchids and proteas, rises above central Mbeya to the 2,656-metre (8,714ft) **Loleza Peak**, which can be ascended in two hours along a footpath starting on Hospital Hill Road. The more challenging 2,827-metre (9,275ft) **Mbeya Peak** is more easily climbed from the out-of-town Utengule Coffee Lodge.

Mbeya was founded in 1927 to service a gold rush centred on **Chunya ❷**, reached by a rough but scenic 72km (45-mile) road that skirts the eastern slopes of the Mbeya range. It is part of a circuit that can be completed over a

⊘ **Main Attractions**
Kitulo National Park
Ngosi Crater Lake
Daraja la Mungu
Matema Beach

Map on page 202

The fish eagle perches high to spot its prey.

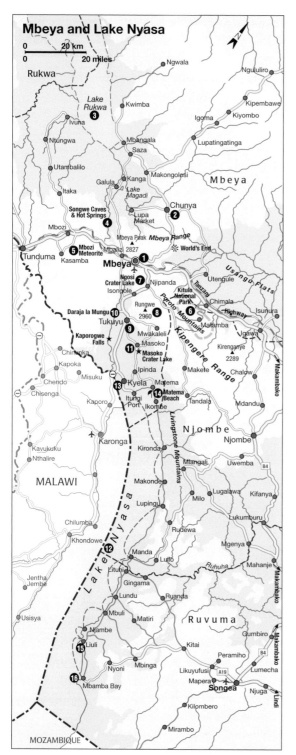

Mbeya and Lake Nyasa

0   20 km
0   20 miles

Rukwa

Lake Rukwa ❸

Ngwala
Nguuliro
Kwimba
Kipembawe
Igoma   Kiyombo
Ivuna
Ntungwa   Mbangala   Lupatingatinga
Saza
Utambalilo
Galula   Kanga   Makongolosi   M b e y a
Itaka   Lake
Magadi
Songwe Caves   Chunya
& Hot Springs   Lupa   ❷
❹   Market
Mbozi
Mbeya Peak   Mbeya Range
Mbozi   Mbalizi 2827   ☀ World's End
Tunduma   ❺ Meteorite   ❶
Kasamba   Mbeya
Ngosi   Utengule   Usungu Flats
Crater Lake ❼   Njipanda
Isongole   Kitulo   Chimala
National
Rungwe   Park   Highway   Isunura
Daraja la Mungu ❿   2960 ❽   Matamba
Tukuyu   Igawa
Kaporogwe   Mwakaleli   Kirenganye
Falls   Masoko   2289
Chimonka   ❶❶   Masoko   Makete   Chalow
Kapoka   Crater Lake
Chendo   Misuku   Ipinda   N j o m b e
Chisenga   Kyela   Matema   Njombe
❶❸   Matema
Kaporo   Itungi   Beach   ❶❹
Port   Ikombe   Tandala   Mdandu
Karonga   Kironda   Njombe
Kavukuku   Mlangali   Uwemba
Nthalire   Makonde   Lugalawa   Kifanya
MALAWI   Milo
Lupingu   Lukumburu
Chilumba   Rudewa
Khondowe   Mgenya
❶❷   Manda   Luifo   Mahanje
Lituhi   Ruhuha
Jentha   Gingama
Jembe   Lundu   Ruanda
Usisya   Mbuli   Matiri   R u v u m a
Njambe   Gumbiro
❶❺ Liuli   Kitai
Peramiho
Nyoni   Mbinga   Likuyufusi
❶❻   Mapera   Songea
Mbamba Bay   Njuga
Kilombero
Mirambo
MOZAMBIQUE

(map labels: Lake Nyasa, Livingstone Mountains, Poroto Mountains, Kipengere Range, Tanzam Highway, Makambako, Lindi)

---

day in a private four-wheel-drive in the dry season. About 22km (14 miles) out of Mbeya, the **World's End Viewpoint** affords expansive views over the arid Usungu Flats.

A longer, more southerly road back to Mbeya runs through Makongolosi and Saza to Mbalizi on the Tanzam Highway. About 5km (3 miles) east of this road, near Kanga, **Lake Magadi** is often rose-tinted with flamingos between July and October. The **Galula Mission**, around 8km (5 miles) past Kanga, has a curious wooden church built in the 1920s.

LAKE RUKWA

The roads around Chunya offer views across **Lake Rukwa ❸**, a vast alkaline sump set in an inhospitable arm of the Rift Valley, all but bereft of human habitation. The Rukwa Floodplain supports plentiful game, including the localised puku antelope and high densities of hippos and crocodiles, as well as incredible concentrations of water birds.

Rukwa is a genuine wilderness, and any expedition there should be self-sufficient in spare vehicle parts, fuel, food, drinking water and camping equipment. From Chunya, a two-hour drive northwest through Saza and Mbangala leads to the fluctuating lake shore, as does a rough track from Galula Mission to Totoe. A third approach crosses the Ufipa Plateau west of Sumbawanga (on the Tunduma–Mpanda road).

AROUND SONGWE

From Mbeya, follow the Tanzam Highway west for 25km (16 miles) to **Songwe** township, then turn left through a limestone quarry dotted with local kilns. After 10km (6 miles), you will arrive at the pink-marble quarry that houses the **Songwe Caves and Hot Springs ❹**. Eroded into a limestone cliff, the caves harbour a colony of six bat species, which stream spectacularly out of the entrance at dusk.

Further west along the Tanzam Highway, a right turn 30km (18 miles) ast Songwe leads to the **Mbozi Meteorite ⑤**, a 12-tonne block of dense nickel-iron alloy listed as the eighth-largest celestial body ever found on the earth's surface.

KITULO NATIONAL PARK

From Chimala, a small town straddling the Tanzam Highway 78km (48 miles) east of Mbeya, a thrillingly scenic southbound dirt road navigates 57 hairpin bends en route to Matamba, gateway town to the 1,300-sq-km (502-sq-mile) **Kitulo National Park ⑥**. Locals refer to Kitulo as Bustani ya Mungu (God's Garden), an apt name for what is the first national park in East Africa gazetted primarily for its floral wealth. The plateau is best visited between November and May, when the rains transform the grassland into a dazzling floral kaleidoscope. Bright-orange red-hot pokers reach skyward from the crags above a carpet of multi-hued lilies, asters, geraniums and orchids punctuated by otherworldly giant lobelias and pretty protea shrubs. Large mammals are scarce, but blue swallow, Denham's bustard and mountain marsh widow top a long list of endangered or localised birds. The Kitulo plateau is most easily visited in a four-wheel-drive from Chimala, but a second, rougher approach road from Isongole (in the Poroto Mountains) is possible.

THE POROTO MOUNTAINS

A nippy, surfaced 140km (87-mile) road runs southeast from Mbeya to Kyela (near Lake Nyasa), passing for most of its length through the scenic **Poroto Mountains**. The highlight of the Poroto region is **Ngosi Crater Lake ⑦**, brooding at the base of a 300-metre (980ft) deep volcanic caldera. The turn-off to Ngosi is signposted from **Isongole** on the main Mbeya–Kyela road. You can drive the first 5km (3 miles) from the junction, but the final two-hour ascent to the crater rim is on foot only.

Towering over the northern horizon of Isongole, the 2,960-metre (9,711ft) **Mount Rungwe ⑧** is a volcano that last erupted in around 1800, though a spate

Sukuma herdsman in the Rukwa Region.

of 30-odd earthquakes in the vicinity since 2009 suggests that further seismic activity is likely. Rungwe's uninhabited higher slopes, protected within a forest reserve, are home to several monkey species (see box) as well as the rare Abbott's duiker, while the higher moorland is dotted with colourful ground orchids and protea scrubs. During the dry season, a reasonably fit person should be able to climb to the peak and back within a day. The easiest ascent is from Kagera Estate Timber Camp, on the northern foothills 18km (11 miles) by road from Isongole.

THE BRIDGE OF GOD

Midway between Mbeya and Kyela, the main surfaced road snakes through **Tukuyu** ❾, an attractive small town founded in the southern foothills of Mount Rungwe during the German colonial era.

From Tukuyu, follow the Mbeya road for 6km (4 miles) to Kyimo, then turn left. After 10km (6 miles), you'll reach the remarkable **Daraja la Mungu** ❿ (Bridge of God), a solidified lava flow

The Bridge of God.

spanning the Kiwira River to form a natural bridge wide enough to walk across. The nearby **Kijungu Boiling Pot** consists of a small waterfall that tumbles into a circular pothole before flowing under another small natural bridge. Further down river, the 20-metre (66ft) high **Kaporogwe Falls** plunge over a basalt ledge into the **Kiwira Gorge**. To get there, follow the Kyela road south from Tukuyu for 5km (3 miles), then turn right onto a track signposted for the Lutengano Moravian Centre.

South of Tukuyu, an alternative route to the surfaced Kyela road is the well-maintained dirt road to Ipinda. Both roads wind in a leisurely fashion through fertile green hills dotted with the tidy Nyakyusa homesteads that the 19th-century explorer Joseph Thomson called 'perfect Arcadia', the charming views enhanced by tantalising glimpses of Lake Nyasa in the Rift Valley below. Some 19km (12 miles) out of Tukuyu, the Ipinda road skirts **Masoko** ⓫, a pretty market village perched above a deep, green crater lake. This, incongruously enough, was a German military

base in World War I. The stone court-house on the crater rim started life as a garrison, while the occasional old coin that washes up on the shore helps fuel a rumour that a stash of German gold and other valuables was dumped into the lake when defeat became inevitable.

LAKE NYASA

The climatic contrast between the breezy Poroto highlands and **Lake Nyasa** ⑫, set at 437 metres (1,434ft) in the Rift Valley floor, could hardly be more dramatic. Nor, for that matter, could Lake Nyasa itself.

Known as Lake Malawi south of the Malawian border, Nyasa runs for 585km (364 miles) through a stretch of the Rift Valley hemmed in by a sheer escarpment rising sharply from the shore. The lake's trademark sandy beaches, studded with giant baobabs and whispering palms, resonate with the high eerie cry of the fish eagle, while the startlingly clear tur-quoise water supports the world's great-est diversity of freshwater fish.

Many seasoned African travellers regard Nyasa to be the most beautiful lake on the continent, but no such eulo-gies have ever been directed at **Kyela** ⑬, a substantial but overwhelmingly scruffy town, 10km (6 miles) from the lake shore at the southern terminus of the surfaced road from Mbeya. From Kyela, a 15km (9-mile) road leads north to Ipinda, connecting with the back road from Tukuyu via Masoko, then after another 27km (17 miles) to **Matema Beach** ⑭ on the northern tip of Nyasa. Serviced by a handful of low-key beach lodges, Matema is the closest thing to a resort on this part of the lake, yet it retains a refreshingly unspoilt, rustic African character. To bask in the deliciously warm water that laps Matema Beach, gazing up at the Livingstone Mountains rising to 2,500 metres (8,202ft) within 4km (2 miles) of the shore, is bliss. And there's plenty in the area to occupy more energetic travellers.

Lyulilo, east of Matema, is the site of a famous Saturday pottery market, while the nearby **Pango Cave** was an important sacrificial site before the missionaries arrived. Thirty minutes from Matema by local canoe, the village

⊘ **Fact**

The Kisi women of Ikombe make their nationally renowned pots by hollowing out a ball of clay, then rotating it manually to smooth the edges, before applying a feldspar finish that gives the product a distinctive creamy hue. Attractive souvenirs, Kisi pots sell locally for a fraction of their price in the cities.

Matema village and traditional houses on the shore of Lake Nyasa.

of **Ikombe** is the main source of the region's distinctive pale Kisi pottery, sold at Lyulilo for distribution all around the country. A canoe is also the best way to reach the swampy **Lufirio River Mouth**, 3km (2 miles) west of Matema, which provides excellent viewing for birds, crocodiles and hippos.

THE INLAND NAVY

A ferry service circumnavigates the Tanzanian portion of Lake Nyasa once a week, departing from **Itungi Port** (near Kyela) on Thursday and returning on Sunday. Geared primarily towards locals, the Nyasa ferry makes few concessions to luxury, but it does provide a fabulous overview of the scenic northern lake shore, punctuated by regular stops at isolated ports where the ship is greeted by a rapturous fleet of local boats. **Liuli** ⑮, the penultimate stop, is dominated by an impressive rock formation from which its German name of Sphinxhafen was derived. Bizarrely, Liuli was the site of the first naval encounter of World War I. London's *The Times* proclaimed 'Naval Victory on Lake Nyasa', rather overstating the more farcical reality. Captain Rhoades took the only British ship on the lake to fire on the only German ship while it was in dry dock. The German captain, a long-time drinking buddy of Rhoades, rowed out in a dinghy to leap on board the British ship and berate his old pal, only to find himself a prisoner of war – a war that he was unaware had been declared.

The ferry service terminates at **Mbamba Bay** ⑯, a pleasant lake-shore port on a palm-lined beach near the Mozambique border, and ideally positioned to catch the legendary sunsets over the lake.

Aside from the ferry, the only escape route from Mbamba Bay is a scenic 170km (106-mile) road that winds treacherously uphill to **Songea**, a large town notable for its small museum (daily 9.30am–6.30pm), dedicated to the Maji Maji Rebellion. From Songea, a superb surfaced road runs for 350km (217 miles) – passing through the undistinguished highland town of **Njombe** – to Makambako, at the junction of the Tanzam Highway.

The shore of Lake Nyasa.

🔍 THE TAZARA RAILWAY

Built by the Chinese during the socialist 1970s, this railway stretches from Dar es Salaam to central Zambia through the remote wilderness of southern Tanzania.

It must be the cheapest and most comfortable game drive in all of Africa. Snaking through mountains, over rivers and stretching out over the savannahs of Tanzania and Zambia, the TAZARA rail line takes in rugged terrain, rural villages and passes through the heart of the Selous Game Reserve. Giraffe run alongside the carriages, hyenas drink from nearby waterholes and elephants wander happily along the track.

First-class passengers are treated to comfy beds, an adequate bar and a waiter who brings breakfast, lunch and dinner to your cabin during the 40-hour trip between Dar es Salaam and New Kapiri Mposhi. The view is fantastic and the ride relaxed, but the roots of this line lay in much higher hopes.

After the Rhodesian Unilateral Declaration of Independence in 1965, landlocked Zambia found itself in a potentially desperate position, totally reliant on getting its copper out to the sea. The only available route was through white-dominated Rhodesia and South Africa. Presidents Kaunda of Zambia and Nyerere of Tanzania, both key players in the nationalist movements, acted quickly and began making plans to construct the TAZARA rail line.

This umbilical cord linking the newly emergent black nations would allow Zambia access to the Indian Ocean, and breathe life into Tanzania's southwest corridor, an area rich in agricultural and mineral potential but isolated from the country's main cities.

Such potential needed heavy funding. China, one of socialist Tanzania's closest allies, donated US$400 million, as well as expertise and equipment, to assist in building the lines. With more than 100 bridges and two dozen tunnels needed, it was no small task.

In 1967, the surveys began along the 1,860km (1,160-mile) line. Construction started in 1970. The line was inaugurated only six years later, in July 1976.

Though passenger trains were part of the proposed service, its prime purpose was for freight, hauling copper from the mines in northern Zambia and returning to Dar with fuel, fertiliser and goods. Only in 1986 did the line report an operating profit.

While for several decades the future of this train service looked uncertain, recent years have witnessed an increase in both freight and passenger traffic. There are currently two scheduled departures from Dar es Salaam every week (Tuesday and Friday), but note that trains do not always run on time and are sometimes delayed for several hours. There are sleeping cars (1st and 2nd class) and a restaurant car on each train. Tickets can't be bought online, only over the phone (tel: 255 22 26 2191) or at the Dar es Salaam railway station. For timetables and fares, visit www.tazarasite.com or www.seat61.com. Also see page 243.

The communities living along the railway line have become dependent on the train for their livelihoods. Farmers sell their goods at the stations and passengers spend valuable currency. Local tradesmen rely on it to transport their goods to the major cities.

The TAZARA rail line offers some splendid views across varied scenery.

The design of the Swahili dhows is little changed since ancient times.

THE SOUTH COAST

The journey to the south coast is not easy, but it's worth the effort in order to explore an enchanting area that encapsulates the traditional Swahili lifestyle.

With its sticky tropical ambience and generous quota of postcard-perfect beaches and atmospherically time-worn ports, the 600km (370-mile) coastline that stretches from Dar es Salaam south to the Mozambican border shares most of the elements that have made Zanzibar such a popular post-safari chill-out destination. What it lacks, however, is a tourist infrastructure comparable to Zanzibar's.

True, the main coastal road has improved greatly in recent years, but many side roads are bumpy dust-bowls that transform into impassable quagmires at the height of the rains. What's more, aside from Mafia Island (which has few travel links to the facing mainland) there are just a handful of hotels along the entire south coast that loosely conform to the description 'idyllic beach resort'. Indeed – while certain areas are beginning to open up – as a whole, the region is not much better suited to package holidays than it would be to dedicated ski parties!

Nevertheless, this remote part of Tanzania has much to recommend it to travellers seeking genuine insight into Swahili culture past and present. It is not merely that the area's assortment of ruined and living settlements provides a cross-section of coastal trade and history over the past millennium. There is, too, a pervasive aura of

cultural continuity hanging over this forgotten corner of Tanzania, the feeling that while its front foot stretches gamely towards the future, the other one remains firmly planted at the cusp of the 19th and 20th centuries.

KILWA

The south coast has not always been the backwater it is today. Exhibit one for the defence, and unquestionably the region's one 'must-see' attraction, is the extensive, ruined medieval port of **Kilwa**, described in 1331 by

Map on page 210

Main Attractions
Kilwa Kisiwani
Kilwa Kivinje
Mikindani
Mafia Island

Aerial view of the fort on Kilwa Kisiwani.

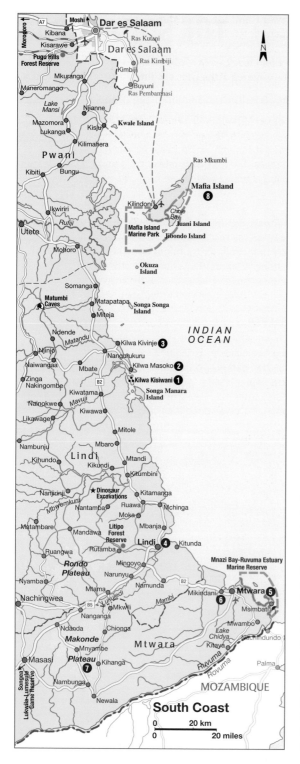

the insatiable Arab sightseer Ibn Buttata as 'one of the most beautiful and well-constructed towns in the world'. For three bountiful centuries before the arrival of the Portuguese, Kilwa was the greatest trade emporium on the coast south of Mogadishu, the site of the first coin mint in sub-equatorial Africa, as well as of a clutch of buildings that stand at the pinnacle of Swahili architectural achievement. Every year, at the peak of the monsoon winds, the island's small harbour bustled with commercial activity, as fleets of ocean-going dhows sailed from the sultanates of Arabia and great empires of Asia to purchase or barter for Kilwa's legendary stockpiles of gold, sourced from Great Zimbabwe.

The ruins of Kilwa lie on **Kilwa Kisiwani ❶** (Kilwa on the Island), divided by a narrow estuarine channel from the rather nondescript mainland port of **Kilwa Masoko ❷** (Kilwa Market). Connected to Dar es Salaam by occasional flights and an adequate 300km (180-mile) road, Kilwa Masoko is dotted with a few comfortable (through far from luxurious) beach hotels and numerous guesthouses. The opening of a local tourist information office on the market square in 2015 is the most visible sign that tourism is being taken seriously by local authorities, who are making great efforts to promote the district's cultural heritage and natural sites.

For tickets to visit the island, visit the Department of Antiquities office in the administrative buildings. The dhow trip across the channel can take anything from 10 to 45 minutes, depending on the prevailing winds and currents; allocate at least half a day for the expedition.

The shoreward side of Kilwa Kisiwani is dominated by an imposing, partially collapsed fort known locally as the **Gereza**, built around 1800 during a brief Omani occupation of the island, and entered via imposing wooden

Zanzibar doors. A short footpath leads uphill past the fort, through a cheerful fishing village, to the abandoned medieval trading centre, studded by semi-collapsed mosques and palaces, as well as the ornately carved tombs of a succession of powerful sultans.

The singularly lovely **Great Mosque** is the most inspired Swahili building of the medieval period. Its exquisite domed roof, supported by bays of precisely hewn arches, remains largely intact a full seven centuries after it was constructed. Ten minutes' walk east of the main ruins, on a rise overlooking the beach, stands the **Husuni Kubwa**, the isolated and ostentatious palace – complete with sunken audience court and swimming pool – where the Sultan of Kilwa played host to Ibn Buttata in 1311.

KILWA KIVINJE

Kilwa's decline, precipitated by a Portuguese naval bombardment in 1505, was sealed 50 years later when the cannibalistic Zimba raided the island and corralled its 3,000 residents to devour at their leisure. The area enjoyed a revival in the early 19th century, with the arrival of a group of Omani settlers who stayed briefly on the island before founding the mainland port of **Kilwa Kivinje** ❸ (Kilwa beneath the Casuarina Trees); this was the terminus of the slave caravan route to the Lake Nyasa hinterland.

During the 20th century, Kilwa Kivinje degenerated into a fascinating time warp of alleys lined with decaying balconied Omani mansions, leading to a mangrove-lined waterfront dominated by the hulk of a disused German boma (colonial office). Spend time in Kilwa Kivinje, and its fading architectural grandeur starts to feels curiously anomalous – as if the Omani ghost town had been superimposed on a randomly selected overgrown fishing village. Decidedly strange but satisfyingly authentic, Kilwa Kivinje will

reward any traveller who wishes to spend a few days absorbing the slow pace of a traditional Swahili settlement – ruled today, as in medieval times, by the vagaries of the tides and the winds.

LINDI

Some 230km (140 miles) south of Kilwa, **Lindi** ❹ is the most substantial settlement on the coast between Dar es Salaam and Mtwara. Lindi was founded on the north bank of the Lukuledi River Estuary at about the same time as Kilwa Kivinje, but it was not an especially significant port during the Omani era, and the only major structure dating from this time is a tall stone jail near the seafront. The gridlike layout and architectural style of the run-down town centre speak of a degree of prosperity during the early colonial period, evidently curtailed by the emergence of Mtwara as the main regional harbour in the 1950s.

Immediately north of the centre, a curving, sandy beach runs into a busy, traditional dhow harbour. Regular motorised ferries run across

Interior of the 14th-century Great Mosque, Kilwa Kisiwani.

the estuary to the fishing village of **Kitunda**. Local fishing boats can be rented to explore the estuary upstream or to visit the fruit-bat colony on the offshore **Bat Island**. Further afield, some 30km (19 miles) east of Lindi and accessible by dirt road, the **Litipo Forest Reserve** shelters a rich variety of birds of the coastal forest biome, while a trio of lakes bordering the reserve harbour a few hippos and are sporadically visited by elephants.

MTWARA AND SURROUNDS

Linked to Lindi by a blissfully smooth stretch of tarmac, **Mtwara** ❺ is a substantial harbour town of 135,000 residents, situated 20km (12 miles) north of the Mozambique border. It was founded in 1947, when its deep-water harbour was developed to service the disastrously misconceived post-war Groundnut Scheme (see page 53). As a consequence, Mtwara has never really grown to flesh out its ambitious skeleton. The nominal town centre, main market area, residential suburbs and harbour are all divided from each

other by open fields. The town is not overly endowed with character, but the lovely beach, friendly atmosphere and adequate facilities ensure that it's an agreeable place to break your journey.

Straddling the Lindi road 10km (6 miles) north of Mtwara, the tiny village of **Mikindani** ❻ is where David Livingstone set off on his final expedition into the African interior. A plaque commemorating Livingstone's 'reputed dwelling place' is nailed to the wall of a balconied two-storey house which, while rather picturesque, has several architectural quirks suggesting it was constructed nearly a century after the explorer's death. However, Mikindani does have several genuinely interesting German- and Omani-era relics, most impressively the fortified 19th-century **German Boma**, immaculately restored to its whitewashed pomp by the British charity Trade Aid in 1998, and now a hotel.

Committed to opening up the far southeast to all levels of tourism, Trade Aid (www.tradeaiduk.org) can also arrange trips to (or advise independent travellers about) several obscure

Untouched nature at Mafia Island.

⊙ MAKONDE CARVINGS

The Makonde, whose homeland straddles the eastern border of Mozambique and Tanzania, have a matrilineal society unusual for this part of Africa. They are best known for their carvings, which are traditionally sculpted by men only, and relate to a complex ancestral cult of womanhood.

Makonde sculptures achieved renown in the 1950s after a carving workshop was founded in Dar es Salaam. The genre has expanded to include complex sculptures embracing several human figures and symbolising abstract concepts such as *Ujamaa* (national unity) and good and evil.

In Dar es Salaam, which is now the main centre of commercial carving, outstanding works sell for high prices to collectors. It is harder to visit traditional carvers on the Makonde Plateau in situ without good local contacts.

but rewarding local attractions, including the forested **Rondo Plateau**, the superb **Msimbati Beach**, the **Lukwika-Lumesule Game Reserve** and crocodile-infested **Lake Chidya**.

Inland of Mtwara, the **Makonde Plateau 7** is home to the most celebrated traditional sculptors in East Africa. The main town of the Makonde is **Masasi**, situated at the base of the plateau among tall granite outcrops reminiscent of parts of Zimbabwe. The breezy highland town of **Newala** is distinguished by a stirring sweeping view across the Ruvuma River. It is also the last – or first – Tanzanian town passed through by travellers crossing to or from Mozambique via the Unity Bridge, which spans the Ruvuma River and opened in 2010.

THE MAFIA ARCHIPELAGO

Linked to Dar es Salaam by regular flights, Mafia is more realistically viewed as a stand-alone upmarket destination than as an extension of the south coast's rough-and-ready travel circuit. The archipelago, which lies some 20km (12 miles) east of the Rufiji River Delta, is comprised of the 50km (30-mile) long **Mafia Island 8** as well as a dozen smaller islets and numerous coral outcrops. The only settlement of any substance is **Kilindoni**, the main port on Mafia Island, and site of its only airstrip. Elsewhere, the isles are scattered with rustic fishing villages, while a cluster of top-notch and very exclusive lodges lies along **Chole Bay**, 12km (7 miles) by road from Kilindoni.

Mafia is East Africa's premier diving, snorkelling and game-fishing venue. The extensive offshore reefs, protected within an 820-sq-km (317-sq-mile) **marine park**, are comprised of 50 genera of coral and harbour some 400 species of fish. Recommended for their colourful coral formations and kaleidoscopic shoals of small reef fish are the **Kinasi Wall** and adjoining **Chole Wall**, near the outlet of Chole Bay, while a

12-metre (40ft) coral pinnacle within the bay is a reliable place for sighting giant cod and moray eels. Further afield, sharks and giant tuna haunt the **Dindini North Wall** and **Forbes Bay** on the main barrier reef. Snorkellers are also well catered for: the two larger coral islets in Kinasi Pass host a volume and variety of reef fish that compares favourably with any site in East Africa.

Nor does Mafia lack historical interest. A short dhow trip across Chole Bay leads to **Chole Mjini** (Chole Town), where a stand of ancient baobabs houses the disintegrating walls of several 19th-century mansions, built by wealthy Omani merchants who held slave plantations on the main island (then known as Chole Shamba – Chole Farm). Further afield, on **Juani Island**, the ruined city of **Kua** was founded at about the same time as Kilwa, and is one of the few medieval ports in East Africa to have been inhabited continuously into the 19th century. Nearby **Jipondo Island** is an important traditional shipbuilding centre, where dhows are constructed using traditional tools.

A dhow glides elegantly along the coast.

Mafia Island lighthouse.

ZANZIBAR AND PEMBA

These legendary spice islands still exude an air of mystery and romance that have made them one of the world's favourite honeymoon destinations.

Mention that you are going to Zanzibar and the response will be one of two things: 'Oh, is it a real place, then? Where is it?' or, just as frequently, 'You'll love it, I went there for my honeymoon.' Go into almost any resort hotel along the east coast and you'll find the lovebirds lined up two by two, arms entwined, around the bar or pool, champagne at the ready. If you have the temerity not to be on your honeymoon, you will probably give up and get married along the way, so relentless are the congratulations. It is funny, but you can see why it is so popular – a perfect blend of African charm, Middle Eastern exoticism, picture-perfect beaches, romantic hotels and a sophisticated range of activities, from spice tours to diving. The weather may get slightly warmer or wetter at some times of year, but is basically good all year round. And it is all within easy reach of the Tanzanian mainland or Kenya, should you choose to tack on a safari.

As for the other question: it may be the stuff of legends, even featuring in the tales of Sinbad, but Zanzibar is very definitely real. 'Northerners' – including Mesopotamians, Phoenicians and Romans – were trading along this coast in Biblical times, and Zanzibar is first mentioned, as the Island of Menouthesias, in two landmark Greek documents: *The Periplus of the Erythraean Sea* (*c*.AD 60) and Ptolemy's *Geography* (*c*.AD 150). But it was the arrival of Islamic Arabs and Shirazi (Persian) settlers from the 8th century onwards that changed the face of the region for ever, with the evolution of the KiSwahili language and culture (see page 39). At its apogee in the mid-19th century, Zanzibar was the capital of the entire far-flung Omani Empire and one of the most important cities on the Indian Ocean.

⊙ Main Attractions
Zanzibar Stone Town
Maruhubi Palace
Chumbe Island
Jozani-Chwaka Bay National Park
Dolphin watching at Kizimkazi
Matemwe Beach
Ngezi Forest Reserve

Maps on pages 216, 218, 235

Old lighthouse on Nungwi beach.

Zanzibar

0   10 km
0   10 miles

RISE AND FALL OF A CITY-STATE

Today, Zanzibar is actually the name of an archipelago and semi-autonomous region of Tanzania comprising the two main islands of **Unguja** (usually just called Zanzibar) and **Pemba**, along with a host of smaller islands, some not much more than coral rocks.

Lying only 40km (29 miles) off the mainland, Unguja is about 100km (60 miles) long and 35km (22 miles) wide, while Pemba, 50km (30 miles) to the north, is roughly 70km (45 miles) by 20km (12 miles). The total population of the islands is approximately 1.3 million, of which more than 200,000 live in **Zanzibar City ❶** (usually called Stone Town) and just over 400,000 live on Pemba. The vast majority are Muslim.

After centuries of being batted backwards and forwards by the Arabs, Portuguese and British, in 1964 the locals revolted. Up to 20,000 people died and Sultan Jamshid fled to live the rest of his life in the UK, while many of the Arabs and Indians headed north to Oman, their property confiscated and their businesses nationalised. The new government, under Sheikh Abeid Amani Karume, signed an Act of Union with the mainland, creating modern Tanzania.

At best, it is an uneasy alliance. Having ruled the roost for hundreds of years, the Zanzibaris are uncomfortable about coming second to the mainlanders, and many still retain close ties to Oman. Elections are regularly marked by riots, intimidation and allegations of corruption. In May 2012, the usually peaceful island was rocked when demonstrators allegedly associated with an Islamic secessionist group clashed with police and burned down two churches.

The presidential elections in 2015 were again marred by fraud allegations, forcing a contentious re-run in March 2016. While the opposition boycotted the second vote, incumbent president Ali Mohamed Shein and his CCM (Chama Cha Mapinduzi) party were victorious.

Political tension continues to simmer, and despite Zanzibar's autonomy, many islanders still talk longingly of breaking away again as an independent state. It may yet happen.

STONE TOWN

Stone Town is the most common name for the old heart of Zanzibar City, which stands on a small triangular peninsula first settled by the Portuguese in 1560, although most of the buildings date from the mid-19th century.

Begin your city tour in the **Forodhani (People's) Gardens ❹**, which run along the seafront near the dhow harbour, beside several of Stone Town's most famous monuments. Make sure you come back here at sunset. As the sea turns to gold and billowing dhows creep back to the shore, people gather to watch the world go by, chat and enjoy the warm night air. Originally laid out in 1936 to celebrate the Silver Jubilee of Sultan Khalifa, the gardens underwent a US$2.2 million facelift in 2008, funded by the Aga Khan Historic Cities Programme.

Busy street in Stone Town.

> ⊙ Tip
>
> Stone Town covers a very small area and is best explored on foot. The narrow alleys protect you from the direct sun, but the heat and humidity can still be draining, so stop regularly to drink. If you want to go slowly, do the Creek Road section as a separate walk.

From the gardens, look across the road. To the right of the fort, the **NBC Bank Building** ❸ was once the home of Princess Salme (see page 220).

Tucked out of sight, about a block inland, is the Catholic **Cathedral of St Joseph** ❸ (Cathedral Street), built by missionaries in 1898; it was designed by the French architect M. Bérangier, who was also responsible for the Basilique de Notre Dame de la Garde in Marseille. Inside, it is decorated with tiles, murals and stained glass – none masterpieces, but the overall effect is colourful.

To the right again, **Kenyatta Road** ❸ is the town's main shopping street, while the building with the arch on the far right is the **Zanzibar Orphanage**.

THE ARAB FORT

Back on the seafront, the **Arab Fort** ❸ (daily 9am–10pm), known locally as Ngome Kongwe, is the town's oldest surviving building, built by Omani Arabs in 1698–1701 around the original Portuguese church (1598–1612). With thick coral rag walls, battlements and arrow slits, it is a formidable fortification, but has rarely been put to the test. Instead, over the years, it has done duty as the local prison, railway station (the gatehouse was demolished to allow trains access), tennis club and, today, a museum and cultural centre. Inside are some nice craft shops and a shady café, as well as an open-air theatre which hosts the ZIFF Festival of the Dhow Countries each July (www.ziff.

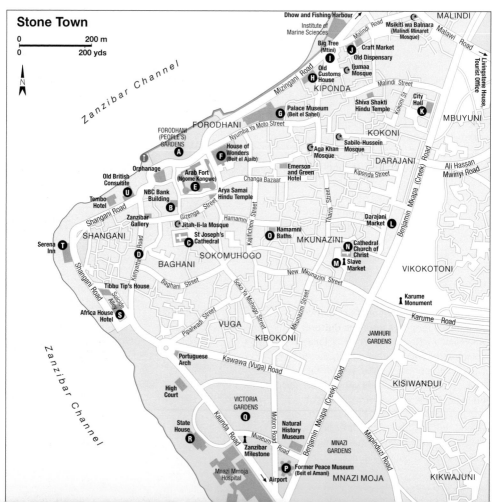

or.tz). On three evenings a week, there are lively cultural events, with dinner and traditional music and dance. There is also a tourist information desk inside the fort, but its opening hours are erratic and it has few resources to give out. The inconveniently located tourist office in Livingstone House (see page 223) is not much help either; however, visitors can find plenty of information about what's on offer from advertising or from their hotels.

THE ROYAL PALACES

Turn right as you leave the fort. Next door, the **House of Wonders ❻** (Beit el-Ajaib; officially closed for renovation, although guardians will let you in for a small fee) was built in 1883 by a British marine engineer for Sultan Barghash, on the site of a 17th-century palace built by Queen Fatima. Inside this huge four-storey structure, girdled by iron balconies, there are only a few cavernous rooms. It was designed purely for ceremonial purposes and was never intended to be a residence. The decoration is magnificent, from the marble floors to the ornate carving on the doors, but it gained its name from its dazzling technology. Not only was this the tallest building in sub-Saharan Africa, but the first to have electricity or a lift, while caged animals in the courtyard helped add spectacle for the people. The clock tower was added in 1896. The cannons at the entrance were captured from the Portuguese in 1622.

In 2005, following extensive renovations, the House of Wonders reopened as the Museum of History and Culture. However, in November 2012, a large corner of the House collapsed, along with its historic iron pillars, threatening the structural integrity of the building. Three years later the roof collapsed under heavy rain. Consequently, the House has been closed (officially at least), and much-delayed renovation works finally started in 2016. It is

possible to enter by paying a small fee, but we would advise against it given that the building is structurally unsafe.

In the late 19th century, the House of Wonders was one of three adjoining palaces connected by high-level walkways. The next along was the Beit el-Hukm (House of Government), and beyond that was the Beit el-Sahel (House of the Coast), built by Sultan Seyyid in about 1830. In 1896, there was an attempted coup, and both the Beit el-Hukm and Beit el-Sahel were destroyed by a British naval bombardment. The **Palace Museum ❼** (Beit el-Sahel; Mizingani Road; tel: 024 223 1158; Tue–Sat 10am–6pm) was built as a replacement, and remained the Sultan's official residence until 1911. It was renamed the 'People's Palace' after the revolution. Today, it is a museum, with an interesting collection of original furniture and costumes, and a room dedicated to Princess Salme (see box page 220), furnished according to her own detailed descriptions. There are plenty of guides in the foyer, if you would like a tour.

The House of Wonders, one of Stone Town's most impressive buildings.

MIZINGANI ROAD

As you continue along the road, a less than riveting collection of warehouses on your left marks the back of the modern dhow harbour and port, built on reclaimed land in 1925. Before they were built, this was prime real estate with many magnificent mansions and offices, most now sadly decaying. The old **Customs House ⊞** shows what can be achieved with some care, having been beautifully restored as a conservation centre by the Stone Town Conservation Authority. It has particularly fine doors with maritime decoration. A little further on is a giant banyan, planted in 1911 by Sultan Khalifa and known simply as the **Big Tree ❶** (Mtini). It is one of the best-known landmarks of the city and a popular meeting place for locals.

The **Old Dispensary ❶** (daily 9am–6pm; free), with its elaborate fretwork gingerbread decoration, rivals the House of Wonders. It was originally built in the 1890s by a local Ismaili Indian trader, Tharia Topan, who donated it to the city to be used as a cottage hospital and dispensary, a role it fulfilled until the 1970s. Restored by the Aga Khan Foundation, it is now grandly but erroneously called the Stone Town Cultural Centre. There is a café and a small exhibition space on the ground floor and a few shops upstairs. Next door you will find a **Craft Market** where you can watch Tingatinga painters and carvers at work. Prices are reasonable.

There is little more to see along Mizingani Road, so your best bet is to dive into the alleys away from the seafront. You will almost certainly get lost, but it really doesn't matter. Every new corner brings something interesting to look at, and the area is so small that it is impossible not to pop out eventually onto one of the main roads. **Hurumzi Street** and **Gizenga Street** are busy shopping thoroughfares which eventually lead back to Kenyatta Road. **Malindi Street** will take you inland to **Benjamin Mkapa Road**, better known to everyone as Creek Road.

CREEK ROAD

When the Portuguese arrived, the little peninsula was effectively an island, cut

Tingatinga painter at work in Stone Town.

off by Darajani Creek. Over the years this silted up, until eventually, in 1957, it was filled in to become Creek Road, a busy, broad road that marks the boundary between the historic and modern cities. Cross the great divide and you'll see a very different town, with housing from shanties to high-rise socialist blocks, all with a great deal of life and very little charm.

At the north end of Creek Road, the **City Hall (K)** belongs firmly to the British era, a flourish of neo-Gothic grandeur that would feel at home in Manchester. Head a few blocks south and you reach **Darajani Market (L)**, which has long since outgrown the market hall, built in 1904, to spread across the surrounding streets. There are few souvenirs on offer, although spices are well to the fore. Instead, take time to enjoy the vibrant colours, salesmen's patter and the extraordinary array of fruit, vegetables and fish on sale. You will be guaranteed to find things you have never seen before, such as Zanzibari apples.

THE SLAVE MARKET

A block south of the market, twice weekly public auctions (Wed and Sun) are held in the small park. Walk through this and you come to a far more chilling sales ground. Only a monument now marks the site of the infamous **Slave Market (M)**, founded in 1811 by Sultan Seyyid and eventually closed in 1873. At the height of the trade in the 1830s–50s, tens of thousands of people were sold (see page 43) to work on the plantations or for shipping to Oman.

In the basement of St Monica's Hostel next door, guides will take you on a harrowing tour through what are purported to be the slave storage chambers, although some maintain that it is far more likely to have been a bathhouse.

Next door is the Anglican **Cathedral Church of Christ (N)** (daily 8am–6pm, English mass Sun 8am), built in 1873

by Edward Steere, Bishop of Zanzibar from 1874 to 1882, and funded by the Universities' Mission in Central Africa. The altar stands on the same spot as the 'whipping tree', to which slaves were probably tied while being sold. The small wooden crucifix to the left of the altar is made from a tree in the village of Chitambo, where David Livingstone died and his heart was buried. There is also a stained-glass window dedicated to Livingstone, whose influence in abolishing the slave trade has earned him a special place in the hearts of the Zanzibari people. Other windows are dedicated to African saints. The mosaics on the altar were donated by Caroline Thackeray (see page 227).

Wriggle down through the alleys behind the cathedral to visit the **Hamamni Baths (O)**, the city's first public baths, commissioned by Sultan Barghash and designed by Persian architect Haju Ghulamhusain, who was also responsible for the Kidichi Baths (see page 225). Sultan Barghash, who ruled from 1870 to 1888,

The Old Dispensary borrowed its gingerbread architecture from 19th-century India.

The covered market hall in Stone Town was built in 1904.

was a great innovator and builder, responsible for the House of Wonders, for bringing piped clean water to all parts of the city, and for buying Zanzibar its own fleet of steamships, which were used during the Haj to carry the local faithful to Mecca, free of charge. In between, the money rolled in from their cargo routes.

THE BRITISH INFLUENCE

Alternatively, carry on south down Creek Road and turn right onto Museum Road to take a look at the remarkable **former Peace Museum ℗**. Built as a World War I memorial, the impressive domed building is modelled (in miniature) on the Ayghia Sophia in Istanbul and was designed by John Sinclair, an architect who worked in Zanzibar for 27 years and is responsible for many of the civic buildings of the British era.

Now walk down Museum Road. At the end, turn right onto Kaunda Road, the main road back to the town centre. On your right, the **Victoria Gardens ℚ** were created by Sultan Barghash for his harem, but given to the people by Sultan Seyyid Houmoud. Sir John Kirk (see page 223) transformed them into a botanical garden. At the centre, **Victoria Hall**, built over the harem baths, was the seat of the pre-independence Legislative Council. Nearby, look out for the green octagonal **milestone** showing distances all over the island – and to London (12,978km/8,064 miles, via the Suez Canal).

Opposite is the **State House ℝ** (no photographs allowed), now the official residence of the President of Zanzibar, but built in 1903 as the British Residency. Both this and the **High Court**, a little further along on the left, were built by John Sinclair. Just at the turning of Kenyatta Road and Shangani Street, an insignificant house on the right was once home to Zanzibar's most famous modern citizen, the late rock idol Freddie Mercury, lead singer of Queen, who was born here in 1946 as Farrokh Bulsara, son of a local accountant. His family came from Persia, via India. Turn down Shangani Street and, two blocks on, the **Africa House ℠** was once the British Club. Now a prestigious hotel, it has an airy balcony restaurant and bar offering one of the city's best sea views, especially at sunset.

Follow the road round and it passes two mansions, carefully restored into fine hotels, the Zanzibar **Serena Inn ⓣ** and **Tembo Hotel**. Just before you reach the archway underneath the orphanage (see page 218) is a mansion that served as the **British Consulate ⓤ** from 1841 to 1874. This was base camp for many of Africa's most famous expeditions, with Speke, Burton, Grant and Stanley all staying here; David Livingstone's body lay here for five days in 1874. After his death in Chitambo, his body was dried and his servants carried it for four months back to the coast and across to Zanzibar, from where it was sent back to England for final burial.

Tall houses line the narrow alleys of Stone Town.

AROUND UNGUJA ISLAND

It is possible to reach every part of Unguja Island on a day trip from Stone Town, but few choose to do so, preferring to match the historic charms of the city with the glories of the beaches. However, some excursions are best done before you leave the city. There are few decent roads on the island, and you may well find yourself having to come back into town anyway.

Just offshore are several small islands. **Changuu Island 2**, also known as Prison Island, was originally used as a lock-up for disobedient slaves by its Arab owner. It was bought in 1873 by General William Lloyd Matthews, a British officer who became Commander-in-Chief of Sultan Barghash's army, and was specifically charged with stopping the smuggling of slaves. Matthews built a house here, but in 1893 it became a prison, while in the 1920s it was used as a quarantine centre for immigrants from India.

The luxurious Changuu Private Island Paradise resort (www.privateislands-zanzibar.com) now occupies part of the island, but it is still possible to visit the colony of Aldabra giant tortoises, imported from the Seychelles in the 18th century. This is one of Zanzibar's most popular excursions. Nearby **Chapwani (Grave) Island 3** has a British cemetery dating back to 1879 and a pleasant swimming beach. **Bawe Island 4** is quiet and fringed by good swimming and snorkelling spots. Once completely uninhabited, it is now the site of the small Bawe Tropical Island resort (www.privateislands-zanzibar.com).

THE NORTHERN SUBURBS

About 2km (1 mile) north of Stone Town, look for a run-down mansion on the right. The **Livingstone House** (Bububu Road; tel: 024-223 3485) is now officially, but ineffectively, the city tourist office. However, it has a more illustrious past. Built in 1860 for Sultan Majid, it was used, like the British Consulate, by various explorers as a base camp, including Burton, Speke, Stanley and Livingstone; the latter lived here while preparing for his last big expedition in 1866.

A kilometre on, a small turning on the left leads to the **Maruhubi Palace 5** (open access, but there is an entrance charge), built by Sultan Barghash in 1882 as the home of his one official wife and 99 concubines. The walled complex, supposedly modelled on English country houses seen by the Sultan during his visit to Europe in 1875, was approached by an avenue of stately mango trees leading to a huge lily pond. Inside were several bathhouses, while stairs of black-and-white marble led to a broad balcony supported on giant pillars. Maruhubi was destroyed by a fire in 1899, but is still Zanzibar's most charming and atmospheric ruin.

The **Mtoni Palace 6** is easy to miss. A short way north of Maruhubi, look for the signpost to Mtoni Marine, a laid-back beach bar and pizza place that is popular with expats. The ruins are on

Sculpture of slaves chained in a pit.

🔍 SWAHILI ARCHITECTURE

Stone Town has a collection of around 2,000 historic buildings. Few of them date back further than the mid-19th century, but they represent one of the world's finest collections of Swahili architecture.

Stone Town's Swahili buildings represent a fascinating cultural marriage between Arab, African and Indian styles. Sadly, many are in a dire state of repair, although the Aga Khan Trust for Culture (www.akdn. org/AKTC) and the local conservation association have embarked on some serious restoration.

The narrow alleys, designed for shade in a time when donkeys were the only form of transport, are organised by quarters *(mitaa)*, usually named after a significant local landmark or the family by which they were founded. Each would have its complement

Doors in Zanzibar are traditionally intricately carved with geometric and delicate floral designs.

of coffee shops, stone benches, mosques and shops to cater for the social, spiritual and physical needs of the community. What can appear to be scruffy, vacant lots are frequently badly maintained grave-yards. Arabs began trading and settling along the coast in the 5th century AD. In Stone Town, however, the real creation of the city began in the 17th century. Some of its earliest settlers were from Hadhramaut in the Yemen, closely followed by other Swahili people from along the coast.

The typical Swahili mansion was plain on the outside, the status of the residents only displayed in the magnificently carved doors. In fact, the door was often bought first and the house built around it. Doors, centuries old, have been handed down through the generations. Typical designs included maritime themes, chains (to symbolise security), Quranic inscriptions and Indian-influenced lotus blossoms.

Inside, the entrance porch *(daka)*, where visitors were traditionally greeted and served coffee, led to a much more ornate courtyard, decorated with carved coral or stucco, surrounded by long, thin rooms. Many of the houses were linked by upper-storey galleries to allow the women to socialise in privacy.

Working-class houses were far more African in style, with wattle and daub used and a thatched roof overhanging a broad veranda, which often served as a shop. The courtyard of the more formal houses became a working yard shared by the whole family and their livestock.

The most significant period of building began when the capital of Oman was moved here in 1840. Many Omani houses were semi-fortified, with crenellated walls. The downstairs rooms became servants' quarters, while the family slept in the airier rooms above. A screen surrounded the public areas of the courtyard, shielding the women from public view.

The houses with outside verandas, many of them sporting intricate fretwork designs, were almost all the property of Indian merchants, who added the balconied upper storeys as living space over the simple Swahili shops. The rows of shuttered windows on the upper levels were designed to catch the breeze.

the beach nearby. This was the first of the Omani royal palaces, built by Seyyid Said, the Sultan who moved the imperial capital from Muscat to Zanzibar in 1840. It was a typical Omani complex, with a number of low, flat-roofed buildings housing up to 1,000 people, surrounding a large pool and courtyard. At one end stood a conical wooden tower, from where the Sultan could survey his fleet. Princess Salme grew up here and describes it in detail in her memoirs (see page 220). All that now remain are the main walls and the roof.

NORTH TO BUBUBU

If you head north from Zanzibar Town for about 10km (6 miles), you'll reach **Bububu** ❼. This little town has only one claim to fame, as the northern end of Zanzibar's only narrow-gauge railway (the southern terminus was the Old Fort in Stone Town), which operated for 24 years between 1904 and 1928.

Turn left by the police station for **Fuji Beach**, about 500 metres/yards from the main road and the nearest

good swimming beach to Stone Town. Turn right, and after about 2km (1 mile) you reach the row of spice stalls which mark the first stop on the spice tour. Take plenty of money for shopping; prices are significantly lower than in town, and the variety of spices on sale, from vanilla pods to cinnamon sticks and weird and wonderful blends for use in cooking, will be difficult to resist. Some of the plants, such as pineapple or ginger, are relatively easily recognised, but even the most insignificant-looking bush may prove to be a source of lipstick or the local headache cure. It would be easy to spend the whole day here. However, there are usually a couple of other stops to look at fruit and nut plantations and local sights of interest.

About 3km (2 miles) from the turn-off, the **Kidichi Baths** ❽ (open access, but there is an entrance charge) were built in 1850 by Sultan Seyyid Said for his Persian wife, Binte Irich Mirza (also called Sherezade). Each of the royal plantations had baths, so that visitors could refresh themselves

Cardamom is one of the spices grown on the island.

Maruhabi Palace, built by Sultan Barghash for his harem.

after a hot, dusty journey. These are the finest and most complete baths surviving on the island, with much of their elegant Persian-style stucco still intact. About 3km (2 miles) further on, the **Kizimbani Baths ❾** were built by the 19th-century merchant Saleh bin Haramil, the first man to plant cloves on the island.

Mangapwani Beach ❿ is about 11km (7 miles) north of Bububu, just off the main road. Many of the spice tours choose to make a day of it and bring their clients here for lunch at the open-air restaurant, run as a satellite of the Serena Inn in Stone Town, followed by an afternoon on the beach.

Those who still have the energy for sightseeing should visit the coral cavern, near the sea, and the slave chamber, about 2km (1 mile) further north. The official abolition of the slave trade in 1873 drove business underground. A local slaver, Mohammed bin Nassor al-Alwi, built these illegal holding pens and auction rooms, away from prying city eyes.

THE SOUTHERN SUBURBS

About 7km (4 miles) south of Zanzibar Town, near the airport, **Mbweni ⓫** is now the city's most exclusive residential suburb, full of grand mansions and millionaires. First settled by the Arabs in the 7th century, the Persians arrived in the 12th century and the Portuguese in the 16th and 17th. In 1871, Bishop Tozer bought the large house of a wealthy Arab family on behalf of the Universities' Mission to Central Africa, to set up an Anglican Mission and village for freed slaves.

The 60-hectare (150-acre) settlement included schools, houses, workshops, sugar, coconut and maize plantations, and had a population of around 250. The original house, with three additional wings added, was turned into St Mary's School for Girls, with between 60 and 85 pupils at any one time. They were taught a mix of academic, religious and practical skills, while less academic girls were given industrial skills that would ensure their future survival.

A ferry arriving at sunset.

Caroline Thackeray (the cousin of William Makepeace Thackeray, author of *Vanity Fair*) arrived in 1877, remaining as headmistress for 25 years. She stayed on the island until she died in 1926 at the age of 83, and is buried in the neighbouring oriental-looking **St John's Church**, built in 1874 by Bishop Tozer's successor, Bishop Steere, who also built the Anglican Cathedral in Stone Town (see page 221).

Although some descendants of the original freed slaves still live in the area, the school eventually closed in 1920 and the buildings sank into ruins, which now stand in the grounds of the Marriott Mbweni Ruins Hotel. Here, they welcome visitors both to the ruins and their fine botanical garden, containing 650 species of indigenous and exotic plants, including 120 types of palm. It is based on the magnificent botanical garden created by Sir John Kirk on land adjacent to the mission, sadly now overgrown and in private hands, so not open to the public. Easily explored along a short nature trail, the garden and adjacent shoreline attract over 60 species of bird.

CHUMBE ISLAND

The Mbweni Ruins Hotel is also where you catch the boat across to tiny **Chumbe Island** ⑫, about 8km (5 miles) offshore. Only about 3km (2 miles) long and 1.3km (0.25 miles) wide, Chumbe is Tanzania's first privately run marine park, guarding a 1.1km (half-mile) long reef containing an extraordinary 200 species of coral and 400 species of fish. Until the building of the eco-lodge which manages the reserve, the only buildings on the island were a ruined mosque and the lighthouse. The lodge is run on strict ecological principles, and the design of the basket-weave chalets is one of the most fascinating aspects of a visit. Tours include snorkelling, beach and forest walks, all led by trained naturalists. Look out for giant fossil clam shells and, more alarmingly, giant live coconut crabs. The only way to visit is as a guest of the lodge. It is not cheap, but profits go to

A Kirk's red colobus monkey, found only in Zanzibar's few remaining forests.

the upkeep of the reserve and a strong education and research programme, which includes free visits for local school children.

JOZANI FOREST

To reach the south and east of the island, take the main road east from Stone Town. About 21km (13 miles) from town, a small turning on the right signposts **Unguja Ukuu** ⓭, the oldest known settlement on the island, dating to the 8th century AD, and thought to have been founded by Swahili people fleeing from violence on the mainland. It was abandoned again in the 10th century. Only attempt to go there if you have plenty of time. The site is about 6km (4 miles) from the main road, but it seems far longer. The road winds through the villages, within touching distance of doors, gradually getting smaller until it virtually disappears. Once you get there, all you will find are a few bits of wall.

Back on the main road, another 11km (6-mile) drive leads you to the 50-sq-km (19-sq-mile) **Jozani-Chwaka**

Bay National Park ⓮ (daily 7.30am–5pm; forest paths closed in the rainy season), which was gazetted in 2004 mainly to protect the endemic Zanzibar red colobus monkey. Although Jozani is usually billed as the last remnant of indigenous forest on the island, once there, you discover that while some of it is original, much of it has actually been replanted – the land was a working timber plantation in the 1930s and 1940s. However, it doesn't really matter; it is still a magical place.

There is an excellent interpretation centre next to the car park, from where guides lead forest walks. In addition to the many trees, climbers and other plants, wildlife includes around 50 species of brightly coloured butterflies, over 40 species of bird, including the rare but spectacular Fischer's turaco, Sykes' (blue) monkeys, and small antelope such as the endangered Aders' duiker and suni. However, the undoubted stars of the show are the habituated Zanzibar red colobus monkeys, which often hang around in bright sunlight

Pupa in Jozani Forest.

ⵔ UNDER THREAT

First identified and catalogued by Sir John Kirk (see page 223), the Zanzibar red colobus *(Procolobus kirkii)* is one of Africa's prettiest primates, with its vivid chestnut coat, white shirtfront, bushy tail and Victorian whiskers. It is also one of the rarest, found only in Zanzibar, where it has evolved in isolation from other similar species since the late Pleistocene. Unlike most other monkeys, it and other colobus species have only four elongated fingers and no thumb. Uniquely among primates, colobus monkeys all have four stomachs, designed for digesting the tough leaves and unripe fruit on which they live.

The Zanzibar red colobus is a very social creature, living in forested areas in large troops of 30–50, led by one to four adult males. They live for about 20 years. Gestation takes six months, and females produce a baby every two years.

Their Swahili name, *'kima punju'*, means 'poison monkey', and the monkeys are associated with evil – which doesn't help their chances of survival.

The population of Zanzibar red colobus is estimated at between 1,500 and 3,000, of which about half live in the Jozani Forest, where several troops are used to human visitors. The monkeys are susceptible to human diseases, so anyone who has a cold is asked not to visit.

near the car park for maximum photographic impact. On the far side of the road, a 1km (half-mile) dirt track leads down to a mangrove swamp, laid out with boardwalks.

Just before you reach Jozani-Chwaka Bay National Park, you will find the **Zanzibar Butterfly Centre** ⑮ (ZBC; www.zanzibarbutterflies.com; daily 9am–5pm). The sanctuary includes a butterfly display and guided tours of the botanical garden, and aims to encourage the conservation and proliferation of butterfly species indigenous to the area and also protect the local environment. The ZBC works closely with the national park and NGOs to assist local development projects, particularly those that are involved in conservation and poverty alleviation.

ZALA PARK

The main road to the south of the island branches off just after Jozani Forest. The BP petrol station at the crossroads is the last you will meet if heading south or east, so take

advantage of it. A couple of kilometres south of the crossroads, on the right, look out for the easily missed sign for **Zala Park** ⑯ (daily 8.30am–5pm; donations), a scruffy-looking but fascinating community project started by a local teacher with a passion for science and biology. His main aim is to educate Zanzibari children about the island's wildlife and ecology, and to that end he has gathered a small collection of animals that are either endangered, seen as food, or feared through superstition. Among them are some tiny suni antelope (your best chance to see these shy forest dwellers); tortoises and terrapins; two dozen species of snake; chameleons, thought by locals to presage death if they drop on your head; land crabs, said to bring divorce with them into a house; and the plated lizard, whose bite can supposedly only be cured by sleeping with your sister! There is also a nature trail through the forest to a mangrove pool and a tour of the local village, which now owns the park.

Mangroves on the beach.

Thank the humble parrotfish for the magnificent sand. It chews up coral and expels it as a fine white powder.

A Savanna vine snake.

DOLPHINS

Head south and turn right at the T-junction for **Kizimkazi** ⑰ in the southwestern corner of the island, where children mob the tourists asking for pens, selling shells and trying to look winsome enough for handouts. They are undeniably cute, but it is sad to see them developing the pattern of expectation that is so far refreshingly absent elsewhere on the island. Their efforts are directed at the many tour groups now visiting the village to go **dolphin watching**. The coast around here has several caves that are favourite dolphin calving grounds, and some 100 bottlenose and 50 humpback dolphins have taken up permanent residence. Trips run year-round and visitors have an excellent chance of sighting pods of 20–30 animals.

There may be an opportunity to swim with the dolphins before the boats move to a nearby coral reef for snorkelling. These trips are very cheap if you hire your own boat locally; the price is doubled if you go on an organised excursion, although transport to Kizimkazi and lunch at one of the two simple restaurants which flank the bay will be thrown in. Some of these tours have a reputation for harassing the dolphins, so choose carefully.

Kizimkazi is also home to what is technically the oldest mosque on the island still in use. It was originally founded in 1107 by Sheikh Abu Mussa Al-Hassan bin Mohammed, but was virtually rebuilt in 1770. Inscriptions on either side of the mihrab mark the two dates. Among the surrounding graves are several said to belong to relatives of the Prophet, including the one-handed Sheikh Omar Ali and the one-legged Sayyid Abdallah Said bin Sharif. The mosque is extremely plain, looking more like a barn from the outside. Non-Muslims should enter only if invited.

MAKUNDUCHI

Return to the T-junction and take the other fork for **Makunduchi** ⑱, in the far southeastern corner of the island. This is one of the few major coastal villages virtually untouched by tourism, and a wonderful place to experience

true Zanzibari culture, with the women wading the shore, digging for crabs and octopus or using the coral rocks to husk coconuts. Along the roads you will see lines of women with bundles of wood on their heads, while the smaller side roads through the village offer an intimate glimpse of daily life in the small palm-thatched houses, many with surprisingly elegant carved doorways.

In July, during the Shirazi New Year, Makunduchi is the site of Zanzibar's most famous – and strangest – festival, **Mwaka Kogwa**, when the local men challenge past foes with banana leaves. The contestants then flail one another until hopefully they make amends. Meanwhile, the townswomen dance around the banana-beating men singing songs. A house of spirits is constructed and set on fire to burn away the misery of the previous year. The evening sees fewer banana beatings and plenty of drinking and dancing with new-found friends.

The road up the east coast is extremely poor, and it is better to retrace your route back through Jozani.

THE SOUTHEAST COAST

As you head across to the eastern half of the island, the landscape changes dramatically from the lush farmlands and woods of the west to dry, scrubby grassland that clings precariously to the coral rock. However, this is also where you will find all the best beaches – mile upon mile of powder-soft, snow-white sand, the shallow shelving water an almost surreally bright turquoise. Offshore, breaking waves mark the line of the coral reef, beyond which the water changes to a rich indigo. If you are very lucky and have a good pair of binoculars, you can watch the humpback whales spouting and breaching as they migrate.

Only one thing potentially mars the perfection – from mid-November through to mid-February, the prevailing winds can wash ashore huge quantities of sludgy brown seaweed, which disappears again with the start of the rainy season. Inevitably, anywhere this idyllic is resort-land, lined for much of its length by hotels to suit a variety of budgets, from small backpacker

⊙ Tip

While the British think of Zanzibar as a luxury holiday, the Italians regard it as a mass-market destination, and the island has several large, noisy young Italian resorts. If you are after peace and quiet, you need to check not only your own hotel, but also its neighbours.

Meeting the local children is always a pleasure.

guesthouses to upmarket hotels. Most offer, or will organise, tours to Stone Town and the spice plantations, snorkelling, diving and a range of water sports. The main road east from Jozani stops at the village of **Paje** , from where a slow, bumpy, crater-filled dirt road leads north and south along the coast. It is only about 12km (7 miles) from Paje to the tip of **Ras Michamvi**, but it takes over an hour to drive. Along the way, you pass a wide variety of resorts, including that famous honeymoon hotspot, **Breezes Beach Club** (www.breezes-zanzibar.com).

THE EAST COAST

There are no connecting roads between the southeast coast and the east coast, so once again, head back towards Stone Town, from where a road leads due east as far as **Chwaka** ⑳, a large attractive fishing village and former slaving town, with a lively fish market and one or two small guesthouses. Along the way, look out for the **Dunga Ruins** ㉑ (daily 8am–6pm), signposted off the road near Dunga village, 14km (9 miles) east of

Stone Town. Built by the Swahili *Mwinyi Mkuu*, King Mohammed, in 1846–56, the still-imposing walls are persistently rumoured to have had live slaves buried in the foundations, and human blood used to mix the mortar.

About 8km (5 miles) further on, near Jendele village, is the **Ufufuma Forest Habitat** ㉒ (mob: 0777-276620/491069; www.ufufuma.wordpress.com), a tiny remnant of indigenous forest with a good variety of birds and small animals, including Sykes' and red colobus monkeys. Also ask your guide to take you to the Shetani spirit caves, used by traditional healers.

The so-called road north along the coast from here is nigh on impassable, so return to Stone Town again and head north on the Bububu road. At **Selem**, the main road forks inland through **Mahonda** from where there is a turning east to **Kinyasini** and further on to **Kiwengwa** ㉓, a tiny village surrounded by a clump of resorts.

To reach the more northerly resorts, head north at Kinyasini to **Mkwajuni**, where a road to the east connects with

Handler holding a Southern African Rock Python.

the sandy track leading to **Matemwe** ㉔. This is perhaps the most enchanting of all the beaches on the Unguja coast, its white sand framed by jagged coral rocks, looking like mini-Himalayas. Seaweed-drying frames are strung between whispering coconut palms, and children play happily between the blindingly white coral-rag houses and the outriggers of the beached canoes. There are several places to stay nearby.

About 5km (3 miles) offshore, **Mnemba Island** ㉕, run as a private marine sanctuary by &Beyond Mnemba Island is a picture-perfect tropical island with superb diving and snorkelling (see page 236).

THE NORTH COAST

At the far northern tip of Zanzibar Island, **Nungwi** ㉖ and **Kendwa** feel like real backpacker destinations, with small guesthouses scattered among the villagers' homes. Foreign children play happily alongside the locals, while the beach rings to the sound of sawing and the thunk of hammer on wood as the dhow-builders work in the shade of the coconut palms. To get there, head north on the main road from Mkwajuni. There are several large resorts in the area. The only 'sight' is the **Mnarani Natural Aquarium** (www.mnarani.org), where green, loggerhead and leatherback turtles are bred in a natural lagoon for eventual release back into the wild.

PEMBA

Pemba, 80km (50 miles) northeast of Unguja, is the place for those looking to get away from it all. For the moment, the island has only a couple of small upmarket hotels and a handful of guesthouses catering to hard-core dive enthusiasts. Savour it while you can.

Physically, the island is built of rock, not coral, so is far hillier and more densely forested than Unguja, with peaks rising to 1,000 metres (3,280ft). It is also much poorer: its people survive on a meagre diet of cassava, rice, fish, tomatoes and onions and earn their living almost entirely on farming and fishing. Around 80 percent of Tanzania's cloves are grown here; the

Matemwe Beach is one of the finest on Unguja island.

⊘ DOLPHINS

The most common marine mammal off the coast of East Africa is the Indo-Pacific bottlenose dolphin *(Tursiops aduncus)*, which is typically around 2.8 metres (13ft) in length and weighs up to 250kg (550lbs). It gets its name from its bottle-shaped beak; other distinguishing features are a dark 'cape' over its back and a slightly hooked dorsal fin. It feeds on fish and squid, usually catching them near the surface. It is a very social animal, found in pods of between 10 and 100 in the sea around Zanzibar. A powerful, acrobatic swimmer, it is often seen bow-riding and leaping alongside vessels. In Kizimkazi, it might be seen alongside the Indian Ocean humpback dolphin *(Sousa plumbea)*, a smaller species (1.8–2.4 metres/6–8ft) with a distinctive dorsal hump.

roads are lined by drying mats, and the air is heavily scented with their delicious aroma.

Many people work far away, in Dar or even Oman, while back at home society is polarised, with the north largely Arab and the south mainly African. Politically, the island is extremely active – many of the riots surrounding the 2012 elections happened here, and there is a strong movement to disassociate from the mainland. However, within the local community Islam and Christianity live comfortably side by side, also rubbing along astonishingly well with the island's third great tradition. Pemba is reputed to be one of the great witchcraft centres of the world. Few will talk about it, but the tradition lives on, with voodoo practitioners visiting from as far afield as West Africa and South America.

CHAKE CHAKE

There really is very little for visitors to see here. The capital and home of the airport is **Chake Chake** ㉗, roughly halfway up the island, on the west coast. It is as old as Stone Town, but remained a backwater under the Omanis and has few historic buildings, other than a less than exciting fort. However, it is a pleasant place, with a lively market, and there are several ruins close to the town.

The **Pujini Ruins** ㉘, 10km (6 miles) to the southeast, consist of a few scattered remains of a 14th-century town, including part of the ramparts, a few houses and a mosque, purportedly built by a local tyrant, Mohammed bin Abdul Rahman, known as the *Mkame Ndume* (Milker of Men) because of his harsh treatment of his subjects.

At the 11th-century Swahili city of **Ras Mkumbuu** ㉙, 20km (12 miles) west and most easily reached by boat, are a mosque, some houses and pillar tombs. This was one of the most important towns in East Africa in its heyday.

TO THE SOUTH AND NORTH

Mkoani ㉚, 38km (24 miles) south of Chake Chake, is the island's main ferry port. Across the bay, reached by boat,

Seaweed farming in the Indian Ocean, Paje.

a remote and exclusive resort called **Fundu Lagoon** (www.fundulagoon.com) is set on the picture-perfect white sand of Wambaa Beach.

Wete ③, 30km (19 miles) north of Chake Chake, has some fine colonial architecture, but is most interesting during the clove season, when the local port is busy with big ocean-going dhows.

Head north for a further 20km (12 miles) to the **Kigomasha Peninsula** to find Pemba's finest onshore attraction, the **Ngezi Forest Reserve** ③ (daily 8am–4pm). There is a network of footpaths across the reserve, a 1,500-hectare (3,700-acre) remnant of primeval rainforest, mangrove swamp and coral scrub, offering the opportunity to see a fascinating variety of endemic species, including the Pemba green pigeon, Pemba scops owl and Pemba flying fox (a large fruit-eating bat that came close to extinction between 1996 and 2003, but now numbers around 20,000 in the forest). Also present is a small population of Zanzibar red colobus,

which were introduced from the neighbouring island in the 1970s. There are a couple of fine beaches, at **Vumawimbi**, on the east coast, and **Verani**, on the west coast.

The main reasons people come here are offshore. Much of the coast is lined by mangrove swamps, with relatively few sandy beaches to rival Zanzibar. However, the island is virtually surrounded by magnificent coral reefs, which provide some of the finest dive sites in Africa. **Misali Island ③**, off the west coast and easily reached from Chake Chake or Mkoani, is a tiny place (only 1km by 500 metres/1,100 by 550 yards), ringed by coral and protected as a marine reserve.

It has superb diving and snorkelling (see page 237), while onshore are fine beaches, some set aside as turtle breeding grounds, and forest and mangrove swamps which support a rich array of birdlife. Captain Kidd is rumoured to have used it as a hideout in the 17th century, but it is now the site of the exclusive Pemba Misali Sunset Beach Resort.

Diver in a shoal of glassfish.

CORAL DIVING

Tanzania's coral gardens offer some of the world's most rewarding diving, with hundreds of species of colourful reef fish living alongside marine turtles, rays and eels.

Before your depth gauge even starts to register, you feel the current pulling you towards the mainland. Descend to 25 metres (82ft), adjust your buoyancy and you're off, sweeping along the huge reef wall with the deep blue of the open ocean on your left. Navigating video-game style, you steer around the obstacles where the reef juts out, spot the eagle rays and turtles as they glide the other way, take time to inspect the caves and holes with their morays and lion fish, before being spat out into the washing machine which spins you around as you try to take hold for some decompression time. This is

Exploring the underwater delights of Pemba.

Deep Freeze, drift diving at its best, catching the incoming tide through the gap between Uvinje and Fundo Islands on the west coast of Pemba.

On a good day, you can see the sandy ocean floor 70 metres (230ft) below. The Zanzibar archipelago and Mafia Island, to the south, have an excellent combination of shallow water reefs for less experienced divers and high walls and deep channels for the more adventurous. Both the soft and hard corals are in relatively prime condition, despite El Niño, and the variety of reef fish and larger pelagics is as good as anywhere. You won't encounter as many of the glorious colours of the Red Sea or the Barrier Reef, but you won't find hordes of other dive boats either. In Pemba and Mafia, you will have the site to yourselves. You won't find many sharks, but large rays, turtles, whale sharks and whales are wonderful compensations.

ZANZIBAR ISLAND

Zanzibar Island (Unguja) is the largest of the islands but has the least impressive diving. Two main areas are worth consideration. There are four or five smallish reefs about 30 minutes from Stone Town where the coral is in good condition but marine life is limited. With nothing deeper than 20 metres (66ft) and often nothing bigger than a parrotfish, they are fine for a warm-up dive. The highlight is a wreck, thought to be the *Pegasus*, which lies 40 metres (131ft) down, a 15-minute speedboat ride from town. No coral has developed, but there are huge shoals of barracuda and jacks, and what remains of the deck is littered with lionfish. Another recommended site is the Boribu reef, at 15 metres (49ft).

OTHER ISLANDS

Mnemba Island, some 5km (3 miles) off the northeast coast, near Matemwe, offers enough variety for two to three good days. The reef has a range of good inner and outer wall dives, and some beautiful coral gardens. The best diving is on the south side, where strong currents mean excellent drift dives. The hard corals are in excellent condition, and you will find honeycomb, pillar and brain, clouded with shoals of sergeant fish, fusiliers and wrasse. The island is now a marine sanctuary. Good sites include Kichwani (20 metres/66ft), Aquarium (20 metres/

66ft) and Big Wall (25 metres/82ft). The highlight of the year is when the migrating whale sharks stop over in about March. They range in size from 5 to 12 metres (16 to 39ft), and there is nothing more graceful or harmless in the oceans.

Pemba has more interesting, more varied and more spectacular diving than anywhere else in East Africa. The coastline is dotted with tiny, uninhabited islands surrounded by almost unlimited dive sites, while on the far side, the 800-metre (2,620ft) deep Pemba channel provides world-class deep-sea fishing. There is excellent drift diving along the big walls, and some huge independent bommies teeming with reef fish. **Njao Gap** in the north hosts table-top coral, sea whips and gorgonian sea fans with giant groupers, Napoleon wrasse, titan triggerfish and regular darting pelagics wahoo, jacks and giant trevally. In the south, **Misali Island** is the coral jewel in the crown, with shallow water reefs in pristine condition so even snorkellers can indulge. Recommended sites include Manta Point (30 metres/100ft), Murray's Wall (35 metres/115ft), Deep Freeze (40 metres/130ft), Trigger Corner (25 metres/80ft) and Chillies Wall (35 metres/115ft).

Live-aboard enthusiasts should take a trip down the east coast, with its strong currents, large pelagics, fantastic soft corals and the likelihood of large shoals of hammerhead sharks. At the right times of year, you can encounter schools of pilot whales and the awesome humpbacks.

Mafia Island, 150km (90 miles) south of Zanzibar, has some sites that rank alongside those on Pemba. Most of the diving is focused around Chole Bay, and from September to March, it is possible to dive the walls outside the reef that protects the bay. There are three types of dive sites here. The sloping reefs (12–25 metres/39–82ft) are home to small coral bommies, huge moray eels, ribbontail rays, nesting turtles and guitar sharks. The coral walls stretch down 10–25 metres (33–82ft), with visibility around 30 metres (98ft), and caves, caverns and gullies to explore. Here you will encounter dolphins, huge groupers defending their caverns, large turtles, reef rays and the occasional bull shark.

The coral gardens, at a maximum of 20 metres (66ft), provide the best hard corals in East Africa, with brain and staghorn in abundance, and crocodile fish, turtles and stripe barracuda among the colourful reef fish. Recommended sites include Kinasi pass (24 metres/79ft inside reef), Mlila (23 metres/75ft outside), Juwani North (28 metres/92ft outside) and Milimani (18 metres/59ft inside).

Colourful coral reef, Zanzibar.

📷 THE SWAHILI

Inhabiting the coast and oceanic islands of East Africa, the Swahili are Tanzania's most culturally distinctive people, thanks to their long history of maritime trade with Arabia and Asia.

Culturally, the Swahili display strong Arabic influences. These include the adoption of Islam since medieval times (the oldest known Islamic structure in East Africa dates to the 11th century). Indeed, the very name Swahili derives from an Arabic word meaning 'coastal'.

The KiSwahili language, like most in Tanzania, is part of the Bantu linguistic group, but its enduring importance as a lingua franca – initially of coastal trade, later along caravan routes into the interior – has led to a relatively simplified grammar and a liberal peppering of Arabic words.

Dhows, their design adapted from Arabian vessels, are used widely along the Swahili Coast, not only as fishing vessels, but also as the main mode of transport between the mainland and the islands, and for shipping goods. Best known is the graceful *jahazi*, with its distinctive billowing triangular sail. There is also the all-purpose keel-less *dau la mwao*, while a dugout canoe or double-outrigger canoe may be used in creeks and harbours.

The ocean is integral to the Swahili way of life. Fishing features prominently in the local economy, with spears, hand lines, nets and basket traps all commonly used for this purpose. Also of considerable economic importance is the ubiquitous coconut palm, various parts of which are used for food, drink and oil, as well as forming the raw material for building, thatching, rope-making and plaited basketwork.

Traditional Swahili dhow at sunset, Zanzibar.

Muslim hats for sale in the market, Stone Town.

Muslim girl, Pangani.

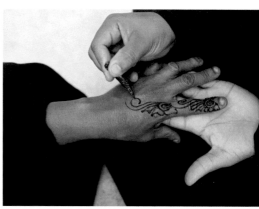

Swahili woman painting hands with henna.

Arts and architecture

The most conspicuous manifestation of Swahili artistic tradition is the stone architecture of ruined cities such as Kilwa, or living ports like Bagamoyo or Zanzibar's Stone Town. This architecture is notable for its tall narrow designs, gracious arches and features such as mangrove-pole ceilings and multiple niches. While an Arabic influence is easily detected, local innovations include the medieval pillar tombs whose closest regional counterparts are the phallic medieval stelae erected in parts of southern Ethiopia.

The origins of the poetic Swahili literary tradition are rather obscure, since the earliest works were passed down orally. Certainly, the tradition is hundreds of years older than the earliest extant Swahili document, an epic poem called *Utenzi wa Tambuka* (Story of Tambuka), written in Arabic script in Pate in 1728.

Taarab music is something of a hybrid, fusing Swahili lyrics with Arabic melodies. Many modern performers supplement traditional instruments – the lute-like *udi* and the *darbuk* drum – with the likes of guitar, violin and keyboards. Others have taken things a step further by assimilating elements of Bollywood, R&B, and hip-hop into their sound.

A traditional Swahili meal, including crab.

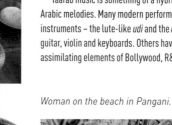

Woman on the beach in Pangani.

Antique Swahili pot, Zanzibar.

TANZANIA & ZANZIBAR

TRAVEL TIPS

TRANSPORT

GETTING THERE

By air

Tanzania is well served by international airlines. The most important hub for international flights is Dar es Salaam's Julius Nyerere International Airport, but there are also some international flights to Kilimanjaro International Airport, which lies about halfway between the towns of Arusha and Moshi, and Zanzibar International Airport, on the island of the same name.

Coming from the UK or elsewhere in Europe, airlines offering connections to Tanzania include British Airways (from London), KLM (from Amsterdam) and Swiss (from Zurich). It may be cheaper, however, to look at flying with African carriers such as Ethiopian Airlines (via Addis Ababa), Kenya Airways (via Nairobi) or Egypt Air (via Cairo), or the likes of Air India and Emirates.

Travelling to Tanzania from within Africa, South African Airways (SAA) operates daily flights from Johannesburg, and Ethiopian Airlines and Kenya Airways also have a good network of intra-African flights.

There are no direct flights from North America or Australia. Coming from North America, it is most common to fly via London or elsewhere in Europe, though it is also possible to route via elsewhere in Africa with SAA, Ethiopian Airlines or Kenya Airways. Coming from elsewhere, the main regional port of entry is Johannesburg, which is connected to several major centres in Asia, Australia and South America by SAA and other international carriers.

Airport taxes, where applicable, are now included in the ticket fare as a matter of course.

Airports

Dar es Salaam
Located 15km (8 miles) west of the city centre, Julius Nyerere International Airport (airport code DAR; www.taa.go.tz) is well staffed, with a foreign exchange bureau, ATMs, wheelchair facilities, many taxi stands and hotel information. Flight information is more difficult to come by. The best option is to contact the airline directly. Otherwise, contact the airport on 022-284 4095.

Zanzibar
Zanzibar International Airport (airport code ZNZ; tel: 024 223 3979), 5km (3 miles) south of Stone Town, has money-changing facilities and is well served by taxis and local buses (dala dalas). Taxis to town cost around US$15–25, much more than buses, but are worth the price as Stone Town is very easy to get lost in. If you've pre-booked at a reputable hotel or one of the beach resorts, transfers should be provided.

Kilimanjaro
Kilimanjaro International Airport (airport code JRO, but often referred to locally as KIA; tel: 027-255 4252; www.kilimanjaroairport.co.tz) is roughly 45km (28 miles) east of Arusha, halfway to Moshi. Taxis are available, and some airlines run a hotel shuttle service. Most safari companies organise pick-ups and drop-offs.

International airline offices

Dar es Salaam
British Airways
Dar es Salaam Movenpick Royal Palm Hotel, Ohio Street
Tel: 022-211 3820/1
www.britishairways.com

Egypt Air
Mezzanine Floor, NHC House, Samora Avenue
Tel: 022-211 0131
www.egyptair.com

Emirates
6th Floor, Haidery Plaza, Ali Hassan Mwinyi Road
Tel: 022-211 6100/1/2
www.emirates.com

Ethiopian Airlines
TDFL Building, Corner of Ohio Street and AH Mwinyi Road
Tel: 022-211 7063
www.ethiopianairlines.com

Kenya Airways
Upanga Road
Tel: 022-211 9376–7
www.kenya-airways.com

KLM
1st Floor, Viva Towers, Ali Hassan Mwinyi Road
Tel. 255 216 3914/5
www.klm.com

Qatar Airways
4th Floor, Diamond Plaza, Samora Avenue and Mirambo Street Junction
Tel: 022-219 8301
www.qatarairways.com

South African Airlines
Raha Towers Building, Maktaba Street
Tel: 022-211 7044–7
www.flysaa.com

Swiss
Luther House, Sokoine Drive
Tel: 022-211 8870/1–3
www.swiss.com

Arusha
Ethiopian Airlines
Boma Road
Tel: 027-250 4231

Rwandair
Swahili Street
Mob: 0732-978558
www.rwandair.com

By sea

Though Tanzania is a major shipping centre, the passenger trade consists mainly of internal ferries.

Some cruising companies have discovered the beauty of a cruise here, including Hayes and Jarvis (www.hayesandjarvis.co.uk).

By rail

The TAZARA rail line, originating in Zambia, is the only passenger train that crosses the borders of Tanzania (see page 207). The train departs from Kapiri Mposhi, north of Lusaka, if all is going well, on Tuesday and Friday, taking around 40 hours to reach Dar es Salaam (trains for Kapiri Mposhi also leave on Tuesday and Friday). This is a beautiful journey, passing through the Selous Reserve and offering the opportunity to see many animals near the tracks. The first-class sleeper is very reasonably priced. However, the service is somewhat erratic and there are often long delays en route. It is best to book in person at Kapiri Mposhi (New) Station, and double-check exact departure times and whether food and drinks will be available on board the train.

On a far more luxurious note, **Rovos Rail** runs an all-inclusive, annual rail tour originating in Cape Town and using the same railway track from Zambia to Dar es Salaam. See www.rovos.co.za for more details.

Bus/coach

It is possible to travel by bus from neighbouring countries into Tanzania, and the costs are a fraction of the air fare. However, be warned that a journey on bumpy African roads can mean many hours of discomfort, not to mention a few days' recovery time. Once you arrive at Ubungo bus terminal in Dar es Salaam, you must keep your wits about you: pickpockets are rife and you risk being ripped off by unscrupulous taxi drivers (also see page 245). For these reasons we recommend taking regional flights, but for intrepid travellers, here is the bus/coach information.

From Kenya: the main border town between Kenya and Tanzania is Namanga, located about halfway between Nairobi and Arusha. Regular shuttle buses connect the two cities and take 4–6 hours. There is also the option of going on to Moshi. Daily coaches also travel between Nairobi and Mombasa to

Arusha and Dar es Salaam. Public buses and *dala dalas* are also an option from the quieter border posts of Horohoro, Taveta, Illassit, Bologonya and Sirari.

From Malawi: travellers entering Tanzania from Malawi must pass over the Songwe River bridge southeast of Mbeya. Bus services between Lilongwe and Dar es Salaam, and Lilongwe, Mzuzu and Mbeya depart several times each week. Travelling directly, it takes just over 30 hours to reach Dar from Lilongwe.

From Mozambique: overland transport to Tanzania from Mozambique is fairly limited despite completion of a bridge over the Ruvuma River near Newala in 2010. Unless you have a private vehicle, the best option is the ferry at Kilambo (south of Mtwara); however, foreigners must pass through Kitaya to get their passport stamped.

From Uganda: you can cross into Tanzania at Mutukula, northwest of Bukoba. Buses connect Kampala to Dar es Salaam via Nairobi several times a week.

GETTING AROUND

By air

In addition to the three international airports – Dar, Kilimanjaro and Zanzibar – there are dozens of other local airports and airstrips. The most significant of these is Arusha Airport (airport code ARK), which lies on the southwestern outskirts of town, and is the main hub for light-aircraft flights to the northern national parks, as well as boasting regular connections to Zanzibar and Dar es Salaam. Air travel is a major form of internal transport due to the long distances and the poor quality of many roads. Most of the national parks have at least one airstrip, and the larger ones have several. Several domestic airlines and charter companies offer scheduled flights and special services all over the country.

Domestic airlines
Auric Air
Tel: 255 688 723 274
www.auricair.com
Small line connecting Mwanza and Dar es Salaam to several off-the-beaten-track destinations including

Bukoba, Iringa, Pemba, Ruaha, Selous and Songea.
Coastal Aviation
Tel: 255 752 627 825
www.coastal.co.tz
This established airline offers scheduled services into most national parks as well as Arusha, Dar es Salaam, Mwanza, Kilwa, Mafia, Pemba, Pangani, Tanga and Zanzibar.
Precision Air
Dar es Salaam
Diamond Plaza, Mirambo Street/ Samora Avenue
Tel: 022 219 1000
www.precisionairtz.com
Arusha
Safari Hotel Building, Boma Road
Tel: 027-254 5489
Zanzibar
Muzammill Centre Building, Mlandege Street
Tel: 024-223 4521
Tanzania's premier domestic airline, with flights to Arusha, Bukoba, Dar es Salaam, Kigoma, Kilimanjaro International, Mtwara, Musoma, Mwanza, Tabora and Zanzibar. Precision also operates regionally to Kenya, Comoros and UAE.
Regional Air Services
Tel: 255 784 285 753
www.regionaltanzania.com
Reliable scheduled and charter services throughout Tanzania.
ZanAir
Tel: 024-223 3670
www.zanair.com
Very dependable company with scheduled and chartered flights to and from the mainland. Primary supplier of emergency medical flights from Zanzibar.

Air charter companies
Flightlink Air Charters
Dar es Salaam
Tel: 255 782 35 44 48/49/50
www.flightlink.co.tz
Tanzanair
Dar es Salaam
Tel: 022-284 3131/3
www.tanzanair.com
Zantas Air Charters
Arusha
Tel: 255 688 434343
www.zantasair.com

By boat

There are regular ferries between Dar es Salaam, Zanzibar and Pemba. Dar es Salaam Boat Terminal is opposite St Joseph's Cathedral.

Ferry to the Kigamboni Peninsula, Dar es Salaam.

Coastal ferries

It's easy to book tickets to Zanzibar on the day of travel – the ferry companies have ticket offices at the ferry terminal, off Sokoine Drive. The price for visitors is higher than that advertised for locals. Several operators cover the route, but safety has become a serious issue with the cheaper companies after two overcrowded boats sunk, killing thousands of passengers, in 2011 and 2012. It is thus strongly advisable to go with the better and more reputable companies, including:

Azam Marine
Zanzibar
Tel: 024-223 1655
Dar es Salaam
Tel: 022-212 3324
www.azammarine.com
The pick of the ferry operators, with an air-conditioned booking office at the ferry jetty, and an easy-to-use online booking service. Normal ferries and catamarans run between Dar and Zanzibar a few times daily, plus services between Zanzibar and Pemba five times a week.

Lake ferries

Marine Services Company Ltd
Weekly trip along Lake Tanganyika from Kigoma to Mpulungu in Zambia, on the MV *Liemba*, a renovated 1919 German ship. Theoretically, it leaves Kigoma on Wednesday afternoon and Mpulungu on Friday morning, arriving back in Kigoma on Sunday

morning. Foreigners must pay in hard currency. No advance booking. There are also regular ferry services on lakes Victoria and Nyasa. For details, go to www.mscl.go.tz.

By bus

The Ubungo bus terminal, located 5km (3 miles) from the centre on Morogoro Road, Dar es Salaam, is the starting point for domestic services to the Southern Highlands, the Northern Safari Circuit, Morogoro, Dodoma, Mwanza, Singida and Shinyanga. It is not the most pleasant place to hang around in: avoid it at night and keep a close eye on your belongings during the day. If you need a taxi, you can get a better deal from one of the many drivers outside the gates.

Major inter-city bus companies

There are two grades of buses on the **mainland**. The most common are brightly coloured vehicles run by locals with the furnishings of a small village on top and no room inside. These are the cheapest – foreigners are charged more but are guaranteed a seat, whereas many locals stand, even during eight-hour journeys. A trip on one of these is certainly an experience, but not everyone's idea of a pleasant one.

The other category is 'luxury' buses. These are similar to, but not quite so good as, National Express in the UK or Greyhound in the USA.

They serve most main routes, cost more (but are still reasonable), and – most importantly – are usually air-conditioned. Following the collapse of the much-missed Scandinavia Coach Line, the best lines in this category are **Akamba Bus**, **Dar Express** (tel: 255 754 049 395), Mtei Express (mob: 0755-717117) and **Royal**.

Most country buses on **Zanzibar** start from Creek Road. Buses travel to Jambiani, Paje and Bwejuu; Makunduchi and Kizimkazi in the south; Matemwe and Pwani Mchangani on the east coast; the slave caves in Mangapwani; Nungwi in the far north of the island; and Kiwengwa. From Mwembe Ladu Hospital, you can take a bus to Chwaka, Uroa and Pongwe.

A shared minibus is the normal way around Zanzibar for budget-conscious tourists. The trip between Zanzibar Town and any of the northern or eastern beach resorts should cost less than US$10 per person. You have to arrange this in advance, however, so you can be fitted into the schedule. Talk to any minibus driver (they scout hotels and guesthouses between 8 and 9am) for more information. A taxi will be much more expensive.

By train

Tanzanian Railways Limited (www.trl.co.tz) runs services from Dar es Salaam to Mwanza (through Dodoma) and to Kigoma. In 2016,

⊘ Bus travel times (in hours)

Town	Dar	Morogoro	Iringa	Mbeya	Dodoma	Arusha	Moshi
Dar	—	3.5	7	11	7–9	9	8
Morogoro	3.5	—	3.5	4	5–7	***	—
Iringa	7	3.5	—	4	9–12	—	—
Mbeya	11	4	4	—	13–16	—	—
Dodoma	7–9	5–7	9–12	13–16	—	***	—
Arusha	9	***	—	—	***	—	1
Moshi	8	—	—	—	—	1	—

*** There are regular services between Arusha and Dodoma/Morogoro, but the road is very poor.

a new 'deluxe' service with modern coaches was introduced. Check timetables and fares via the website. The train service from the TAZARA Station in Dar es Salaam to Zambia (www.tazarasite.com; see page 207 and see page 243) stops at Mbeya, near the border. In 2015 the government announced plans to build several new railway lines across the country by 2021, and to transform Tanzania into a regional transport hub.

Dar es Salaam stations

Central Railway Station
Corner of Railway and Gerezani streets
Tel: 022-26 2191 or 255 78 7099 064
www.trl.co.tz
Domestic services only.

TAZARA Station
Corner of Nelson Mandela Expressway and Nyerere Road
Tel: 255 713 354 648
www.tazarasite.com

City transport

You can easily make your way around Arusha or Stone Town on foot, and both are safe to walk around by day. In the evening, walking is less advisable. In Dar es Salaam, the centre can be negotiated on foot, but many outlying areas are better reached by taxi or shuttle bus.

Buses

In Dar es Salaam, the first part (of six) of the new bus rapid transit system (BRT), connecting the city centre with its outskirts, became operational in 2016. Co-financed by the government, African Development Bank and the World Bank and operated by Dar Rapid Transit Agency (DART), it consists of three trunk routes with a total length of about 21km (13 miles), with dedicated bus lanes and 29 stations, linking Kimara in the east with Kivukoni (city centre).

The Chinese-made Golden Dragon buses operate between 5am and 11pm, providing express and local services. The second stage of the project – a 19km (12-mile) long section from Kilwa to Kawawa south via Kivukoni is currently under construction, due for completion by 2019. Once all stages are finished, the BRT network will be 130km (80 miles) long. For details, go to http://dart.go.tz.

Taxis

The larger cities all have a plentiful supply of taxis that come (usually) at a reasonable price. It is safest not to use unmarked cars. Always negotiate the fare before getting in. Expect a town-centre journey to cost the shilling equivalent of US$5–10.

In Arusha, licensed taxis have black serial numbers on the door and should charge US$4–8 in town.

Taxis rarely cruise when empty, so you will need to find a taxi rank or ask someone to call you a cab; most cafés, restaurants, shops and offices are willing to do this. Many cabbies now have mobile phones, so if you got good service, you can take the number and call again.

Reputable hotels usually provide transfers from the nearest airport. If this service isn't available, approximate taxi rates are as follows: from Zanzibar Airport to Stone Town US$8–15; from Kilimanjaro International Airport to Arusha US$50 (per car with a maximum of 4 passengers); from Julius Nyerere International to Dar es Salaam city centre US$15–20.

Dala dala

The most common form of local transport is the *dala dala* or shared taxi. These often-creaky minibuses and vans usually leave from ranks scattered across the city and run on roughly set routes. They wait to leave until full, but can be waved down beside the road. Reluctant to turn anyone away, they are piled high with people inside, and some passengers even cling to the fenders outside. Fares are extremely low (usually around US$0.20), but the accident rate is high, and they are not recommended if you have luggage or for any long journey.

Driving

To drive in Tanzania, you need an International Driving Licence, available from motoring organisations before you leave home. Your national licence will not be sufficient.

Drive defensively. Traffic is on the left, as in Britain, and while there are official speed limits, the reality is that people drive as fast as possible.

The TAZARA railway line running past the Udzungwa Mountains.

Fortunately, the state of Tanzanian roads often keeps this down to a crawl, but when it does not, beware. Drivers frequently fail to signal, while others signal right to warn following traffic against overtaking due to oncoming traffic, and left when it is safe to overtake. In rural areas, watch out for children or animals running out in front of the car. Driving after dusk should be avoided: cars often do not have lights, and there is also more danger of being robbed.

Roadblocks

You will meet frequent police roadblocks. These are money machines for the local cops as much as they are a serious attempt to check papers or get unsafe vehicles off the road, and bribery is the general order of the day. The good news is that as long as your papers are in order and you are polite, tourists are infrequently asked to pay the fine/bribe. If you have a local driver, he may need help paying up.

Fuel

Filling stations are usually found on the edge of town or at major route intersections. They are relatively infrequent, so fill up when you can. Fuel is cheaper than in Europe, and more expensive than in the US. It is unlikely that you will be able to pay with plastic and even if you do, there will be a hefty surcharge. Many filling stations are shut on Sundays.

Automobile Association of Tanzania
Azikiwe Street, Dar es Salaam
Tel: 022-215 1837
Email: info@aatanzania.org
The AA offers the usual services for members, such as international driving permits, discounted accommodation rates and insurance, travel advice and breakdown cover.

Independence Torch, Morogoro.

Local buses are cheap but the accident rate is high.

Car hire

Few tourists to Tanzania hire cars. For a variety of logistical and cost-related reasons, it is more conventional to book an entire safari with one company, which will arrange all transfers, flights and provide a vehicle with driver as required.

However, there are some internationally franchised car-hire companies in Dar es Salaam, as well as a few small, local outfits. Prices and the quality of the vehicles can vary, so it is worth shopping around.

In Zanzibar, most car-hire operators are one-man bands with a couple of vehicles. It is best to ask your hotel, tour operator or a local travel agent to sort out your car hire for you.

Some companies offer only chauffeur-driven services, although self-drive is becoming more common. Rates depend on the vehicle type and insurance, but start from around US$35 per day. If you plan to drive yourself, you need a home or International Driving Licence to rent any vehicle, including a scooter. If you don't have a credit card, you will be asked to leave your passport and a cash deposit with the rental company.

If you are travelling out of the city, it is strongly advised that you use a four-wheel drive with good ground clearance. Make sure your vehicle has insurance and a valid road permit. Also check that it has a spare wheel and basic tool kit. If you are planning to travel long distances, it is worth carrying spare fuel, oil and water, and a basic survival kit, including food, water and a blanket.

In addition to the car-hire companies listed below, most tailor-made tour operators in Tanzania also offer chauffeur-driven car hire (see page 260).

International car-hire firms in Dar

Avis
22 Uporto Road
Tel: 022-276 1277
www.avis.com

Europcar (Inter Rent)
Dar es Salaam Serena Hotel
Ohio Street
Tel: 022-266 4722
Mob: 0782-299000
www.europcar.co.tz

Local car-hire firms in Dar

Green Car Rentals
Nkrumah Street
Tel: 022-218 3718
Mob: 0713-227788
www.greencarstz.com

Local car-hire firms in Arusha

Arusha Naaz Rent a Car
Tel: 027-250 2087
Mob: 0754-282799
www.arushanaaz.net

Serena Car Hire
Mob: 0784 525 700/0789 188 027
www.serenacarhire.com

A

Accommodation

Tanzania has a wide range of accommodation to suit every kind of traveller. There are superb luxury lodges at one end, dingy, cockroach-infested dives at the other, and a growing number of options in between. These include campsites, mostly located within national parks, B&Bs (known locally as 'board and lodgings', often offshoots of local bars), and traditional wooden *bandas* (chalets), found mainly on the coast and in the mountains. Travellers on a budget will also find a handful of hostels with a shared kitchen and dormitories. Zanzibar has by far the widest choice of places to stay, and prices for every budget. Note that camping is not allowed on the islands.

Hotel visitors in Tanzania pay 18 percent VAT: check this is included in the rate quoted when you reserve your room. During high season (June to September), room rates are hiked up, so be sure to confirm the price for the time of year you intend to visit. Most large and medium-sized establishments accept credit cards; cash is required for smaller, budget hotels.

Admission charges

Daily entrance fees are charged for all national parks and other reserves. These are usually valid for a 24-hour period, and non-citizen rates are steep by international standards: US$100 per person for Gombe Stream, US$80 for Mahale Mountains, US$70 for Kilimanjaro, US$75 for Selous, US$60 for Serengeti, US$45 for Arusha, Lake Manyara or Tarangire, and US$30 for most other parks. Non-resident children and students (5–15 years) pay US$10–20, depending on the

park, while citizen rates amount to around US$2–4 per day. Fees are regularly increased so check the website (www.tanzaniaparks.go.tz) for the latest details. As of mid-2016, an 18 percent VAT is added to park fees, as well as to other tourist services (guides, accommodation, etc.).

Park entrance fees are normally included in the price of an organised safari. However, independent and self-drive travellers will need to pay them directly. For most national parks, they can be paid with a Visa or MasterCard, or with a TANAPA smartcard, but not with cash.

For the Ngorongoro Conservation Area (NCA), the charge is US$60 per person per 24 hours, plus a service fee of US$250 per vehicle every time you visit the Ngorongoro Crater. This can be paid only with a preloaded NCA smartcard, which can be issued and loaded with cash at the Exim Bank in Arusha or Karatu. Independent travellers will need to calculate their fees carefully (see www.ngorongorocrater.go.tz for full details), as they will be refused entry if the card is not loaded with enough cash, but will not get a refund on any excess.

Admission charges into archaeological sites and museums run by the Department of Antiquities are quoted and payable in local currency, but typically work out at US$3–20 per person. Many locally run establishments ask for a donation, and what the average tourist would consider a small contribution is often very much appreciated.

B

Budgeting for your trip

Budgeting for your visit to Tanzania very much depends on the sort of experience you are looking to have.

Whether you are a backpacker or a luxury client, it is a relatively expensive country, one that seldom offers the shoestring prices of Asia. The key in regard to budgeting is thorough research: find out as much as you can about all the options. Tour operators can book your entire trip right down to the last detail and this makes budgeting a whole lot easier.

It is imperative that you put aside extra funds in case of emergencies. Communication, technology and health-care facilities are nowhere near Western standards in most parts of Tanzania. The best cover you can have in any sticky situation is the means to pay your way out. This, coupled with good travel insurance, should allow you the peace of mind to enjoy your trip no matter what happens.

There are two price brackets for almost all accommodation: resident rates (includes Tanzanians and expatriates) and non-resident rates (everyone else). Non-resident rates are generally quoted in US dollars but payable in Tanzanian shillings. Resident rates are quoted in local currency and always lower. Many establishments catering to tourists have strong seasonal variations in price, with peak season generally regarded as falling from June to early January, so be sure to confirm the price for the time of year you intend to visit.

Prices for accommodation cover the whole gamut. Budget hotels and guesthouses with basic amenities start at around US$20 for a simple room. Luxury five-star lodgings range from several hundred to sometimes thousands of dollars per night. Lower to mid-range hotels fall somewhere in between, depending on facilities and level of comfort. Generally, accommodation in the national parks is far pricier than in towns or on beaches. Zanzibar is more expensive than resorts on the mainland.

Safari vehicle with African elephant, Tarangire National Park.

If you are willing to do as the locals do, you can eat heartily for a pittance. African staples such as *ugali* (maize) with fish or meat stew, *chipsi mayai* (chip omelette) or even the more lavish pilau rice can be purchased for a couple of bucks. International cuisine, served at most high-end hotels, is substantially more expensive than local food.

It is never advisable to drink the tap water anywhere in Africa, so include bottled water as part of the budget for your entire trip. A 1.5-litre bottle of purified water retails US$0.65.

Transport comes in a variety of forms; the cheapest option is to travel by local bus *(dala dala)*; price depends on the distance you are travelling. This can be anything from a few hundred shillings for a few stops in an urban setting to several thousand shillings for much longer distances.

A network of buses covers most intercity routes – the best company is Dar Express, which operates several services daily between Dar es Salaam, Arusha and a few other major centres. A ticket from Dar to Arusha costs around US$15. There are other bus companies, but most are of dubious quality and on the whole considered unsafe to travel with.

Prices for private hire cars with a driver and taxis are negotiable and depend on the distance you are travelling and the level of your bartering skills. Self-drive is a good option if you are a confident driver. Prices in high season from local hirers start at around US$50 a day plus insurance. Going through a more recognised hirer such as Hertz comes with a higher price tag, but offers better quality assurance in terms of safety and cover.

To give an idea of average costs, a 500ml local beer typically costs around US$1.30 at a local bar and US$3–4 at more touristy places, while a glass of house wine (usually of the boxed variety) costs around US$3–5 and a bottle of wine anything upwards of US$20.

A main course at a local restaurant might cost US$4, while a smarter place catering to tourists would typically be in the ballpark of US$5–15 for a main course.

Most organised or bespoke tours include all transfers, but taxis are generally inexpensive: you shouldn't pay more than US$10 for a cab ride within central Dar es Salaam or Arusha.

C

Children

Many Westerners are too timid to take their children to destinations outside of Europe and North America, especially those with less-developed tourist infrastructure. This is a great shame: not only will they have a brilliant time, but it is a massive learning experience, and Zanzibar also has some of the world's best beaches. Give children a project for the trip, such as a travel diary, to keep them interested and involved. Most Africans adore children, and will help you keep an eye on them; having kids with you can open doors of communication, and local children will immediately involve them in their games and activities. All you need to take are some common-sense precautions.

Babies

Taking babies into this environment is not advisable. They won't like the heat, you may find it difficult to get baby food and supplies once out of the major towns, and they won't remember it anyway. It is unsafe to have babies on safari (most operators will not accept them). Their cries are said to resemble those of wounded animals and may attract predators. An even greater risk would be exposing a baby – or any child too young to describe symptoms – to the risk of malaria, which is prevalent almost throughout Tanzania.

Health

From the age of four or five onwards, things become far easier, but there are specific health considerations to watch out for.

Children are more susceptible to illness than adults. They also get dehydrated more quickly, so be sure to give them plenty to drink.

Be extra careful of children's delicate skin in the African sun. Large quantities of sunblock and a good hat are essential equipment.

The other main risk is malaria: seek advice before travelling on what anti-malarial medication is suitable for your children; see page 253 for further information.

There are lurking dangers not found back home. Make sure children wear shoes whenever they are out of the house, and that they wash their hands frequently, do not scramble over rocks without checking where they put their hands, or start playing with any strange insects or wildlife they might meet before it is checked out by someone in the know. If they are scratched, take it seriously and use antiseptic, as bacteria can breed fast in the heat. If they are bitten or stung, get expert advice immediately.

Food for children

Food on offer in Tanzania tends to be quite plain and frequently involves chips, so there shouldn't be any problems finding something suitable. Tourist hotels usually provide special children's menus (some also have kids' clubs). Bottled water and sodas are available everywhere.

Travelling

One of the biggest problems in travelling with children is simply the many long hours spent en route – even the charms of a Land Rover can pall quickly. Take plenty of drinks, sweets to suck or chewing gum, and emergency food rations. A supply of music, audio books and games is essential. Try not to schedule long journeys on consecutive days.

Safaris with children

Older children on the whole enjoy safaris. Most safari companies advise against taking children under six years on safari, and some luxury lodges ban under-12s. It is considered that they will be bored, and cannot sustain the quiet concentration needed for game viewing. Other lodges accept younger children but insist on the family having a private vehicle to view game. A few enlightened operators offer special child-friendly safaris.

On trekking safaris, children need to be at least 14 years old to keep up with the rest of the group. Younger kids just don't have the stamina.

Climate

Tanzania's hottest months are from October to February, and the main rainy season from mid-March to late May. Heavy downpours during April and May are often accompanied by violent thunderstorms, particularly in the highlands. There is also a short rainy season in November and December. The coolest months, June to September, are also the most pleasant.

Tanzania's varied geography creates drastic climatic differences within the country. Coastal areas are hot and humid, with an average daytime temperature of 30°C (86°F). The central plateau has hot days and cool nights. The hilly area between the coast and the northern highlands averages a pleasant 20°C (68°F) from January to September, while mountainous areas (including Kilimanjaro, the Usambara Mountains and the northern and southern highlands) register lows of 12°C (54°F) in May–August. Mount Kilimanjaro is snowcapped year-round, although climate change means more ice is melting each year.

When to visit

There is no truly bad time to visit Tanzania, but certain seasons are preferable for certain parts of the country. The worst time to visit the coast is over April and May, which together account for about 40 percent of the average annual rainfall, while the most comfortable time of year is the relatively cool period from June to October. Inland, the long rains (late February to early June,

peaking in April) are also a poor time to hike on Mount Kilimanjaro.

Game viewing on the northern circuit is good throughout the year. The most important park is the Serengeti, and seasonal movement of the wildebeest migration might well influence when you visit. Popular months include February and March, when the wildebeest calve in the southern Serengeti, while for those who can afford to stay at the premier lodges in the northern Serengeti, August to October is when you are likely to catch Mara river crossings. Those who place a higher premium on a wilderness experience than on individual wildlife sightings might prefer to aim for the low season of April to early June, when you catch the likes of the Serengeti and Ngorongoro Crater at their least crowded.

By contrast, the southern and western parks are a lot more seasonal, and best avoided during the rainy months of late November through to May, when roads often become impassable and many lodges and camps close.

For birdwatchers, the best time to be in Tanzania is the northern winter (October to May), when many resident species are in full breeding colours, and more than 100 species of Palaearctic migrant are present.

What to wear

If you'll spend most of your time on safari, bring a small, select wardrobe for all seasons. Light and casual is the clothing code for the coast and on safari. Clothing should be loose and comfortable – natural fibres help your skin to breathe in the heat. Don't bother bringing rainwear, even if the safari is timed for the rainy season. If necessary, a light waterproof can be picked up locally.

For safaris, bright colours are bad news. Not only do they attract tsetse flies, but vivid reds and oranges may disturb some animals on walking safaris. It is better to wear neutral colours such as beige and khaki. However, there is no need to splash out on the full professional hunter khaki outfit – any light clothing in muted colours will do, plus, of course, a hat for protection against the sun. Soil in Tanzania is often red and dusty, so clothes get grubby quickly.

On safari, shoes need to be sturdy and ideally should cover your ankles, for protection against snakes and sharp branches. The more of your

body that is covered the better, as tsetse flies and mosquitoes will attack the uncovered bits.

Women will probably find cotton dresses cooler and more comfortable than trousers, particularly for daytime. If you prefer to wear trousers, make sure they are baggy enough to allow plenty of ventilation. The local dresses or loose blouses are available in an infinite variety of designs and are good value. The *kikoi* and *kanga* – local wraparound sarongs – are also useful.

On the coast and Zanzibar, bikinis are usually worn by tourists on the beaches, but topless or nude bathing is totally inappropriate, and it is considered respectable to cover up once off the beach. Clothing should be modest and respectable – this part of Tanzania is predominantly Muslim and you should keep shoulders and knees covered in towns and other public places. Brightly coloured *kangas* do the trick nicely.

For footwear, comfort should take precedence over style. Solid walking shoes or boots are useful in most places apart from the beach. They protect against ankle-biting snakes, and they also make for good protection on African transport, where nearly all bags end up on toes at some point. Closed shoes are recommended when walking through towns and cities as many areas are quite dirty and infections on blistered toes, etc, are commonplace. Take beach shoes for walking on sand and in the surf, where you can meet anything from rough coral to sea urchins.

Life is generally informal, but it is a good idea to bring at least one set of smart clothes if you are travelling on business. You are advised to bring any specialist gear you may require

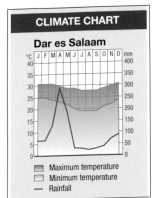

CLIMATE CHART

Dar es Salaam

- Maximum temperature
- Minimum temperature
- Rainfall

(snorkelling, sports gear, hiking, camping equipment) as local supplies are limited and below par.

A hat, sunscreen and sunglasses are crucial protection from the blazing sun.

Crime and safety

Before leaving home

For travel advice, log onto www.gov. uk/government/organisations/foreign-commonwealth-office for official UK Foreign Office advice. If in the US, go to https://travel.state.gov/content/passports/en/alertswarnings.html.

Make scans of all important documents, including your passport, visas, insurance documents and vaccination certificates. Carry the scans on your laptop or smartphone, and email copies to an e-mail address you can access during your trip. This will help ensure speedy replacement should they be stolen. Also, leave a copy of everything at home, with someone you can contact if you get into difficulties.

Theft

Tanzania is a very poor country, so it is no surprise that tourists can be the target of crime. Be alert and cautious.

Street crime is fairly common in larger cities. The main threats are pickpockets and muggers. It is asking for trouble to wear expensive jewellery or watches – if there is anything that you could not bear to lose, leave it at home. Leave your passport, tickets and excess money in the hotel safe (not in your room) unless you have to take them.

If you need them or are in transit, consider wearing a concealed money belt and keep a little 'giveaway money' separately. Most opportunist thieves will probably be content with that and won't look any further.

Children playing in the sea, Zanzibar.

Don't walk the streets or on the beach after dark – take a taxi.

On the road

Do not drive at night, and do follow local advice. Do not stop for hitchhikers, and if you see or are involved in an accident, drive on to the nearest town and report it, rather than stopping to help.

Touts and guides

In Zanzibar, use only guides authorised by the Commission for Tourism – they will have an identity badge.

Although sometimes annoying, most touts who approach you are honest – if persistent – salesmen for safari companies. Beware, however, of the few who aren't. Several scams are on the go, so don't give money upfront until you have checked out the situation. Ignore anyone who approaches you on the street offering to change money. There is no black market in Tanzania, and these guys are looking to cheat you.

Drugs

There is a drug problem in Zanzibar. Beware of touts who approach you off the ferry – many are just looking for money for their next hit. There are tough penalties if you are caught partaking.

Political tensions

Although Tanzania is a largely peaceful country, political tensions might occasionally run high, particularly on Zanzibar, which has a prominent separatist movement. Travellers should avoid political gatherings as they can turn violent.

The ominous shadow of Al-Qaeda fell over Tanzania with the American Embassy bombing in 1998, but no such incident has occurred there since. You should be safe, but be aware that there may be pockets of anti-Western sentiment.

Customs regulations

Duty-free limits for those over the age of 19 are: 1 litre of spirits; 580ml of perfume; 200 cigarettes; 50 cigars or 250 grams of tobacco.

D

Disabled travellers

Disabled travellers to Tanzania face many practical difficulties and a frustrating lack of facilities, but are often amazed at the help and understanding that they get from local people. At the airport, everything is done manually – ie, you are physically lifted on and off the plane; wheelchairs are available once you are on the ground. On the beaches, there are no planks for wheelchair users. Many streets in Stone Town are cobbled. Accessible hotels are few and far between, although in Dar, most of the upmarket hotels have limited facilities.

Safaris can be a good option for disabled travellers, as you spend so long in vehicles. However, they do tend to be more expensive for disabled travellers because they have to be booked from abroad – and the cheaper companies don't tend to advertise internationally. Many smaller lodges have scattered rooms in inaccessible places, but the larger lodges, such as the Serena and Sopa chains, can usually accommodate people in wheelchairs if given advance warning. Abercrombie and Kent (www.akdmc. com) offers a (pricey) flying safari.

The tourist office should be able to provide a list of local tour operators who accommodate disabled travellers; they include the following:

Dar es Salaam

Takims Holidays and Safaris
www.takimsholidays.com
Kearsleys Tours and Travel
www.kearsleys.com

Arusha

Ranger Safaris
www.rangersafaris.com
Information can also be obtained from the following organisations:

In Tanzania
Tanzania Federation of Disabled People's Organisation (SHIVYAWATA)
Ubungo Mawasiliano Tower Area – Sinza C No.33, Off Simu 2000
Tel: 022 276 22 33
www.shivyawata.or.tz

In the UK
Disability Rights UK
Ground Floor, CAN Mezzanine, 49-51 East Road, London N1 6AH
Tel: 020 7250 8181
www.disabilityrightsuk.org

In the US
SATH (Society for the Advancement of Travel for the Handicapped)
347 Fifth Avenue, Suite 605, New York, NY10016
Tel: 212-447 7284
www.sath.org

E

Embassies and consulates

Tanzanian embassies abroad
Australia
2/222 La Trobe Street, Melbourne VIC 3000, Australia
Tel: +61 (0) 8 9221 0033
www.tanzaniaconsul.org
Canada
50 Range Road, Ottawa, Ontario, K1N 8J4
Tel: (613) 232-1509
www.tzrepottawa.ca
South Africa
822 George Avenue, Arcadia 0007, Pretoria
Tel: +27-12-342 4371/93
www.tanzania.org.za
UK & Ireland
Tanzania High Commission, 3 Stratford Place, London W1C 1AS
Tel: 020-7569 1470
www.tanzaniahighcommission.co.uk

☉ Emergency numbers

Ambulance/fire/police:
(mainland) 112
Ambulance/fire/police:
(Zanzibar) 999
Police: 022-211 7362 (Dar es Salaam), 027-250 3641 (Arusha), 024-223 5669 (Zanzibar)
Flying Medical Service: (Arusha) +255 759 367 367; Flying Doctors: (Arusha) +255 719 881 887, 745 716 581, or 684 818 071.

USA
1232 22nd Street NW, Washington DC 20037
Tel: (202) 884-1080
www.tanzaniaembassy-us.org

Foreign embassies & consulates
If you are going far off the beaten track, it is a good idea to register with your embassy when you arrive in Dar es Salaam.

Dar es Salaam
Australia
Australians should contact the Canadian embassy.
Canada
38 Mirambo Street (Cnr Garden Avenue)
Tel: 022-216 3300
www.canadainternational.gc.ca
Ireland
353 Toure Drive
Tel: 022-260 2355
www.dfa.ie/irish-embassy/tanzania
South Africa
Mwaya Road, Msasani
Tel: 022-260 1800
www.dirco.gov.za
UK
Umoja House, Garden Avenue
Tel: 022-229 0000
http://ukintanzania.fco.gov.uk
USA
686 Old Bagamoyo Road
Tel: 022-229 4000
http://tanzania.usembassy.gov

Etiquette

In Tanzania, greetings are very important, and not to be rushed. Africans often spend minutes holding hands after first greeting each other. It is considered bad manners to rush abruptly into a query without first observing the social niceties.

As in Asia, people eat and shake hands with their right hand. Using the left is considered dirty, as this is normally used for toilet purposes. Putting your feet up on a table or stool is considered rude. Physical displays of affection between sexes are frowned upon, as are open displays of anger and impatience. Realise that things often take longer in Africa, and be philosophical and always polite if you want to get a favourable response from officials. Part of the African experience is to slow down to African time – you'll wonder what all the stress and rushing about are for when you get home.

☉ Electricity

Mains electricity is 230V at 50Hz. British-style round or square three-pin plugs are in common use, so a travel adaptor is advised for electrical equipment with two-pin or other plugs (though many rooms in upmarket hotels have at least one such adaptor). Most game lodges and camps depend on generators and/or solar power for their electricity, so there may be limited charging points and hours, and it is important you charge up regularly in order that batteries don't run so low they require immediate charging.

Elderly people are shown a great deal of respect, particularly when being greeted.

Despite the nation's poverty, Tanzanians place a high premium on being clean and neatly presented. Tourists who dress scruffily will receive less respect than those who are well groomed. You can wear shorts in tourist areas, but they are considered childish. Jacket and tie are recommended for meeting senior officials – if in doubt, dress conservatively.

Remember that a large part of the coast and the islands of Zanzibar are Muslim. In these and other areas, it is appropriate for women to wear discreet, long, loose-fitting clothes. Local women are often uncomfortable in the company of men. Modest clothes and bare feet are required for entry to mosques. Most mosques are not open to non-Muslims, so never enter unless specifically invited.

F

Festivals

Mainland Tanzania has a limited selection of festivals, but a few worthwhile ones are held annually on Zanzibar.

February
Sauti za Busara
www.busaramusic.org
Arguably East Africa's most prominent music festival celebrated its thirteenth anniversary in 2017. Centred upon the waterfront Old Fort,

Fort, it offers three evenings of non-stop live music. The emphasis is on local artists, but musicians from elsewhere on the continent also feature.

June–July
Zanzibar International Film Festival (ZIFF)
www.ziff.or.tz
Also centred on the Old Fort, this prestigious film festival, also known as the Festival of the Dhow Countries, was established in 1997. Its focus is the most recent and cutting-edge releases from Africa and the Indian Ocean region.
Zanzibar Cultural Festival
Held in late July in the aftermath of ZIFF, this celebration of traditional Swahili culture involves *taarab* music, traditional dances, and other arts and crafts performed by cultural troupes from different countries. It is held in various venues around Zanzibar Town.
Mwaka Kogwa
Held in the Zanzibari village of Makunduchi over the last week of July, this colourful traditional festival is one of the oldest celebrated on the island, ringing in the Shirazi New Year. Men challenge foes of the past year with banana leaves. The contestants then flail one another and hopefully make amends. Meanwhile, the town's women dance around the banana-beating men singing songs. A house of spirits is constructed and then set on fire as villagers run around the burning misery of last year. Activities are accompanied by much drinking and dancing. Visitors are welcome, and traditionally seen to be harbingers of good fortune.

August–September
Jahazi Literary & Jazz Festival
www.jahazifestival.org
A long weekend dedicated to open-air events such as jazz concerts, poetry readings, storytelling, great debate and cultural walks through Stone Town.

G

Gay and lesbian travellers

Tanzania and Zanzibar are culturally conservative. Open displays of affection are frowned upon even between straight couples. Don't assume, if you see men holding hands, that they are gay; this is a common display of affection between straight males. According to the 2007 Pew Global Attitudes Project, 95 percent of Tanzanian residents believe that homosexuality should not be condoned by society. And gay relationships are not only taboo but effectively illegal, since all same-sex sexual acts are against the law and carry a prison sentence. In practice, for the discreet gay couple, there should be no problem. Although it has no 'scene' (straight or gay), Zanzibar is actually a popular gay destination.

H

Health and medical care

Since health risks are higher in Africa and medical care often inadequate, it is vital that your travel insurance policy is comprehensive and includes emergency evacuation and repatriation. Have a dental check-up before you go and get a spare pair of prescription glasses if you wear them. If you are on medication, make sure you carry enough to last you, plus a prescription and letter from your doctor, to show to border officials who may suspect you of smuggling drugs.

Health advice
In the UK, detailed health advice, tailored to individual needs, is available from MASTA (Medical Advice for Travellers Abroad) online at www. masta-travel-health.com. Traveller advice is also available on the NHS website, www.fitfortravel.nhs.uk, or check with your doctor.

Two other important medical contacts are **AMREF** (African Medical and Research Foundation; www. amref.org) and **IAMAT** (International Association for Medical Assistance to Travellers; www.iamat.org). The former offers emergency regional evacuation by the Flying Doctors Society of Africa (tel: +254 20 6000090; www.flydoc.org), which offers visitors a two-month membership for a small fee. IAMAT provides members (membership is free) with health information and a list of approved doctors all over the world, including Tanzania.

Inoculations
Consult your doctor about inoculations at least two months before you leave. A **yellow fever** inoculation is no longer required unless you are travelling from an infected area, but there is a risk on the Tanzanian mainland, so it is strongly advisable to have one. **Diphtheria** and **tetanus** vaccinations are also a good idea. Boosters are required every 10 years after a trio of injections while young. **Typhoid** is recommended for stays over two weeks.

A series of inoculations exists for **hepatitis A** and **B**. For hepatitis A, long-term protection (10 years) is available by an initial injection followed by a booster at 6–12 months. For short-term protection, an injection of gamma globulin will protect you immediately for up to six months, depending on dosage.

Meningitis inoculations are recommended and should protect you against the major forms of the disease. **Polio** inoculations are strongly recommended.

Protection against **tuberculosis** is recommended for those living in the area for over three months, though the risk to tourists is low.

Rabies vaccinations are usually only given if you are likely to be in close contact with animals during your stay (e.g. working in a game farm or reserve) or if you are going to a remote area. A full course of three injections takes several weeks to administer. If you are bitten by any animal that might have rabies, you should seek the post-exposure shots as soon as possible.

Guard your vaccination record as carefully as your passport.

First-aid kit
The following items should be in your first-aid kit: strong mosquito repellent; malaria prophylactics; sting-relief cream; antihistamine pills; plasters, antiseptic wipes and spray for blisters and cuts; syringes; Imodium for diarrhoea. Also, take your own condoms and tampons (if required).

Hygiene
Many areas in Tanzania are subject to regular outbreaks of cholera and dysentery due to poor sanitation and hygiene. Be conscientious about washing your hands regularly with soap and water. Most good hotels will provide bottled or filtered water.

Elsewhere, use bottled, boiled or otherwise purified water for drinking and brushing your teeth. Avoid ice and take care with juices as their water sources may be suspect. Milk should be avoided as it is often unpasteurised. You may also be better off avoiding uncooked vegetables, salads, unpeeled fruit or frozen products unless properly prepared. Wash all fresh food thoroughly in boiled or bottled water before you eat it.

Sun protection

The African sun is strong: sunblock and a head covering are essential – a wide-brimmed hat is ideal. If your skin is fair, use sunscreen whenever you are going to be out in the sun. Even if you have dark skin, you are still at risk if out all day – particularly if you are going to be swimming or snorkelling. The water reflects the sun's rays, multiplying the effect, and the coolness of the water is deceptive.

Most first-time visitors experience a degree of heat exhaustion and dehydration that can be avoided by drinking lots of water and slightly increasing the amount of salt in the diet. Dehydration is more serious in children, so monitor their intake of liquids carefully.

Health risks

HIV/AIDS

Aids is a major problem in Tanzania, with around 4.7 percent of adults HIV positive; the rate of infection is falling thanks to government programmes such as Aids-awareness campaigns and screening of blood donors. Avoid high-risk activities such as unprotected sex. Make sure your first-aid kit includes syringes and avoid receiving blood transfusions, except in case of dire emergency and preferably only after consulting your consulate or embassy.

Altitude sickness

This is likely to be encountered only by those who are trekking up Mount Kilimanjaro or Mount Meru. It is impossible to predict who will be affected and how severely – it takes little consideration of fitness. Mild altitude sickness will bring headaches, lethargy, dizziness, difficulty sleeping and loss of appetite. Further ascent should be avoided

at this stage as the sickness may become more severe without notice and include symptoms of breathlessness, coughing that may produce frothy pink sputum, vomiting and unconsciousness. In this case, immediate descent is necessary or it may lead to fatal pulmonary oedema. The good news is that a rapid descent to a lower altitude will cure the symptoms as rapidly as they came on.

Some tips to avoid acute mountain sickness:

Ascend the mountain slowly, giving your system time to adjust. Unfortunately, many treks on Mount Kilimanjaro and Mount Meru, especially the budget ones, are geared for getting you up and down quickly. Take the longest route possible if this is your first high-altitude experience and don't hesitate to ask your guide to go more slowly. Try sleeping at a lower height than your maximum height that day. Not only does this give you a nice downhill trot at the end of the day, but it allows your body to adjust more easily.

Drink lots of fluid and avoid heavy foods. Avoid alcohol and sedatives, as these further reduce the blood's ability to absorb oxygen.

Bilharzia

Avoid swimming in fresh water: even large lakes such as Lake Malawi/Nyasa are known to harbour bilharzia parasites, which live in snails that like reedy, still water. Fast-flowing, very cold or clear water should be safe. If in doubt, rub yourself dry thoroughly with a rough towel and ask for a test on returning home. There is a relatively straightforward treatment to this disease if it is caught in time.

Remember that fresh water may also harbour crocodiles and hippos.

Diarrhoea

This curse of the long-distance traveller usually clears itself up within a few days. If there is no sign of improvement within 48 hours, it could be caused by a parasite or infection, and you should see a doctor.

The best way to avoid tummy bugs is by being fastidious about using purified or bottled water to drink and brush your teeth with. Watch out for ice in drinks. If you are felled, stop eating anything but dry toast or biscuits (preferably salty), but carry

on drinking plenty of bottled water. Coca Cola and ginger ale are both a good way to inject calories and help settle the stomach. Avoid alcohol, coffee, tea and any dairy products other than yoghurt. Dehydration is the biggest risk, particularly with chronic diarrhoea, which is most dangerous to children, who become dehydrated more quickly than adults. Rehydration requires salt and sugar as well as liquid.

Malaria

Malaria is one of the most serious health risks in East Africa. Seek advice from your doctor or a tropical institute two months before your departure on the most suitable medication for you and your family.

In the UK, the **Health Protection Agency** publishes a document on malaria prevention, which can be downloaded at www.gov.uk/government/organisations/public-health-england. In the US, the **Center for Disease Control** (CDC) in Atlanta (tel: 404-498 1515/800-311 3435; www.cdc.gov) issues health advice to travellers.

The most commonly recommended prophylactics are Lariam (which can have unpleasant, and in rare cases dangerous, side effects); the antibiotic doxycycline (which can cause photosensitivity in some people); and Malarone (which has few side effects and is effective).

None of these offers 100 percent protection, so it is wisest to avoid getting bitten in the first place. The malaria-carrying female anopheles mosquito is only active between dusk and dawn. At these times, avoid perfumes and aftershave; make liberal use of insect repellent containing DEET; and wear light-coloured clothing that covers arms and legs. Sleep in mosquito-proof quarters (i.e. rooms with mosquito screens on the windows and under a mosquito net impregnated with permethrin).

It is important to remember that initial symptoms of the most dangerous form of malaria are rather similar to those of common flu, for instance aching joints, headaches and a quickly rising temperature. If you start displaying these or other flu-like symptoms at any stage within six months of your return home, you should consult a doctor immediately – be sure to tell them where you have been travelling.

It is also important not to panic unduly. Millions of people visit and live in Africa without getting malaria. Furthermore, providing you seek medical assistance quickly, it is easy to treat.

Automobile accidents

Car crashes are a leading cause of injury among travellers in East Africa, so walk and drive defensively, wear a seat belt and avoid travelling at night.

Bugs and beasties

Many **snakes** in Africa are poisonous, though most will leave you alone and are as anxious to avoid you as you are to avoid them. If walking in thick grasses or undergrowth, wear sturdy shoes and thick socks, and always walk heavily – most snakes will feel the vibrations and get out of your way. The black mamba is the only snake that is aggressive enough to attack, while the puff adder relies on camouflage and is easy to step on inadvertently. If you are bitten, keep the affected part as immobile as possible and seek immediate help.

Many of the huge **spiders** that freak out visitors are harmless – some are even mosquito-munching friends. However, it is best to keep a safe distance unless you are certain. Be aware of children's curiosity overcoming common sense. Check the bed and the toilet seat before sitting down, shake out your shoes before putting them on, and never put your hands on a rock or into a crevice without checking it for occupants first.

Tsetse flies can be a terrible annoyance, and some carry trypanosomiasis (sleeping sickness). With an appearance and a painful, extremely itchy bite similar to a horsefly's, they tend to swarm and are attracted to the heat of a car and the colours black and blue. If infected by sleeping sickness, symptoms include swelling five days after the bite and a fever two or three weeks later. Treatment should be sought immediately, as it can be fatal.

Sea creatures

Sharks can be a hazard along the coast. Make sure you know the local situation before you go swimming or diving.

Although not deadly, the **jellyfish** around Zanzibar can give a nasty sting, so keep an eye out when gazing at the wonders of the deep.

Use beach shoes when wading off the shore, not only to guard against rough coral rock or shells, but in case you step on a sea urchin. If you get stung, bitten or cut by anything in the shallows, try to identify what caused it and seek medical help.

Health care

Air ambulance services

If someone is seriously injured or has a life-threatening disease, the closest hospital with reliable staff and equipment up to Western standards is in Nairobi, an hour and a half's flying time from Dar/Zanzibar. The bureaucracy of insurance claims takes time, so if you think a condition is serious, sort it out as early as possible.

Dentists

We do not recommend seeking dental treatment in Tanzania or Zanzibar. Visit your dentist before your trip if you have reason for concern. For dental emergencies, the Swedish-run Three Crowns Dental Clinic in the Dar es Salaam Serena Hotel (tel: 022-213 6801), the International Dental Clinic (tel: 255 762-612 712), or the Nordic Dental Clinic (tel: 022-213 6664) are your best bet.

Doctors

Oyster Bay Hospital
Haile Selasie Road, Dar es Salaam
Tel: 255-266 7932
Regency Medical Centre
Alykhan Road, Upanga, Dar es Salaam
Tel: 022-215 0500
www.regencymedicalcentre.com
Zanzibar Medical Group
Kenyatta Road, near Vuga Road, Stone Town
Tel: 024-223 3134
Flying Doctors
Nairobi (emergency), tel: +254-6992299 / 6992000 or +254-733 639088 / 736 359362 / 722 314239. For information on membership, visit www.flydoc.org.

Hospitals

Try to avoid a stay in any Tanzanian hospital if possible. Away from urban centres, medical care diminishes rapidly in quality, although some mission hospitals manage to maintain good standards of care. Even in the main areas, patients with severe injury or illness are often flown by

air ambulance straight to Nairobi. For less serious conditions, the following are suitable:

Dar es Salaam
Aga Khan Hospital
Ocean Road
Tel: 022-211 5151
Mob: 0744-777100
www.agakhanhospitals.org
International School of Tanzania (IST) Clinic
Haile Selassie Road, Msasani Peninsula
Tel: 022-260 1307/8
www.istclinic.com

Arusha
Arusha Lutheran Medical Centre (ALMC)
Old Moshi Road
Mob: 0736-502376
www.almc.habari.co.tz

Moshi
Kilimanjaro Christian Medical Centre (KCMC)
Sokoine Road, 2km (1.25 miles) north of the town centre
Tel: 027-275 4377/80
www.kcmc.ac.tz
A clinic in the foothills of Mount Kilimanjaro (about 40km/25 miles east of Arusha) with a good reputation.

Pharmacies

Pharmacies in the major towns of Tanzania and Zanzibar are generally well stocked with Western-brand medicines. Medication in villages is limited. Be sure to check the expiry dates before purchasing medicines. Keep receipts on hand for any purchases, as your travel insurance should reimburse you.

Dar es Salaam
Moona's Pharmacy Ltd
Cnr Samora and Mkwepu streets
Tel: 022-212 9983
JD Pharmacy Ltd
Uhuru Street
Tel: 022 218 2980

Arusha
Moona's Pharmacy Ltd
Sokoine Road
Mob: after hours 0744-309 052
Mob: 0754-334567

Zanzibar
Shamsu
Creek Road
Open until midnight

Darjani Pharmacy
Creek Road
Tel: 024-223 9255
Open daily 8am–10pm

I

Internet

There are numerous cafés and bureaux where you can access the internet, which is by far the most reliable form of communication in Tanzania. Rates are inexpensive in most establishments, although some upmarket hotels charge heavily for a service that's no better than anywhere else. Wi-fi is extremely limited, and where you do find it, is often patchy. In areas with mobile network coverage, it is also possible to access internet inexpensively through a mobile phone, tablet or laptop using a local SIM card or portable USB modem (for Telephones see page 258).

M

Maps

Most travellers will be adequately supplied by the maps in this book describing the hubs of Tanzania and Zanzibar. If you would like something more detailed, the best whole-country maps on offer include one by German publisher Harms IC Verlag, who also do detailed regional maps of popular areas (available in the UK at Stanfords, www.stanfords.co.uk). In North America, the Canadian *International Travel Maps Tanzania* is widely available. Various local publishers have produced detailed maps of Zanzibar and the national parks, and these are widely available in Arusha and, to a lesser extent, Moshi, Zanzibar and Dar es Salaam. Tanzania maps are also available at www.omnimap.com.

Media

Television

Most luxury hotels in Tanzania have satellite television, most commonly one of the packages offered by the South African multi-channel service DStv, which usually includes CNN, BBC and various sports and movie channels. Local stations often broadcast only in Swahili and seem to have a fondness for subtitled Chinese dramas and films. Another channel is STAR TV, broadcasting in English and Swahili from Mwanza, receivable in Arusha and Dar es Salaam. Broadcasting since 1994, ITV is the main station. There is a flourishing DVD market that far exceeds the cinema scene. Quality is bad, however, as most discs are pirated.

Radio

Radio used to be the primary source of news and entertainment for most Tanzanians, but it is rapidly being usurped by television. The sounds of Swahili broadcasts can be heard on public transport and in shops and offices. Clouds (FM88.50), TBC Taifa (FM87.50) and Radio Free Africa (FM98.90) are among the most popular radio stations.

Newspapers and magazines

A wide range of newspapers is available in Tanzania, especially in cosmopolitan Dar es Salaam. National dailies include the *Guardian, Daily News* (www.dailynews.co.tz) and *Citizen* (www.thecitizen.co.tz). Also worth trying for international news are the Kenya-based *Nation* (www.nation.co.ke) and *East African* (www.theeastafrican.co.ke). 24Tanzania (http://24tanzania.com) is another good online source of news in English. Foreign editions of UK papers are on sale at luxury-hotel newsstands and occasionally on the street.

Highly recommended free magazines while on the road include the monthly *Dar es Salaam Guide* (www.darguide.co.tz) and *What's Happening in Dar* (http://whatshappeningtz.com). Both provide up-to-the-minute activity listings and travel information. Copies are found at hotels, restaurants and shops throughout Dar es Salaam, Arusha and Zanzibar.

Money

Currency

The Tanzanian shilling (TSh; often written /=) is the national unit of currency. It is divided into 100 cents, which are rarely used. Notes come in 500, 1,000, 5,000 and 10,000 denominations. Coins are 50, 100 and 200. There are smaller coins, but these are seldom used.

Exchange

You should have no problem changing US Dollars, Euros or the UK Pound Sterling cash into local currency in major towns. US dollars are by far the most widely recognised international currency in Tanzania, though be aware that bank notes printed before 2006 are unlikely to be accepted due to the high number of forgeries in circulation, and US$100 and US$50 banknotes get a significantly higher rate than smaller notes.

Money can be exchanged at most banks and private bureaux de change (the latter known as locally as 'forex bureaux'); the former sometimes give marginally better rates but the latter are more efficient and keep longer hours. There are literally dozens

Drinks at sunset on the shore of Lake Manyara.

of forex bureaux in major centres such as Arusha, Moshi, Dar es Salaam and Zanzibar, as well as in most towns close to a land border. There is no black market, and any moneychangers who approach in the street are likely to be working a scam of some sort.

Banks and ATMs

All the larger towns have banks, though in smaller towns, opening hours and services may be limited. Most of the larger bank chains now routinely have 24-hour ATMs where local currency cash can be drawn against a Visa (or MasterCard) credit or debit card, usually to a maximum daily equivalent of between US$200 and US$400. Visa and MasterCard are also accepted for entrance payments at most national parks, and by the majority of upmarket hotels and tour operators. There are no such facilities in very remote areas, however, where you may need to carry all cash with you. Note that vendors other than Visa and MasterCard are not recognised in Tanzania. It is also wise to have a second card as a backup in case your primary one is lost, stolen or rejected.

Major bank groups represented in Tanzania, all with ATMs outside most branches, are as follows:

Barclays Bank
www.barclays.co.tz
Six branches in Dar es Salaam, most usefully on Ohio Street and in the Slipway Mall, as well as one in Zanzibar Stone Town, one in Arusha and one each in Dodoma, Iringa, Mbeya, Morogoro, Moshi, and Tanga.

Standard Chartered
www.standardchartered.com/tz/en/
Three branches in Dar es Salaam, mostly usefully in the International House Branch on the corner of Shaaban Robert Street and Garden Avenue, but also branches in Arusha and Mwanza.

National Bank of Commerce
www.nbctz.com
The best represented bank, with dozens of branches in Dar es Salaam, most usefully on the corner of Azikiwe Street and Sokoine Drive. It also has several branches in Arusha, in Babati, Bukoba, Dodoma, Geita, Iringa, Karatu, Kigoma, Mbeya, Mtwara, Musoma, Mwanza, Tabora, Tanga, Tukuyu, Tunduma and Zanzibar Stone Town.

National parks

Less busy than those in neighbouring Kenya, Tanzania's national parks and game reserves provide some of the world's best destinations for viewing wildlife in their natural habitat. Numerous tour operators can organise tailor-made safaris, either by vehicle, on foot, on horseback or by balloon. Accommodation is either in luxury lodges or designated camping sites – there is little middle ground.

Timing your trip and careful planning are important. The Serengeti is at its best when the migration is around (see page 172). Some areas, such as the Mahale Mountains National Park, are accessible only by plane or boat. In some parks, such as the Arusha National Park, it is possible to drive around without a guide, but those on foot must take an armed guide or ranger. Night-game drives are possible in Ruaha or in private game reserves, but are not allowed within the parks on the Northern Safari Circuit.

Tanzania National Parks (Tanapa) is a government organisation with headquarters in Arusha. It gazettes, manages and protects the country's national parks.

Tanapa (Tanzania National Parks)
PO Box 3134
Arusha
Tel: 027-250 3471/4082
www.tanzaniaparks.go.tz

Fees for foreigners to enter Tanzania's national parks are quite high, in the region of US$35–100 per adult per day, plus 18 percent VAT. The fees generate money to support the infrastructure and to distribute in the local community, but they will eat up a large portion of your travel budget.

Not all the main game reserves are full national parks, for a variety of reasons. Ngorongoro is owned and run by a separate local authority. Parts of the Selous allow hunting, so cannot follow park rules. However, you will be expected to obey the same rules and guidelines, both for the good of the animals and your own safety.

In many national parks, you will not be allowed through the gates without a guide/ranger to protect you against predators (and protect the animals from you).

National park rules

Do not disturb any animals or birds.
Do not cause any noise or create a disturbance likely to offend or annoy other visitors.
Do not pick any flowers or cut or destroy any vegetation.
Do not discard any litter, burning cigarettes or matches.
Do not bring a pet into the park.
Do not bring a firearm into the park.
Do not feed the animals.
Some parks require a guide before entering.
Some parks do not accept children

Banking facilities are available in most towns.

under seven years old (check before travelling).

If walking in a park, stay strictly on the main trails.

Safety in the bush

Tourists are reminded to maintain a safe distance from animals and to remain in vehicles or other protected enclosures when venturing into game parks. Always follow the advice of the guide, who will know the area and the animals inside out.

O

Opening hours

Business hours are becoming much more varied, as more of Tanzania's economy becomes privatised. Here is a rough guide to hours practised.
Offices: Mon–Fri 8am–noon, 2–4.30pm, Sat 8am–12.30pm, if open.
Government: Mon–Fri 8am–4pm.
Garages/shops: Mon–Fri 8.30am–5.30pm, Sat 8.30am–12.30pm.
Banks: Mon–Fri 8.30am–5pm, Sat 9am–2pm.
Post offices: Mon–Fri 9am–5pm, Sat 9am–noon.

P

Photography

Regardless of your ambitions as a photographer, you will find an unlimited number of subjects to shoot: the beaches of Zanzibar, old charms of Dar and Stone Town, Mount Kilimanjaro, the animals and, most importantly, the people.

Bear in mind the differences in light. Midday can produce harsh shadows; the narrow alleys in the old towns are always in deep shade; and you may spot that elusive leopard only at dawn or dusk.

The most important piece of equipment is a zoom lens. When you are out on safari, the animals seem close enough to touch, but photograph them with a wide-angle lens and they look miles away. A good zoom will really bring your photos to life.

Avoid photographing anything that may be considered strategic, such as bridges, police stations, etc. If in doubt, ask.

Photographing people

Be sensitive when taking photos of local people. You would have to get far off the beaten track to find anyone shocked to see a Mzungu (white person) with a camera. Some will want to pose, while others will run for cover; the more entrepreneurial will want money. The Maasai will make it extremely clear that unless they get money, anyone attempting a sneaky shot will be in trouble.

There is no doubt that the best option is to get to know the people around you. While this may seem too big a task, Tanzanians are very friendly and generous and much easier to get to know than busy city-dwellers back home. However, there may not be time when blowing through a small village, in which case you must decide: photograph and ask, or ask and then photograph.

Few Tanzanians are neutral about the camera's eye. If you take a picture without asking, you may get more natural images, but may face the subject's wrath. Some Muslims, particularly women, may be genuinely upset. However, you'll probably be presented with the invoice of an open hand. If you ask first, it will prevent any possible insult and will mean you have some control over the price. However, if people say no, you must be prepared to accept their decision. If they say yes, you will lose the spontaneity that first caught your eye. Often people will simply ask for a copy. If you agree and take their address, make sure you send them one. It will be a valued present.

Postal services

The postal service is generally reliable but slow. At best, airmail to European destinations takes five days. It takes mail a couple of weeks to reach Dar es Salaam from Europe/North America, and much longer if going to a smaller village.

Do not send valuable items or money through the post. Courier services (in larger cities only) take less than 24 hours to reach European destinations.

Dar

The main post office is on Azikiwe Street.

Public holidays

New Year 1 January
Zanzibar Revolution Day 12 January
Karume Day 7 April
Good Friday and **Easter Monday** Variable
Union Day 26 April
Workers' Day 1 May
Saba Saba (Peasants' Day) 7 July
Nane Nane (Farmers' Day) 8 August
Independence Day 9 December
Christmas Day 25 December
Boxing Day 26 December

Islamic festivals

The dates of these festivals vary from year to year:
Eid El Fitr End of Ramadan
Eid El Haji Celebrates sacrifice of Ismail with pilgrimages to Mecca
Maulid/Maulidi Day Prophet Mohammed's birthday.

Arusha

The main post office is on Boma Road, near the Clock Tower. The Meru branch is on Sokoine Road.

Zanzibar

The main post office in Stone Town is outside the city centre in the direction of Amani Stadium. The most convenient post office is on Kenyatta Road.

R

Religious services

Tanzania has places of worship for all the main religions, as well as a wide range of lesser-known faiths and denominations.

Dar es Salaam

Catholic
Cathedral of St Joseph
Sokoine Drive
www.daressalaamarchdiocese.or.tz/st-joseph-cathedral

Hindu
Hindu Temple
Kisutu Street

Islamic
Al Jumaa Mosque
Cnr Indira Ghandi and Kitumbini streets

Lutheran
Azanian Front Lutheran Church
Cnr Sokoine Drive and Maktaba Road
www.azaniafront.org

Arusha

Anglican
St James Church
North of Uhuru Monument
Tel: 027-250 3448

Hindu
Maharaj Temple
Morning 7.30–8am; evening 6–6.30pm
www.baps.org/Global-Network/Africa/
Arusha.aspx

Lutheran
Lutheran Church
Goliondoi Road
English service: Sun 7.30–9am, 9–
10.30am, 10.30am–noon
www.elct.org

Zanzibar

Anglican
Cathedral Church of Christ
Off Creek Road

Catholic
Cathedral of St Joseph
Cathedral Street

St Joseph's Cathedral, Dar es Salaam.

S

Shopping

The city and town centres usually have markets which sell curios such as African drums, jewellery, Makonde carvings and an endless supply of colourful *kangas* (wraparound dresses) at very reasonable prices. Tingatinga paintings, batik prints and *bao* board games are also very popular. In Zanzibar, local spices are added to this and well worth the price, especially the saffron, which is very cheap. Beware the teas and coffees. There is an endless assortment with multiple names. All, sadly, taste similarly bland once at home. Another popular item is the embroidered *kofia* (traditional Muslim head covering), seen on nearly all Zanzibari men.

Be aware that many of the items sold here are not from Tanzania, but come from all parts of Africa – the ethnic jewellery is likely to be Ethiopian, the pink-and-cream soapstone is from Kenya, most other stone, along with much of the batik and beadwork, is from South Africa and Zimbabwe, the embroidered textiles are from West Africa. However – if its exact provenance doesn't matter to you – it is still beautiful, cheap and well worth buying.

Student travellers

If you are a student, it's a good idea when travelling to carry an International Student Identity Card (ISIC), which offers discounts and benefits in over 100 countries including Tanzania. To apply, go to www.isic.org.

STA Travel is a travel company that caters to students and young people. Their Tanzania branch is:
STA Travel/Escape – Student & Adventure Travel
Tel: +255-758 82 83 84/85
www.escape-tanzania.com

T

Telephones

Most resort hotels provide internet services, as do small shops – just as reliable and half the price.

International calls from landlines are very expensive, unless you use an internet phone. They are also rather inefficient, for which reason many mobile numbers (which always start with 06 or 07) serve as fixed lines within Tanzania because the landlines are so bad – indeed, there are now more than 100 mobile phones in the country for every landline.

Although mobile phones are much more reliable than landlines, and the network is good, even extending into most national parks, roaming charges on non-Tanzanian SIM cards can be very high. For this reason, it's worth considering buying a Tanzanian SIM card (which costs less than US$1 and gives you a local number) and airtime cards. International text messages are very cheap (US$1 will buy you around a dozen text messages to anywhere in the world) and international calls work out at around US$1 for three to four minutes.

This can be arranged in a few minutes through local providers such as Vodacom (www.vodacom.co.tz) or Airtel (www.africa.airtel.com), which have shops in all major centres, as well as through the Zanzibar specific provider Zantel (www.zantel.co.tz). Note that a local SIM card, if set up properly, can also double as an inexpensive internet provider.

Regional dialling codes

The international dialling code for Tanzania is 255. Regional codes are as follows (omit the initial zero if calling from abroad):
Arusha 027
Chake Chake (Pemba) 024
Dar es Salaam 022
Dodoma 026
Iringa 026
Kigoma 028
Mbeya 025
Mkoani 024
Morogoro 023
Moshi 027
Mtwara 023
Mwanza 028
Tabora 026
Tanga 027
Wete 024
Zanzibar 024

International codes

Dial the international prefix 00 and then the country code, followed by the number:
Australia 61
Canada 1
Ireland 353
New Zealand 64
South Africa 27
US 1
UK 44

Important numbers

Directory Enquiries: 991
International Directory Enquiries: 0900
Emergency numbers: see page 251.

Tipping

Tipping is optional here. You'll never insult anyone in Tanzania by giving them a tip. Nor will you end up with New York-style rage if you fail to do so.

Rates are roughly as follows:
Porters: TSh1,000 per bag.
Taxis: Taxi drivers have a hard life – if the service has been good, a tip is a good idea.
Bar staff: 5–10 percent.
Waiters: around 5 percent. A Western-style 15 percent tip at an expensive restaurant would probably equate to a week's wages, so modify things a little. Leave cash, rather than adding it to the bill.

Prices rise steeply on safari, when you should be prepared to pay 6–10 percent of the total cost of the safari (minus air fares). Split this between the guide, driver, cook and cleaning staff, with more generally going to the first two.

If climbing Kilimanjaro, you need to budget around US$200. Some operators include the tips in the price of the climb (see page 148).

Toilets

The Swahili word for toilet is *choo*. Toilets are either Western-style (sit down) or Asian-style (squat). Cleanliness and facilities depend largely on what type of establishment you are in. Mid- to high-end hotels are much more likely to have clean Western-style toilets complete with toilet paper. Toilets in cheaper hotels and guesthouses, however, tend to be seatless, paperless and often squat. Public toilets are few and far between and of varied hygienic standard.

It is a cultural, and in some cases religious, practice for most locals to wash (with the left hand) after going to the toilet rather than use paper. It is also more hygienic given the tropical climate. There is usually a plastic container and a water source in the toilet for this purpose. Washing your hands thoroughly afterwards eliminates any bacteria. Keep a roll of toilet paper in your bag at all times if that is your preferred option.

Tour operators

The following operators can all arrange a broad variety of safaris and Zanzibar stays. See page for specialist operators based in Tanzania.

UK

Expert Africa
Tel: 020 3405 6666; (USA) +1 800 242 2434
www.expertafrica.com
Highly regarded Africa specialists with an expertly designed Tanzania programme concentrating on the smaller lodges and camps along the northern safari circuit, as well as on more remote parks such as Selous, Ruaha, Mahale and Katavi. Also very strong on Zanzibar and Mafia archipelagos. Good value and hands-on knowledge.
Rainbow Tours
Tel: 020 3131 4927
www.rainbowtours.co.uk
Specialist in Africa and the Indian Ocean, offering tailor-made tours to Tanzania and Zanzibar.
Tribes Travel
Tel: 01473 890499

www.tribes.co.uk
This award-winning Fair Trade Travel company offers tailor-made and small group holidays throughout Tanzania. From classic safaris to walking safaris guided by Maasai, Kilimanjaro climbs and relaxing breaks on Zanzibar or Mafia.

USA

Africa Dream Safaris
Tel: (US toll free) 877 572 3274
www.africadreamsafaris.com
This award-winning outfit arranges customised northern circuit safaris for serious wildlife enthusiasts and photographers, using intimate tented camps and avoiding circuits that tend to suffer from overcrowding.

South Africa

South Africa & Beyond (Formerly CC Africa)
Tel: +27-11-809 4300
Europe: +49 89 1392 7690
US: +1-888 882 3742
www.andbeyond.com
Owners of some of Tanzania's most exclusive lodges, including Mnemba Island in Zanzibar and the extraordinary Ngorongoro Crater Lodge, &Beyond operates superb lodges and personalised fly or drive safaris.
Wild Frontiers
Tel: +27-11- 702 2035
www.wildfrontiers.com
An excellent, competitively priced Johannesburg-based tour operator with 25 years of experience

⏱ Time zone

Tanzania operates to East Africa Time, which is GMT+3 throughout the year. That means it is three hours ahead of the UK (two hours ahead during British Summer Time), eight hours ahead of New York (seven hours during daylight saving time) and 11 hours ahead of Los Angeles (10 hours during daylight saving time). Being so close to the equator, Tanzania experiences a limited seasonal variation in the length of the day, particularly in the north, where sunrise falls at around 6am and sunset at around 6pm throughout the year.

arranging general and specialist safaris to all corners of Tanzania, as well as island beach stays and Kilimanjaro climbs.

Tanzania

Awaken to Africa
Tel: (US and Can toll free) 1-888-271-8269; Tanzania 011-255-754-387-061
www.awakentoafrica.com
This small but dynamic operator, managed by enthusiastic Tanzanian-US owners, offers customised upmarket safaris and is particularly sensitive to the needs of photographers.

Fair Travel Tanzania
Mob: 0786-025886/8
www.fairtraveltanzania.com
Strongly committed to ecologically sound safaris that pay fair wages to drivers and other staff, this recommended mid-range option is also very competitively and transparently priced.

Fourways Travel
Main roundabout, Station Road, Mwanza
Tel: 028-254 0653
www.fourwaystravel.net.
Mwanza's leading travel agent for the Lake Victoria area: hotel bookings, local and international flights, Serengeti safaris, car hire, local excursions.

Kearsleys Travel
Tel: 255 22 213 7713
www.kearsleys.com
Now operating offices in Arusha and Zanzibar as well as Dar es Salaam, this is the oldest safari company in Tanzania, established in 1948, with dynamic management, well-maintained vehicles, and heaps of experience on both the northern and southern safari circuits.

Nomad Tanzania
Tel: 255 787 59 5908
Emergency only: 255 784 208343
www.nomad-tanzania.com
Operating some of the most exclusive camps in Tanzania, Nomad is particularly recommended for safaris taking in Selous Game Reserve and Mahale and Katavi national parks, where it has operated for almost two decades. It

☉ Weights and measures

Officially metric, although some imperial measurements are still used.

also organises top-notch Serengeti safaris. Exclusive and expensive.

Nyika Treks and Safaris Ltd
TFC Centre, Arusha
Mob: 0754-393331
www.nyikatreks.com
Nyika means wilderness, and that's exactly what this (mainly) budget company offers. It specialises in camping and lodge safaris via truck or camel, hiking (with donkeys carrying packs) and night drives in the southern circuit (which are not allowed in the northern circuit). It also offers five-day camel safaris (budget) on Maasai land near Mount Meru, and trekking at the Ngorongoro Crater. It has links with a tour operator in Zanzibar and companies offering tours to Selous, etc., in the south. Also offers some cultural tourism programmes in Arusha.

Roy Safaris
Serengeti Street, Arusha
Tel: 027-250 8010/2115
www.roysafaris.com
This is a family-run company offering tours throughout Tanzania. It specialises in tailor-made photographic safaris, cultural tours, mountain trekking and beach holidays.

Wayo Africa
Mob: 0784-203000
www.wayoafrica.com
Specialising in guided walking safaris in wilderness areas within the Serengeti and other national parks, this small but environmentally minded operator is recommended to active travellers seeking a genuine bush experience at reasonable rates.

Zanzibar

Most tour operators on Zanzibar offer the full range of local options, including the Stone Town city tour, the Spice Tour, swimming with dolphins and visiting the Jozani Forest. The following are some of the more reputable companies.

Eco & Culture Tours
272 Hurumzi Street
Tel: 024-223 3731
Mob: 0777-410873/462655
www.ecoculture-zanzibar.org

Gallery Tours & Safaris
Gallery House, Mbweni Estate
Tel: 255 774 305 165
www.gallerytours.net
Specialising in high-end, personalised tours around Zanzibar. Services include weddings and

honeymoons, conferences and special-interest tours.

Sama Tours
Gizenga Street, behind the House of Wonders
Tel: 024-223 3543
Mob: 0777-430385/431665
www.samatours.com
This small hands-on operator has been running an excellent selection of motorised and bicycle tours on Zanzibar for years. It's also a good contact for car rental and hotel bookings.

Safari Blue
Mob: 0777-423162
www.safariblue.net
Highly recommended day tours of the stunning Menai Bay Conservation area. Sail by traditional dhow to sandbanks, snorkel coral reefs, watch dolphins, eat a gourmet seafood lunch and sail on traditional outrigger canoe before returning to shore by lantern sail.

Zan Tours
Tel: 024-223 3116
www.zantours.com
One-stop travel resource for Zanzibar.

Tourist information offices

Local

The Tanzania Tourist Board (TTB; www.tanzaniatourism.go.tz) has offices in Dar es Salaam and Arusha. Details are below:

Dar es Salaam (main office)
Utalii House, Laibon Street/Ali Hassan Mwinyi Road
Tel: 022-266 4878/9
Open Mon–Fri 8am–4pm, Sat 8.30am–12.30pm

Arusha
Boma Road, 100 metres from the Clock Tower
Tel: 027-250 3842/3
Open Mon–Fri 8am–4pm, Sat 8.30am–1pm

Zanzibar
Zanzibar Commission for Tourism, Amani Road
Tel: 024-223 3485

Abroad

In the US, Australia and most other countries, the **Tanzania Tourist Board** is represented by the local embassy or high commission.
In the UK, it is represented by:

Tanzania Trade Centre
3 Stratford Place
London W1C 1AS
Tel: 020-7569 1470
http://tanzaniahighcomm.co.uk

V

Visas and passports

All travellers to Tanzania must possess a passport valid for at least six months after the intended date of travel, plus a return ticket.

Citizens of Australia, New Zealand, Canada, the US and of EU member states require a visa to enter Tanzania. It is usually straightforward to obtain a visa on arrival at any international airport or land border, provided you have a valid passport and funds to pay for it, but some operators will suggest you apply in advance. Single-entry tourist visas are valid for three months; multiple-entry visas for six months (US citizens may only apply for the latter). Visas may be extended at the immigration office in any town in Tanzania free of charge.

Visa prices, which vary according to citizenship, do not include additional charges for working or business permits. If travelling on business, you may be required to present a letter indicating the nature of the trip and your business contact in Tanzania. A special pass is required for those wishing to work in Tanzania.

As information on visas changes frequently, it is advisable to contact your nearest Tanzanian embassy before you travel.

Vaccination certificates for yellow fever are needed to enter Tanzania from certain infected countries in Africa and Latin America (check http://tanzaniahighcomm.co.uk for the latest list).

Finally, keep all receipts for visas and ensure all entries are clearly stamped in your passport. Any smudges may be seen as an opportunity for a fine (bribe).

In Dar es Salaam, the Immigration Service is located at:
Loliondo Street Kurasini
Tel: 022-285 0575/6
www.immigration.go.tz
Open Mon–Fri 7.30am–3.30pm

W

Websites

This roundup lists a few of the most useful sources of background

Dress modestly in conservative Zanzibar.

information on Tanzania and Zanzibar.
http://tanzaniahighcomm.co.uk
The website of the Tanzanian High Commission in London, providing details on visa and work permits, business advice and tourist information.
www.cdc.gov
The website for the US Centers for Disease Control and Prevention, with a section on travel health. The site is updated regularly and gives detailed recommendations by region.
www.masta-travel-health.com
The website of MASTA, the UK-based Medical Advice Service for Travellers Abroad.
www.tanzaniatourism.go.tz
The official site of the Tanzanian Tourist Board, providing information on parks, safaris, lodges and tour operators.
https://wn.com/tanzania_news
A classy news resource from the World News Network.
www.zanzibar.co.uk/en
A free information and booking service for travellers who are looking to visit the Zanzibar Archipelago.
www.tanzania.go.tz
The official site of the Republic of Tanzania and Zanzibar, providing all sorts of detailed information on every aspect of the country.
www.arushatimes.co.tz

The website of the weekly from Arusha.
www.zanzibar.net
Informative website on what to see and do in Zanzibar.
www.tanzaniaparks.go.tz
Comprehensive information on Tanzania's national parks.
www.allafrica.com
Current affairs and social commentary with an archival search function.

Women travellers

Travelling as a lone woman is usually perfectly safe and often entertaining. All Tanzanians are relatively conservative: you will be treated with respect, but the moment you are with a man, he will naturally be regarded as the decision-maker. Dress modestly and avoid skimpy clothing (apart from on the beach), particularly in eastern Tanzania and the islands, whose people are predominantly Muslim.

Be relatively formal in your dealings with men. Few African cultures have a concept of platonic friendship between the sexes, and what may be regarded as normal in Europe and the US may well be regarded as a serious come-on here.

If you decide to have sex, remember that there is a high incidence of HIV/Aids in the local populace, and take suitable precautions.

BASIC RULES

KiSwahili (also known as Swahili) is rapidly becoming the international language of Africa and thereby one of the important languages of the world. Although a relatively easy language to pronounce, it does require some effort for the first-time speaker. Every letter in the language is pronounced, unless it's part of a group of consonants. If a letter is written twice it is pronounced twice. Word stress almost always falls on the second to last syllable.

Vowels

a as in 'calm'
e as in the 'a' in 'may'
i as the 'e' in 'me'
o as in 'go'
u as the 'o' in 'too'

Consonants

dh as in 'th' in 'this'
th as in 'th' in 'thing'
gh like the 'ch' of the Scottish 'loch'

☺ Emergencies

Help! Msaada (kusaidia)/saidia/njoo/nisaidie!
Fire! Moto!
Please call the police Mwite/muite polisi tafadhali
Are you all right? U mzima?
I'm ill Naumwa
I'm lost Nimepotea
(Get a) doctor (Umwite) daktari
Send for an ambulance Uite gari la hospitali
There has been an accident ajali/Pametokea ajali
He is (seriously) hurt Ameumia (vibaya)
I've been robbed! Nimeibiwa!
I'd like an interpreter Nataka mkalimani/mtafsiri

ng' as in the 'ng' of 'singer'
ng as in the 'ng' in 'finger'
ny as in the 'ni' in 'onion'
ch as in 'church'
g as in 'get'

WORDS & PHRASES

Yes Ndiyo/ndio
No A-a/hapana
OK Sawa
Please Tafadhali
Thank you Asante (nashukuru)
Sorry Pole
You're welcome Karibu sana
Excuse me Hodi
I don't speak Swahili Sisemba/sisemi Kiswahili (sana)
How do you say ... in Swahili? Unasemaje ... kwa Kiswahili?
Do you speak English? Unasema Kiingereza?
Do you understand? Unaelewa?
I don't understand Sielewi
I understand Naelewa
A little Kidogo
I don't know Sijui
Please write it down Tafadhali niandikie
Wait a moment! Subiri!
Speak slowly, please Tafadhali sema polepole
Enough! Inatosha/Bas!
Good Nzuri
Fine Salama
Where is...? ...iko wapi?
Where is the nearest...? ...ya (la) karibu liko (iko) wapi?
toilet Choo...
Good morning (literally, how's your morning been?) Habari ya asubuhi?
Good afternoon Habari za mchana
Good evening Habari za jioni
Goodnight Lala salama
Goodbye Tutaonana/kwa heri, kwaheri (berphbk)
May I come in (to someone's house) Hodi!
Welcome! Karibu!
Reply: Salama/nzuri/safi/njema

Don't mention it Rica ederim
Pleased to meet you Nimefurahi
How are you? Hujambo (habari gani?)
Fine, thanks. And you? Sijambo, wewe? (nzuri, habari zako/yako?)
My name is... Jina langu ni (naitwa)...
I am British/American/Australian Natoka Uingereza/Marekani/Australia
Leave me alone Usinisumbue/niache
Go away! Hebu!/Toka!
What time is it? Saa ngapi?
When? Lini?
Today Leo
Tomorrow Kesho
Yesterday Jana
Now Sasa
Later Baadaye
Tonight Leo usiku
Why? Kwa nini?
Here Hapa
There Pale
Where can I find... Wapi nawesa
...a newspaper? Gazeti?
...a taxi? Teksi?
...a telephone? Simu?
Yes, there is Ndiyo
No, there isn't Sivyo

DAYS OF THE WEEK

Monday Jumatatu
Tuesday Jumanne
Wednesday Jumatano
Thursday Alhamisi
Friday Ijumaa
Saturday Jumamosi
Sunday Jumapili

NUMBERS

0 sufuri/ziro
1 moja
2 mbili
3 tatu
4 nne
5 tano
6 sita
7 saba
8 nane

9 *tisa*
10 *kumi*
11 *kumi na moja*
12 *kumi na mbili*
20 *ishirini*
21 *ishirini na moja*
22 *ishirini na mbili*
30 *thelathini*
40 *arobaini*
50 *hamsini*
60 *sitini*
70 *sabiini/sabini*
80 *themanini*
90 *tisiini/tisini*
100 *mia*
200 *mia mbili*
1,000 *elfu (moja)*

MONTHS

January *Januari*
February *Febuari*
March *Machi*
April *Aprili*
May *Mei*
June *Juni*
July *Julai*
August *Agosti*
September *Septemba*
October *Oktoba*
November *Novemba*
December *Desemba*

HEALTH

Hospital *Hospitali*
Clinic *Zahanati*
First aid *Huduma ya kwanza*
Doctor *Daktari*
Dentist *Daktari wa meno/Mganga wa meno*
I am ill *Naumwa*
It hurts here *Inaumwa hapa*
I have a fever/headache *Nina homa/ kichwa kinamua*
I am diabetic *Nina dayabeti*
I'm allergic to... *Nina aleji ya...*
I am pregnant *Nina mimba*
I was bitten by... *Niliumwa na...*

DIRECTIONS

Near *Karibu*
Far *Mbali*
Left *Kushoto*
On the left/to the left *Upande wa kushoto*
Right *Kulia*
On the right/to the right *Upande wa kulia*
Straight on *Moja kwa moja*
City *Mji*

Village *Kijiji*
Sea *Bahari*
Lake *Ziwa*
Farm *Shamba*
Church *Kanisa*
Mosque *Misikiti*
Post office *Posta*
North *Kaskazini*
South *Kusini*
East *Mashariki*
West *Magharibi*
How far is...? *Ni umbali gani?*

TRAVELLING

Car *Motokaa*
Petrol/gas station *Stesheni ya petroli/kupata petroli*
Petrol/gas *Petroli*
Flat tyre/puncture *Pancha/kuna kitundu*
My car has broken down *Gari langu limeharibika/ motokaa yangu imeharibika*
Bus station *Stesheni ya basi/kituo cha mabasi*
Bus stop *Bas stendi/pale inaposi- mama bas*
Bus *Basi/bas*
Train station *Stesheni ya treni*
Train *Treni/gari la moshi*
Taxi *Teksi/taxi*
Airport *Uwanja wa ndege/kiwanja cha ndege*
Aeroplane *Ndege*
Port/harbour *Bandari*
Ferry *Meli*
Ticket *Tikiti*
Timetable *Orodha ya saa*
What time does it leave? *Tutaondoka saa ngapi?*
Where do I go? *Nifikeje?*
How long does it take? *Mpaka tufike itachukua muda gani?*
How far is it? *Ni umbali gani?*
Which bus do I take for...? *Niingie katika bas gani kwa kwenda...?*
Please drive more slowly *Endesha polepole*
Stop! *Simama!*

SHOPPING

How much (is this)? *(Hii) bei gani/ni ngapi?*
Can I have? *Nipatie...tafadhali?*
No, I don't like it *A-a, siipendi hii/ sipendi hii*
Do you have any...? *Kuna...?*
Cheap *Rahisi*
Expensive *Ghali*
Big *Kubwa*
Small *Ndogo*

How many? *Ngapi gani?*
Receipt *Risiti*

RESTAURANTS

Waiter/Waitress! *Bwana!/Bibi!*
Menu *Orodha ya chakula*
Breakfast *Chakula cha asubuhi*
Table *Meza*
Bottle (of) *Chupa (ya)*
Fork *Uma*
Knife *Kisu*
Spoon *Kijiko kikubwa (large spoon)*
Salt *Chumvi*
Black pepper *Pilipili*
Soup *Supu*
Fish *Samaki*
Chicken *Kuku*
Meat *Nyama*
Vegetarian food *Wasiokula nyama*
Vegetables *Mboga*
Salads *Saladi*
Fruit *Matunda*
Bread *Mkate*
Drinks *Vinywaji*
Water *Maji*
Mineral water *Maji ya chupa*
Soft drink *Sharabeti/kinywaji baridi*
Beer *Biya*
Wine (red/white) *Mvinyo/divai (nyeupe/nyekundu)*
Coffee (black/with milk) *Kahawa (na maziwa/nyeusi)*
Tea *Chai*

☉ Greetings

Courtesy is rated highly in Tanzania, and greetings should not be rushed. Always shake hands if possible and pay attention to how people greet each other. If you learn nothing else in Swahili, try to master some of the following:
Greetings (to an elder/authority figure): *Shikamoo...*
...elder *Mzee*
...woman old enough to have children *Mama*
...man old enough to have children *Baba*
Reply: *Marahaba*
How are you...? *Hujambo...?*
...Sir *Bwana*
...Miss *Bibi*
Reply: *Sijambo* (or *Jambo* if you want to convert to English)
Hello *Salama/jambo* (*jambo* is mainly used for foreigners – reply *jambo* if you want to speak English, or *sijambo* if want to try out some Swahili phrases).

FURTHER READING

FIELD GUIDES

Birds of Kenya and Northern Tanzania by Dale A. Zimmerman et al. A must for bird lovers sticking to the north of Tanzania.

Field Guide to the Birds of East Africa by Terry Stevenson and John Fanshawe. The best field guide to the country as a whole.

Field Guide to the Reptiles of East Africa by Stephen Spawls, Kim Howell, Robert Drewes and James Ashe. A little esoteric for most, perhaps, but an utterly magnificent field guide.

Field Guide to African Mammals and **Pocket Field Guide to African Mammals** by Jonathan Kingdon. The best guides to the region's mammalian fauna, with the former being more detailed and pricey, the latter more portable and affordable.

The Safari Companion: A Guide to Watching African Mammals Including Hoofed Mammals, Carnivores and Primates by Richard D. Estes. A comprehensive guide to watching and understanding the behaviour of park life.

Field Guide to Common Trees and Shrubs of East Africa by Najma Dharani. **East African Marine Ecoregion** by Matt Richmond and Irene Kamau.

WILDLIFE

Among the Elephants by Ian Douglas-Hamilton. Compelling account of the elephants of Lake Manyara by the king of elephant research.

Mahale: A Photographic Encounter With Chimpanzees by Angelika Hofer, Michael A. Huffman, Gunter Ziesler and Jane Goodall. Photos from Tanzania's Mahale Mountains.

Mara Serengeti: A Photographer's Paradise by Jonathan Scott and Angela Scott. Breathtaking photographic study of the Serengeti and its inhabitants.

My Life with the Chimpanzees; The Chimpanzees I Love: Saving Their World and Ours; In the Shadow of Man; Through a Window: My Thirty Years with the Chimpanzees of Gombe; 50 Years at Gombe by Jane Goodall. Several titles detailing the chimp queen's life and work with the Gombe Stream chimpanzees.

Jane Goodall: The Woman Who Redefined Man by Dale Peterson. A detailed and insightful biography of the founder of the chimp research project at Gombe.

In the Lion's Den by Mitsuaki Iwago (photographer). A photographic essay on the king of beasts.

Serengeti: Natural Order on the African Plain by Mitsuaki Iwago. A visual diary of life and death in the Serengeti.

The Serengeti's Great Migration by Carlo Mari (photographer), Harvey Croze and Richard D. Estes. One of Africa's greatest events depicted in wonderful detail.

Serengeti Shall Not Die by Bernard Grzimek. Where it all started; the account of the struggle to preserve the Serengeti, by the man who made it happen.

Tanzania – African Eden by Graham Mercer and Javed Jafferji. Beautifully photographed A–Z of the wonders of Tanzania.

Wildlife of East Africa by Martin B. Withers and David Hosking. A compact guide with full-colour photographs and detailed descriptions.

HISTORY

Africa: A Biography of the Continent by John Reader. A panoramic history of where human life began.

Africa Explored: Europeans in the Dark Continent by Christopher Hibbert. The lives, journeys and impact of the 19th-century explorers.

The Africans by David Lamb. Part travelogue and part history of a continent at odds with itself. Written by former bureau chief for the Los Angeles Times.

Battle for the Bundu by Charles Miller. The East Africa campaign during World War I.

Cargoes of the East: The Ports, Trade and Culture of the Arabian Seas and Western Indian Ocean by Edmond Bradley Martin and Chryssee Perry Martin.

Empires of the Monsoon by Richard Hall. Ambitious but thoroughly readable history of the countries and trade routes surrounding the Indian Ocean.

A History of Tanzania ed. N. Kimambo and A.J. Temu. Tanzanian-written history of the country, with a refreshingly non-European angle. About the only general history to pay serious attention to what was happening before the Europeans arrived.

No Man's Land: An Investigative Journey through Kenya and Tanzania by George Monbiot. Looking for justice in the area where conservation and land rights meet.

Revolution in Zanzibar: An American's Cold War Tale by Donald Petterson. Eyewitness account of the 1964 Zanzibar Revolution.

The Scramble for Africa by Thomas Pakenham. Masterly unravelling of the complex politics and history involved in Europe's 19th-century land grab.

Tanzania Notes and Records. Contains great period pieces on a wide variety of topics of Tanzanian history and culture. On sale at the National Museum in Dar es Salaam and the Arusha Declaration Museum.

The White Nile by Alan Moorehead. Tale of European exploration of East Africa in the 19th century.

Zanzibar Island Metropolis of Eastern Africa by Major F.B. Pearce.

LIVES AND LETTERS

African Voices, African Lives: Personal Narratives from a Swahili Village by Patricia Caplan. A story of three distinctive villagers, told through their words.

The Leakeys: Uncovering the Origins of Humankind by Margaret Poynter. Biography of the family of pioneering archaeologists.

The Life of Frederick Courteney Selous by J.G. Millais. Biography of the first of the great white hunters.

Livingstone by Tim Jeal. Authoritative biography of the greatest of the explorers.

Memoirs of an Arabian Princess by Emily Said-Ruete. The autobiography of a princess from Zanzibar who eloped with a German to Europe. An intriguing historical portrait.

Tanzania, Journey to Republic by Randal Sadleir. This description of life as a district commissioner in colonial Tanganyika is also a fascinating account of the road to independence.

TRAVEL WRITING

Going Solo by Roald Dahl. Autobiographical account of working for Shell in 1930s Dar es Salaam before joining the RAF.

Kilimanjaro Adventure by Hal Streckert, Kathy Wittert (editor) and Tom Tamoria (illustrator). A climb to Africa's roof.

Kilimanjaro: To the Roof of Africa by Audrey Salkeld. Accompanying coffee-table book to an Imax film on the mountain, with superb photography and authoritative text.

Livingstone's Tribe: A Journey from Zanzibar to the Cape by Stephen Taylor. White former resident of South Africa journeys south from Zanzibar, looking at the people of Africa, black and white.

Safari Living by Gemma Pitcher, photography by Javed Jafferji. Stunning coffee-table book on the design of the country's best lodges and camps.

Sand Rivers by Peter Matthiessen. A private safari in the Selous.

Tanzania: Portrait of a Nation by Paul Joynson-Hicks. Beautiful photographs and well-written text.

A Tourist in Africa by Evelyn Waugh. The comic novelist's journey through East Africa.

FICTION

Antonia Saw the Oryx First by Maria Thomas. A finely composed juxtaposition of two women: one black, one white.

Death in Zanzibar by M.M. Kaye. Torrid romantic novel.

An Ice Cream War by William Boyd. Grimly comic novel set during the World War I East Africa campaign.

Paradise by Abdulrazak Gurnah. Booker and Whitbread Prize shortlisted novel by a prominent Zanzibari writer now living in the UK. You may also want to read his novel *Desertion*, set in Zanzibar in the late fifties.

The Snows of Kilimanjaro by Ernest Hemingway. The master storyteller turns his attention to death and the African bush, where he spent many happy hours hunting.

Zanzibar by Giles Foden. Murder mystery wound up in the true-life events of the bombings of the US Embassies in Dar es Salaam and Nairobi.

Zanzibar Tales: Told by the Natives of East Africa by George Bateman. Collected Swahili folk tales, translated a century ago.

OTHER INSIGHT GUIDES

The classic Insight Guide series combines in-depth features and an exploration of essential sights accompanied by vibrant photography. Insight Guides to Africa include: **Cape Town; Egypt; Kenya; Mauritius, Réunion and Seychelles; Namibia** and **South Africa**.

Insight **Fleximaps** to African destinations include **Cape Town, Marrakesh** and **South Africa.**

☉ Send Us Your Thoughts

We do our best to ensure the information in our books is as accurate and up-to-date as possible. The books are updated on a regular basis using local contacts, who painstakingly add, amend and correct as required. However, some details (such as telephone numbers and opening times) are liable to change, and we are ultimately reliant on our readers to put us in the picture.

We welcome your feedback, especially your experience of using the book "on the road". Maybe we recommended a hotel that you liked (or another that you didn't), or you came across a great bar or new attraction we missed.

We will acknowledge all contributions, and we'll offer an Insight Guide to the best letters received.

Please write to us at:
Insight Guides
PO Box 7910
London SE1 1WE
Or email us at:
hello@insightguides.com

CREDITS

PHOTO CREDITS

akg images 45, 51
Alamy 177TR, 179, 186, 203, 236
Ardea.com 87BR
Ariadne Van Zandbergen/Apa
Publications 1, 6MR, 6BL, 6BR, 7TR,
7MR, 7ML, 7BR, 9T, 9B, 10/11, 12/13,
14/15, 16, 17T, 17B, 18, 19, 20, 21, 22,
23, 24, 25, 28T, 32, 39, 40, 60/61, 62,
63, 64L, 64R, 68, 69, 70, 71, 72, 73, 74,
76, 77, 79, 80R, 81, 82T, 82B, 83TL,
84BR, 84MR, 85TL, 85ML, 85BR,
86ML, 86TL, 87TL, 87MR, 87ML, 88ML,
88BR, 88TL, 88MR, 89TL, 89BR, 90ML,
90BR, 90TL, 90MR, 91TL, 91MR, 91ML,
92ML, 92BR, 92TL, 92MR, 93TL, 93MR,
93ML, 94ML, 94BR, 94TL, 94MR, 95TL,
95MR, 95ML, 96MR, 97, 98/99T, 98BL,
99BL, 99BR, 99TR, 100, 101, 102, 103,
104, 105, 106, 107, 108, 110/111,
112/113, 114/115, 116, 117T, 117B,
120, 121, 122, 123, 125, 126, 127, 128,
129, 130, 131, 133, 134, 135, 136B, 137,
138, 139, 140, 141, 143, 144, 154, 155,
156, 157, 159, 160, 161, 162, 163, 164,
165, 167, 168, 169T, 169B, 170T, 170B,
171, 173, 175, 176/177T, 176BL,
177ML, 177BR, 177BL, 188, 189, 191,
192, 193T, 193B, 194, 195, 196T, 196B,
197, 198, 201, 208, 214, 215, 219, 220,
221T, 221B, 222, 223, 224, 225T, 225B,
226, 227, 228, 229, 230B, 231, 232, 234,
238/239T, 238BR, 238BL, 239BR,
239ML, 239BL, 239TR, 240, 242, 244,
245, 246B, 246T, 246/247, 248, 250,
255, 258, 261, 262
Art Archive 48
AWL Images 176BR
Bigstock 8B, 96BR, 149, 212, 213B
Corbis 28B, 41, 43, 52, 78, 80L
Dreamstime 6ML, 7ML, 67, 85MR,
86MR, 89ML, 95BR, 98BR, 145, 182,
200, 205, 206, 211

FLPA 7TL, 96TL, 178
Fotolia 75, 83MR, 93BR, 181T, 233
Getty Images 31T, 33, 35, 37, 38, 42,
53, 54, 55, 56, 57, 58, 59, 66, 109, 237
iStock 4, 65, 83ML, 83BR, 84ML, 84TL,
89MR, 91BR, 96ML, 99ML, 147, 148T,
148B, 150, 152, 153, 172, 181B, 183T,
184, 185, 187, 217, 230T, 256
iStockphoto 264
James Tye/Apa Publications 136T
Joachim Huber 204
Library of Congress 29
Manyara Ranch Conservancy 8T
Mary Evans Picture Library 44, 46, 47,
50, 199
Photoshot 30, 31B, 34, 49, 86BR, 209
Richard Stupart 207
Robert Harding 235
Shutterstock 166, 183B
Tanzania Tourist Board 213T
TopFoto 36

COVER CREDITS

Front cover: Zebras Shutterstock
Back cover: Mafia Island Bigstock
Front flap: (from top) Maasai herding
camels Ariadne Van Zandbergen/Apa
Publications; African fish eagle Ariadne
Van Zandbergen/Apa Publications;
Swahili dhow Ariadne Van Zandbergen/
Apa Publications; Kikois for sale
Ariadne Van Zandbergen/Apa
Publications
Back flap: Grey Crowned Cranes
Ariadne Van Zandbergen/Apa
Publications

INSIGHT GUIDE CREDITS

Distribution
UK, Ireland and Europe
Apa Publications (UK) Ltd;
sales@insightguides.com
United States and Canada
Ingram Publisher Services;
ips@ingramcontent.com
Australia and New Zealand
Woodslane; info@woodslane.com.au
Southeast Asia
Apa Publications (SN) Pte;
singaporeoffice@insightguides.com
Hong Kong, Taiwan and China
Apa Publications (HK) Ltd;
hongkongoffice@insightguides.com
Worldwide
Apa Publications (UK) Ltd;
sales@insightguides.com
Special Sales, Content Licensing and CoPublishing
Insight Guides can be purchased in bulk quantities at discounted prices. We can create special editions, personalised jackets and corporate imprints tailored to your needs.
sales@insightguides.com
www.insightguides.biz

Printed in China by CTPS

All Rights Reserved
© 2017 Apa Digital (CH) AG and
Apa Publications (UK) Ltd

First Edition 2003
Third Edition 2017

No part of this book may be reproduced, stored in a retrieval system or transmitted in any form or means electronic, mechanical, photocopying, recording or otherwise, without prior written permission from Apa Publications.

Every effort has been made to provide accurate information in this publication, but changes are inevitable. The publisher cannot be responsible for any resulting loss, inconvenience or injury. We would appreciate it if readers would call our attention to any errors or outdated information. We also welcome your suggestions; please contact us at: hello@insightguides.com

www.insightguides.com

Editor: Helen Fanthorpe
Author: Philip Briggs, Melissa Shales and Maciej Zglinicki
Head of Production: Rebeka Davies
Update Production: Apa Digital
Picture Editor: Tom Smyth
Cartography: original cartography Stephen Ramsay, updated by Carte

CONTRIBUTORS

This new edition of *Insight Guide Tanzania & Zanzibar* was edited by **Helen Fanthorpe** and updated by **Maciej Zglinicki**. It draws on the comprehensive work of **Philip Briggs**, a South African travel writer who has written guides to many African countries and contributes regularly to a number of leading South African and British wildlife periodicals. Other previous contributors include **Melissa Shales**, **Jeffery Pike**, **Mary Johns** and **Claire Foottit**. **Ariadne van Zandbergen** took many of the pictures that illustrate this guide.

ABOUT INSIGHT GUIDES

Insight Guides have more than 45 years' experience of publishing high-quality, visual travel guides. We produce 400 full-colour titles, in both print and digital form, covering more than 200 destinations across the globe, in a variety of formats to meet your different needs.

Insight Guides are written by local authors, whose expertise is evident in the extensive historical and cultural background features. Each destination is carefully researched by regional experts to ensure our guides provide the very latest information. All the reviews in **Insight Guides** are independent; we strive to maintain an impartial view. Our reviews are carefully selected to guide you to the best places to eat, go out and shop, so you can be confident that when we say a place is special, we really mean it.

Legend

City maps
Freeway/Highway/Motorway, Divided Highway, Main Roads, Minor Roads, Pedestrian Roads, Steps, Footpath, Railway, Funicular Railway, Cable Car, Tunnel, City Wall, Important Building, Built Up Area, Other Land, Transport Hub, Park, Pedestrian Area, Bus Station, Tourist Information, Main Post Office, Cathedral/Church, Mosque, Synagogue, Statue/Monument, Beach, Airport

Regional maps
Freeway/Highway/Motorway (with junction), Freeway/Highway/Motorway (under construction), Divided Highway, Main Road, Secondary Road, Minor Road, Track, Footpath, International Boundary, State/Province Boundary, National Park/Reserve, Marine Park, Ferry Route, Marshland/Swamp, Glacier, Salt Lake, Airport/Airfield, Ancient Site, Border Control, Cable Car, Castle/Castle Ruins, Cave, Chateau/Stately Home, Church/Church Ruins, Crater, Lighthouse, Mountain Peak, Place of Interest, Viewpoint

INDEX

INSIGHT ⊙ GUIDES

OFF THE SHELF

Since 1970, **INSIGHT GUIDES** has provided a unique perspective on the world's best travel destinations by using specially commissioned photography and illuminating text written by local authors.

Whether you're planning a city break, a walking tour or the journey of a lifetime, our superb range of guidebooks and phrasebooks will inspire you to discover more about your chosen destination.

INSIGHT GUIDES

offer a unique combination of stunning photos, absorbing narrative and detailed maps, providing all the inspiration and information you need.

PHRASEBOOKS & DICTIONARIES

help users to feel at home, when away. Pocket-sized with a free app to download, they go where you do.

CITY GUIDES

pack hundreds of great photos into a smaller format with detailed practical information, so you can navigate the world's top cities with confidence.

EXPLORE GUIDES

feature easy-to-follow walks and itineraries in the world's most exciting destinations, with our choice of the best places to eat and drink along the way.

POCKET GUIDES

combine concise information on where to go and what to do in a handy compact format, ideal on the ground. Includes a full-colour, fold-out map.

EXPERIENCE GUIDES

feature offbeat perspectives and secret gems for experienced travellers, with a collection of over 100 ideas for a memorable stay in a city.

www.insightguides.com

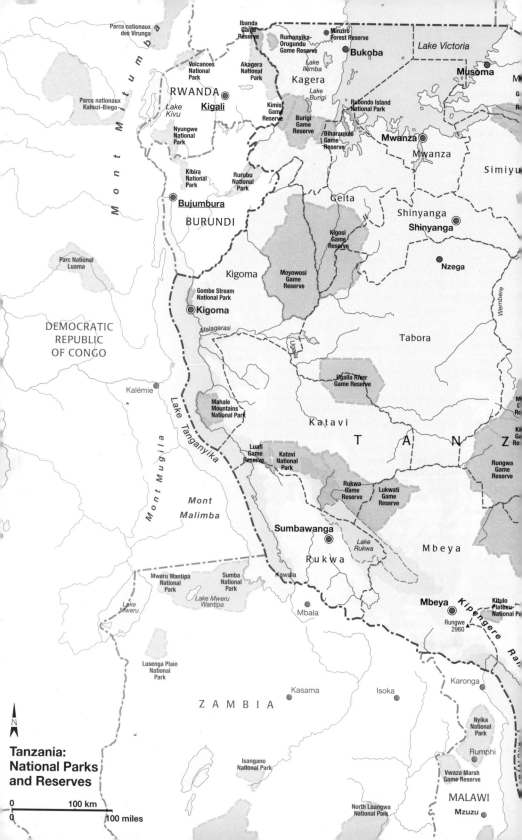

Tanzania:
National Parks
and Reserves

0   100 km

0   100 miles

N